Louis Franci~

THIS IS

𝕸𝖞 𝕾𝖙𝖔𝖗𝖞

Whittlesey House

McGRAW-HILL BOOK COMPANY, INC.

NEW YORK : LONDON

THIS IS MY STORY

PUBLISHED BY WHITTLESEY HOUSE

A division of the McGraw-Hill Book Company, Inc.

PRINTED IN THE UNITED STATES OF AMERICA

To MARY IMMACULATE

Patroness of Our Beloved Land

The Return

ONE FULL year has gone by since my return to Rome. In that act my entire family joined—my wife, formerly a Unitarian, and our three daughters. The intervening hours since our conversion have ripened enough for us to be able, calmly and charitably, to recite the causes for this decision, causes which have to do not only with ourselves but with all of present-day America. In the midst of the peace and joy which is now ours, we can exclaim with the Psalmist: "I will declare my iniquity, and I will be thoughtful of my sin." In our repentance, we can likewise say with David in Psalm 50: "Thou shalt make me hear of joy and gladness. . . . Thou shalt open my lips, O Lord; and my mouth shall declare thy praise."

Writing from our hearts, in this mingled spirit of contrition and rejoicing, we hope that the recitation of our past mistakes will profit others and that the story of our positive act of good will be a source of inspiration to those tempest-tossed. That is the chief aim in the telling of this tale.

It was on the evening of October 10th last that the radio commentators suddenly stated, in all parts of the United States and in Latin America and Europe, that a leading American Communist had again become a Catholic. The Managing Editor of the Daily Worker, organ of the Communist Party of the United States, declared then, "With deep joy, I wish to announce that by God's grace I have returned fully to the faith of my fathers, the Catholic Church." The event was widely commented on, far into the night, and the newspapers the next morning devoted generous and conspicuous space and display to its recitation. Much was made of the continued appearance of the Catholic convert's name on the masthead of the Daily Worker the very morning the newspapers were heralding his abandonment of Communism throughout the length and breadth of the land. All men could note from that phenomenon that he had stood in high regard among the Communist to the very last, that his deed was his own in voluntarily and completely shaking off the Kremlin allegiance and in accepting fealty to Catholicism. "The Daily Worker," drily said a news magazine given to clever phrasing, "was caught with its ideological pants down." After two days of unusual silence, the Communists on their part post-dated their observations by calling their ex-editor's act "frightened" and by heaping some of their run-of-the mill abuses upon his head.

Even before my family and I had reached Notre Dame University, which had given us sanctuary, my mail was flooded with requests that I write and lecture on our conversion. The repercussions from the move had been as wide and deep as the reportage which it received. A Brother of the Sacred Heart, fifty years a teacher, able but humble Brother Ilbertus, heard the news over the radio in the Far South and rejoiced that one of his well-remembered pupils at old St. John's High School in Indianapolis had re-entered the True Fold. A Bishop on the Pacific coast noted that a former classmate had received the grace to turn toward Catholicism and embrace it. Another Bishop of the Northwest, who had learned in advance of what was to take place, expressed his happiness that it had occurred. A labor leader of some national note, absent in Europe, heard of the conversion from the radio there and was glad. One who had faithfully followed the new convert in former labor activities and who was now a captain in the forces of occupation in Germany, learned of the business there and hastened to send greetings. A judge of a leading court of appeals in the Middle West was deeply moved that one whom he had known favorably in his boyhood had taken this great step. A distinguished columnist on a leading Ohio newspaper, who had been a playmate of my early Indiana youth, devoted his contribution of Oct. 12 to a fine if over-laudatory discussion of our boyhood associations. Over against the hundreds of congratulatory messages received, only six expressed dissent and only two of these were personally abusive. With letters so easy to write and passions so readily aroused, this was a recognition of the sincerity of my return to Rome which was much treasured.

It proved impossible, though, to honor the scores of requests to write and speak which accompanied these congratulations. Almost every large agency of opinion in America sought my cooperation in getting my story told, in print and on the lecture platform. It was natural that such requests would be made, but it was also understandable that they should be declined. The act of becoming a Catholic is a solemn and sacred one. All those who have turned to the Church from any prominent or semi-prominent position outside its ranks have paid tribute to this realization by their months of silence and study upon their entry into the Catholic fold. St. Paul spent two years after the "light on the road to Damascus," in retirement in Arabia. The great Augustine went into his "vintage vacation," as he calls it, for spiritual strengthening and intellectual clarification. The saintly John Henry Newman gave over a long period to retreat in his first years as a Catholic communicant. Such an act is essential for the great as well as the small; how much more so for the small in contrast to the great!

My responsibilities to Notre Dame in the first year there dictated a similar course. It was therefore the way of wisdom which led the Rev. J. Hugh O'Donnell, then president of the university, and myself to agree right in the beginning that I would refrain from any public activity of any sort for an indefinite number of months, approximating at least one year from my conversion.

As month followed month in the quietude of Notre Dame, a new duty pressed more and more definitely upon me. My fellow-Americans had wanted to learn more of my experiences, of what is actually involved in being a Communist in America, of the "story behind the story" of my return to the Catholic Church. There were those who were impatient that I did not take to the hustings and to the public prints faster than has been the case. To them it can be said that though a lot of emotional satisfaction may be obtained from rushing before the klieg lights with "exposés" and expletives, this is not the way which generally contributes most to the cause of justice. Nor does it make for that sober presentation of the truth which America's present serious hour of crisis requires. My own discoveries, however, as to the repulsiveness of Communism and my own need for the religious consolations of Catholicism would be of small account were it not that they are intertwined with the whole question of whether America is to march forward as a healthy nation or go into a crippled future. My discovery that the Communist movement in this country, the agent of a foreign power, is committed to the maiming of the American nation and the atomization of the American people is of more concern than to myself alone. My finding once more that the Catholic viewpoint is not only essential for my own welfare as an individual but can be a major aid to America's good health is something that should be shared with my fellow-citizens. These are matters of such great movement that I do have a duty to discuss them, to bring forward what I learned and saw, but to do so quietly, calmly and with wise restraint. Catholic charity, too, counsels such an attitude.

Those who will look in these pages for bitter invective against individual Communists, to the ferreting out of Reds in this place and that, to lurid accounts of countless secret conclaves will be disappointed. Although such conclaves were held and although a strong light must be thrown upon their pernicious conclusions and commands, the case against Communism rises high above such considerations. Many Communists, too, as was the case with myself, enter the "movement" through their sense of justice; they become twisted and crippled personalities through the doctrine of hate which they adopt and the wooden-soldier "discipline" which they are compelled to follow. I have no interest in pillorying them as individuals but in laying bare the gangrene embedded in the "movement" to which they adhere. Rather shall I pray for them to the Mother of that God who cried out two thousand years ago: "Saul, Saul why persecutest thou Me?"—in the hope that they shall be granted the courage to break their chains and be restored to personal integrity.

The ordinary American has no idea of the alien world which exists right here in our own country, as exemplified by the Communist Party. He or she would be astounded to enter the actual life of a leading Communist Party member, and to discover the intellectual strait jacket in which that person is imprisoned. The leaders of that party are in the darkest ignorance as to what is occurring in the country they serve, Soviet Russia, and yet follow every beck and call of those who command them from abroad. Here is a walled-in community, in the midst of free America, whose leadership works secretly in the shadows and is not unfrequently dictated to by the secret police or other agents of a foreign government and even threatened on occasion with removal by such police. And yet, I, a fourth generation American, have witnessed such occurrences with my own eyes and heard them with my own ears.

The real indictment of the Communist conspiracy in America rises far above any petty personalities. What I have found is much deeper and more somber than the naughty acts of some misguided individual. For years I tried to reconcile love for America and the rising knowledge of my need for the Catholic Church with my leading position as a Communist. The war against the Axis made me strive even harder to establish such a reconciliation, It proved to be impossible. The Communist position is irrevocably built on that obscure but malignant dictum of Marx, "Religion is the opiate of the people." The folly of such a position is that history, experience and the aspirations of all human beings reveal religion as the medicine of the people; the Communists propose by force to dash it from the people's lips.

In these pages I will state as simply as I can what occurred during the ten years of my leading position as a Communist. The reader may then judge for himself the correctness of my judgment and the wisdom of my recent decision. That decision has brought me and my family the liberated feeling that comes to one who has just been rescued from long years in jail. The narrative presented in these pages is a history of ideas, not primarily of personal episodes, and yet the thread of such personal experiences must run through the background of the account. Brought forward reluctantly, they will be used with as much economy as is possible and at the same time sustain the discussion.

For what appears in this book neither Notre Dame nor Fordham, the two colleges with which I have been connected since my return to the Church, are at all responsible. I wish to express appreciation, though, for the fine cooperation offered me by these universities in order that I might get out this book. It was the Rev. John Cavanaugh, now president of Notre Dame, who urged me to set down this narrative. And it was the patient advance reading of these pages by the Rev. Francis Cavanaugh, Dean of the College of Arts and Sciences there, which aided much in the completion of the work.

I have not sought here to present a profound study of the philosophy of Communism, nor has there been any attempt to evaluate the activities of the Reds in the labor movement. I hope very shortly to deal with both subjects in separate volumes, beginning with the latter. There has been, even within the limits of this presentation, a certain careful selection in the mountains of material on the Communist conspiracy which I have at hand. Most of the subversive maneuvers in American political life and the Red espionage on political figures in America have been intentionally omitted, since such might have aroused bitter personal controversy in the beginning. And that would have obscured the main moral arising from my experiences. At a future day this information can probably be given to the American people in the most effective way.

It is in the spirit of St. Augustine, then, that this book is written, in "hatred of the sin but in love of the sinner," in that spirit which Monsignor Fulton J. Sheen so well expressed on the occasion of my entry into the Church: "I hate Communism but love the Communists." It was his own devotion to that course which made him of such magnificent aid to me and mine in the hour of test and trial. It is in humility, too, that I write, knowing that but for the grace of God I would be in the place still of those whom in service to the truth I must condemn. It is in apology to all men and women of good will that I set down these words, for having failed so long on my part to see the way and the light.

It is in fervent gratitude to the Mother of God, Mary of the Magnificat, that I give testimony to the truth, acknowledging that but for her amazing assistance I would not tonight close my eyes with the sign of the cross in that peace which the world cannot give.

L. F. B.

Fordham University
Oct. 11, 1946
The Feast of the Maternity of Mary

CONTENTS

THIS IS MY STORY

ONE

Joy to My Youth

I<small>T ALL</small> began in Indiana, more than fifty years ago. My father's house lay back from the dusty road that ran through the south side of Indianapolis to Shelbyville. It was a strange little structure, the quaint and formless extension of an original log cabin. Folks, walking through it, thought they had seen it all and then were surprised suddenly to find that there was another room or two off to the side. Several of its scattered neighbors in that nearcountryside were much more imposing, but few contained the treasures which our family felt lay within its walls. That house, our home, was for us a seat of culture and a haven for the Catholic faith to which we zealously adhered.

The great, wooden-framed "Ecce Homo" of the Christ crowned with thorns, which dominated the center room, proclaimed the banner under which we labored, loved and lived. The whole atmosphere of the place was in accord with that giant picture, to which as little children we looked up with such awe and reverent affection.

The distance from our front door to the church, old St. Patrick's, was long enough—a mile or more. But in the silence of early summer mornings I found it magically short in the frequent walks to six o'clock Mass. There was a peace in the sparsely filled church which beckoned me, as I knew the scene which was to greet me before the tabernacle—the ten or twelve silent figures scattered through the church in prayer, the gentle happiness of the morning sun as it sang out the glory of God through the colored windows. There was the melody in those words with which each Mass begins: "I will go to the altar of God, to God who giveth joy to my youth." There was the rising wonder in the progress of the drama of Calvary, which was being enacted right there in my native Indiana. From outside the first warnings of the day's traffic might be heard, the beat of horses' hoofs upon the irregular bricks; within was the grandeur and solemnity of "*Sanctus, Sanctus, Sanctus, Dominus Deus Sabaoth*—Blessed is He that cometh in the name of the Lord." In those sacred moments the inspiration rushed upon me to lead a full Christian life of peace and benignity, and to make the blessings of Catholicism serve my country.

Our family had been there in Indiana almost from its very beginning as a state; our covered wagon had dragged through the mud of Washington Street among the first settlers of Indianapolis. This was our land, our city; we belonged there—and yet it was not the way we wanted it to be. The voices of the French missionaries, saying this very Mass a long time ago in wilderness and Indian settlement, from Vincennes to the south bend of the St. Joseph, had been lost to thousands of our Hoosier fellows. So many of them had become blinded to an understanding of the faith which was so essential to my own life and well-being.

Could not the peace and beauty which lay within the Church be extended to those who no longer knew what the Church was? That was the burning thought which came to me as the bells rang the solemn notice of the elevation of the Blessed Sacrament, that renewal of the crucifixion scene. Though but a child, I had seen the evil effects of the broken homes which followed divorce; the sufferings and lost-soul feelings of those playmates whose fathers and mothers had severed their marriage tie. I couldn't help comparing their longings for secure home life with the rocklike permanence of the relationship between my father and mother and therefore of our whole family circle. It made an indelible impression on my nine-year-old heart and mind, and brought warmth and the firelight of the hearth to my homage at the altar. That may be dubbed "idyllic" by those who look only for sourness in any history of childhood, but that's the way it was. That's the way it is in the genuinely Catholic family; it's the nearest thing to perfect happiness that can be discovered in what is called in religious parlance "the world." The love of God, I found when very young, makes perfect and permanent the love of man and woman and brings peace to their hearthstone, even though that be represented only by the base burners which heated our home.

My mother's laughter rippled through the house every day, and so with her songs. She sang as she washed the babies' diapers—and five babies came in all—or boiled the apples or pears or grapes in the summer kitchen when the fall season arrived and these fruits were put up. Was it because she was an orphan, this daughter of immigrants from counties Cork and Kerry, and that this place was her haven, her domain? That may have been the cause in part, but its secret lay rather in those words with which she sometimes greeted an occasional quarrel among us children: "Remember, you began the day with the sign of the Cross." She has to be brought soon into any story of my ideas and how they determined the events in my life, for she proved to be another Monica, whose Catholic charity and prayerful patience followed me lovingly until the new dawn of conversion came.

My father was spoken of by countless people as an "unusual man," and so he was. He was a man of deep faith, acquired by conversion after a youth spent sampling everything from agnosticism to Anglicanism. He was also a man of wide reading. How humble was his religious devotion can be no better illustrated than by the promise he made on the day he obtained the position as paying teller at the Capitol National Bank, two years before my birth. To the Mother of God he pledged that were he to remain honest and proficient in that work he would place a bouquet of the finest flowers on her altar at every feast of the Immaculate Conception. And every year for fifty-four years, until his death, the flowers appeared on Our Lady's altar on December 8, and were looked for by some few people who knew of the promise. His culture, handed down from ancestors in western Germany, was attested to by the library which was partly inherited but which he built up over the years out of his humble earnings. His father's cousin was the noted Joseph Budenz, the German author of the first Magyar dictionary and professor of philology at the University of Budapest.

My father's library, a facet of our pride, was much too large for our house; the volumes, from Plato to Pope and Poe, overflowed into all sorts of odd places. They crowded the queer big closet, with its solid wooden door, built into the wall of the center room; they filled the shelves of the quaint closets in the finished attic and were piled on old tables there. In later years, they were more and more to be placed in modern bookcases, but their homely position in my youth did not give them an inferior place. They were, as my father put it, "a more precious heritage than silver and gold."

From the shelves which contained these cherished possessions I was privileged to take, when I was approaching the magical ninth year, the sacred *Tragedies of Shakespeare*. I can still feel the smooth, hard leather and recall the reverence associated with that book. The music of Shakespearean verse charmed my ear and made my pulse beat faster. I was not satisfied until I had learned the first scene from *Hamlet*, reciting it to Father when he came home one summer evening. We agreed then to save every cent and go together to the performance of that play to be given by the noted E. H. Sothern, with Virginia Harned as Ophelia, at English's Opera House the coming winter.

For the next three years, the theater season was a gala time for us. Through the medium of Robert Mantell's associates and other repertoire companies, we were delighted with everything from *King Lear* to *Coriolanus*, and with such productions as Bulwer-Lytton's *Richelieu* thrown in for good measure. These adventures gave life to the world of books and made my father's library a new wonderland. They provided the key to that intellectual treasure which the Catholic layman must possess if he is to bear witness fully to his faith before his fellow-citizens. Through line after line and page after page of the books I devoured, the medley of America and of the influence of Catholicism in America began to be organized into a complete harmony.

Many a summer day of the school vacation was spent over the *History of France* by François Pierre Guizot. It is a work which I cannot recommend unconditionally, but in its vividly written pages I learn that history is more than the mere record of captains, conquerors, and kings; that it is the story of peoples and of "peoplets," that quaint French term which Guizot uses so effectively. It is the pageant of the migrations, struggles, the buildings and the tearings down of those societies of men whose consent is essential in the natural law before the governors can govern.

It was not hard to turn from Guizot to Thomas Jefferson, whose Declaration of Independence told me as a Catholic youth—my rights being again questioned by the remnants of the A.P.A. and the beginnings of the new Ku Klux Klan— that life, liberty, and the pursuit of happiness were guaranteed to all. In our household the political philosophy of Jefferson was held dear. To it the Irish in America had looked for protection and vindication when the Ursuline Convent was burned by the Know-Nothings a half century before. It was that proclamation to the people of far-off lands which led my grandmother's father, Lawrence Eurich, to leave Frankfurt am Main to lumber over the Alleghenies in a prairie schooner, and set up a tent in the newly created capital of Indiana. The magic word "progress," which came so easily to the American tongue in the Nineties, was fondly treasured by my grandmother, but no more so than the traditions of America connected with the third President of the United States. It surprised and shocked me that some of my Protestant playmates sought to trump up a fictitious friction between the Catholic view of the world and Jefferson's outlook. "How could this be," I thought and argued, "when the declaration that governments exist ethically solely by the consent of the governed was first thundered out by the great Jesuits, Cardinal Robert Bellarmine and Francis Suarez?"

I can remember a fervid debate on this topic, when I was fourteen years of age, with a Protestant boy for whom I had considerable respect. I was amazed to learn that he did not know what I was talking about. My astonishment grew when he used the argument that the Catholic Church stood for the divine right of kings, whereas to me, that was the stand of the Protestantizing King James I against which Bellarmine and Suarez wrought so eloquently.

Put on my mettle, I sacked the library for information on the relationship of the Schoolmen's views to the American liberties which were part of my native land. From the *Catholic World* magazine, which came each month to our house, from the English Jesuits' books, the contributions of Cardinal Gibbons and such other sources as I could lay hands on, I formed a rounded-out opinion. From out of the Middle Ages had come the heritage of government by the consent of the governed, the work of a long line of Catholic spokesmen and theologians. Thomas Aquinas and Duns Scotus led the list of those Catholic pioneers in political thought who spoke of the democratic concept long before John Locke had come upon the English scene. Then, at the end of the sixteenth century, other Catholic geniuses had organized these expressions into what could be called the traditional Catholic position on the right of self-government.

There were those who might say that Bellarmine and Suarez had placed political authority in the whole community, as coming from the hands of God, because they saw in that attitude a means to offset the anti-Catholic pretensions and persecutions of Elizabeth's successor. The mighty living fact was, just the same, that it was the first James, as the mouthpiece of opposition to Catholicism, who produced the doctrine of the divine right of kings. The Catholic Church as such, of course I knew, makes no choice between forms of government. But in the heart of America, it brought warmth and strength to my young being to know that the foremost champions of Catholicism had said, in the words of Bellarmine, "It depends on the consent of the people to decide whether Kings or consuls or other magistrates are to be established in authority over them: And if there be legitimate cause, the people can change a kingdom into an aristocracy, or an aristocracy into a democracy, and vice versa as we read was done in Rome."

This search into the origin of the people's rights led to a further understanding: The relationship of the Catholic Church to the so-called social or labor question. One had only to walk down the dusty road from our front door to learn that there was more to be won than free speech, free press, and the other freedoms of our Constitution. The right to life and liberty meant the right to a livelihood, to a decent existence, to associate with one's fellows to gain those ends.

It included—who could say that it did not?—the right to raise a family, to feed and clothe, to educate and lead to worship the children of that family, the foundation of the nation.

Even in those days of "the full dinner pail" and the huzzah through the land for the onward march of factory and foundry, there were laboring people in our very neighborhood who were too poor to live as they should. The headquarters of a considerable number of "international" unions were located in Indianapolis, but in the city itself there was a widespread lack of labor organization. Although in a few moments' walk through the center of the town you could look into the national offices of such old and well-established unions as the International Typographical Union, the United Mine Workers, and the United Brotherhood of Carpenters, the Hoosier capital was also the place from which David M. Parry, the carriage maker, launched the National Association of Manufacturers.

Among Catholics in those days there was mounting talk of the righteousness of labor organizations—an echo of the encyclicals of the thirteenth Leo. During my teens, the understanding grew that the right of association was something that would have to be carried out in life. Many of the Kentuckians, who began to immigrate into the central belt of Indiana, were used—by reason of the lack of labor organization—to break down wage standards previously established. Their own poverty, as they settled in the outskirts of the city far across the Commons from our place, was painfully apparent. When one picked up the *Rerum Novarum* of Pope Leo XIII, which had stirred the world in 1892, these words stood out in answer: "Religion teaches the rich man and the employer that their work people are not their slaves; that they must respect in every man his dignity as a man and as a Christian."

There one also found stated the urgent character of the right to live—that most pressing of the natural rights—and learned from the words of the great pontiff what followed therefrom. "The preservation of life is the bounden duty of each and all, and to fail therein is a crime," says his message on the "Condition of Labor." "It follows that each one has a right to procure what is required in order to live; and the poor can procure this in no other way than by work and wages." Therefore, he argued, the worker's remuneration must be at least "enough to support the wage-earner in reasonable and frugal comfort." From that consideration, too, arises the right and necessity of association to assure that by organized group action the rights to live and to livelihood be attained. Here was brought into the modern world in a pulsing, dynamic way the principles which guided the thought and conduct of the Middle Ages, the just price, the just wage, and their realization through association.

It was a courageous doctrine, for in 1900 the American Federation of Labor had a membership of no more than 1,500,000. Four years later, it was to decline even below that modest figure and was to hover around it for seven additional years. Organization was confined, since the test in the last steel strike at Homestead in 1893, mainly to the skilled crafts. The booming steel, rubber and new born automobile industries were devoid of unionization. So deeply did the words of the *Rerum Novarum* penetrate the consciousness of Catholics that today there are many Catholic labor leaders in America. The Catholic worker, in instance after instance, became the center of organizing activities because he felt deeply the justice in his cause. He understood that he was enacting the drama of social justice in advancing the natural right to association for workingmen.

Nor could Catholics of some education fail to know that early in America's life, the man who had been most instrumental in forming the first Workingmen's Party, Orestes Brownson, was the first outstanding native American thinker to leave the ranks of Protestantism for the Catholic faith. As I thumbed the pages of the *Catholic World*, with its stories of Brownson, my youthful imagination was fired by what he had done. When, on a November morning in 1945, my wife and I came across the slab in the basement Chapel of Sacred Heart Church at Notre Dame, reading, *Hic Jacet Orestes Brownson*, it was like finding an old friend. The knowledge that he, who in the days of Andrew Jackson had urged the rights of the working people and helped to give the Catholic Church a larger place of citizenship in America, had found his last resting place at Notre Dame, made the scene there suddenly warmer and more familiar. It was my father who had first led me to know the former Brook Farmer, because he thought Brownson's spiritual migrations from Presbyterianism via Unitarianism to the Catholic Church were much like his own.

The Catholic workingmen—and specifically the Irish— who had been greeted as "scum" by the *Journal of Commerce* in 1830, and who saw their liberties and their religion challenged by the Know-Nothing movement, were among the vanguard in building the unions in anthracite coal and the nation's railroads. In the record of Catholic life in America, there had blended, then, the rights of the Declaration of Independence, the rights of their Church to function freely in this new land, and the right of association for their daily bread. With this realization and with my mind and heart moved by the words of the papal encyclicals, it is no wonder that in the 1912 files of *The Carpenter*, the official organ of the United Brotherhood of Carpenters and Joiners, can be found fervid arguments from my pen showing that the right to life makes valid the right to organize.

In the Notre Dame library I recently picked up the

October, 1912, issue of that magazine and read again "The Right to Live," written thirty-five years ago by my youthful hand. Its first words were: "There are some rights which all men no doubt do not possess—it is not my purpose to discuss that matter here—but there is one right which unquestionably every man originally has—the right to live. 'Thou shalt not kill' is the first of the Commandments of the Decalogue dealing directly with man's relations with his neighbor. Civil society has rightly and naturally likewise adopted this, protecting in as far as is possible the weak man from the strong."

After more of such argument, the article stated: "And as no man can ordinarily violate this right directly, neither can he do it indirectly. The placing of laborers in insanitary shops and factories, amid poisonous surroundings, which slowly but surely rob them of their existence, then knowingly forcing them to work with carelessly guarded machinery . . . and above all, the paying to them of wages on which they cannot live as men . . . certainly cannot morally be justified. The guarantee which the Constitution of our country has given of the right to 'life, liberty and pursuit of happiness' must be preserved." The article concluded with an emphasis on the dignity of man, which requires that "he must be allowed to live and act and enjoy himself as becomes this dignity—a dignity which shines out greater in one willing to do his share."

From this discussion on the right to live, other contributions in following numbers of *The Carpenter* went on to conclude from this that workingmen had the rights to organize, to strike and to boycott. With some of these thoughts all men of good will may not agree, but they will recognize a serious striving to apply the teachings of the Church and the Schoolmen to the modern world. No one was more aware than the young Hoosier who wrote them that the Church's endorsement of the right to association did not mean approval of everything done in the name of that right.

That was when I was twenty-one years of age and had studied under the Brothers of the Sacred Heart, the Jesuits, and had graduated in law. What these articles stated in an organized form I had already written in part in the years before to the letter column of the *Indianapolis News*. I can remember one of those letters as though it were written yesterday—a reply to the noted and respected Louis Howland, who had derided the Middle Ages because they had so many religious holidays. This, he contended, encouraged idleness. With youthful zeal, I quickly seized on this statement to show that this was one of the good features of the Medieval period and that the nation would be benefited by more leisure for the workers and by shorter hours and stricter observance of holidays.

The use to which I put the words of Leo XIII was duplicated in community after community and in many publications. In fact, studies are being made today—and they should be heartily welcomed—of the effect of the *Rerum Novarum* on American life. The full measure of what took place in this respect could never be estimated, for much of what occurred in obscure little towns or sections of cities will never be unearthed. Some Catholic worker heard the words of the great pontiff in a parish lecture hall, or read them in some local Catholic publication and was made bolder in urging the formation of labor unions. Or a Catholic employer, whose conscience was touched by the papal declarations, more willingly agreed to collective bargaining. Then there were those pioneers in American social legislation, like Monsignor John A. Ryan, who made the issue of the minimum wage and other protective laws understood throughout the nation. Father Ryan's writings, I know, affected me deeply.

There was no workmen's compensation legislation in 1900—or in 1910, for that matter. Both worker and employer were at the mercy of "employer's liability," that archaic survival of the common law. Responsibility for the maiming of workers at machines or in the mines could be established only by proving undue negligence on the part of the employer. Since this was left to the hazards of the law and the whims of judges and juries, it resulted in chaos and injustice. It was only after industrial accidents were made a definite part of the risks and responsibilities of industry—through the Workmen's Compensation Act—that some just measure of protection was afforded those who lost limbs or lives at their work. It was only in 1911 that the first of these laws was adopted in our country—or at least adopted and declared constitutional. The pioneering honors in this field went to California, New Jersey, Washington and Wisconsin—in that these were the states which adopted these acts in 1911 and got them to stick as constitutional. Not the least of the pressures that speeded their adoption was Catholic backing based on the education and agitation in Catholic journals and communities inspired by "The Condition of Labor." The labors of the Central Bureau of the Catholic Central Verein in behalf of this legislation in the Middle Western states is an epic action in itself that deserves recording.

It was this tradition of Catholic interest in the condition of labor which led me, in high-school years, to attend regularly the sessions of the United Mine Workers of America. From time to time, the coal diggers streamed into Indianapolis for the conventions which mapped out the course of their growing union. I shall never forget the eagerness with which I would rush from school at old St. John's in downtown Indianapolis, to see and hear the delegates debate the fate of the men who went into the pits to dig the black diamonds.

They met always in aging Tomlinson Hall, where the city

market was also located. In the gallery of that drab, barnlike structure—so I recall it—the discussions of "industrial democracy" raged. I continued to attend them as long as I lived in Indianapolis, and in later years was there again to cover the conventions.

In Tomlinson Hall, as the years went by, I saw the distinguished-looking John Mitchell in the chair, the inconsequential Tom Lewis, the efficient-appearing John White, the redheaded (and so his opponents said) the erratic Frank Hayes, whom "some of the boys" thought was a dead ringer for Albert J. Beveridge. The conventions were often tumultuous, filled with charges and countercharges, with homely humor and thundering threats. Then came the bushy-browed man from nowhere, John L. Lewis, to take the helm, and the miners met their master. The long drama of the coal diggers' meetings—their Congresses of Labor—as Lewis grandiloquently acclaimed them, constituted for me a profound education in the American workers' lives, hopes and aspirations. But the driving force behind my study, greater even than any inherent curiosity, was the social doctrine of the Catholic Church.

In the moving panorama of these labor parliaments there was one thing to be noted. As time went on, the national origins of the delegates tended to shift to a considerable extent. In the earlier gatherings, the British, Scotch, Welsh and Irish made up the majority of the delegates. Then, the number of Negroes, Slavs and Italians grew. Still later, the second and third generations of all these national streams blended into a melting pot cross section of "Americans all."

This change in the composition of the working population occurred, too, to some extent in the central belt of Indiana. The Slavs, Magyars and Italians were not nearly so numerous in that area as the kinsfolk of Abraham Lincoln from the hills of Kentucky and Tennessee. But from anyone with a growing interest in Catholic social views, both the newcomer from southeastern Europe and the Negro could not fail to receive warm and sympathetic attention. Among those strange-appearing people who dug the sewer through our back yard, and who were contemptuously called by im-provised names, such as John Mike, Nick Steve, and the like, there were many Catholics. The endeavor to get shorter hours at the packing plant in Indianapolis where many of them worked, and in the steel mills at Gary a few. hundred miles to the north, and throughout the nation's iron and steel industries, was a Catholic endeavor. Its primary aim was to assure men and women that they would have the freedom from the seven-day week and overburdening toil that would enable them to practice their religion and worship God. Without wishing to recall too many painful episodes of the past, it was just this issue which Bishop Joseph Busch, of Lead, South Dakota, sought to bring to a head in the copper-mining industry. His stand forcibly brought home to me the interrelation between the protection of labor and the preservation of religion in America. And the campaign to wipe out the slums, particularly for the strangers within our gates from Europe, further strengthened my convictions. For the safeguarding of family life was put to a severe test in crowded, insanitary and vermin-infested hovels.

Although the European immigrant was not so conspicuous in central Indiana, the same could not be said of the Negro. When the underground railroad was established, Indianapolis lay directly in its path. Many Negro slaves escaped from border states to find refuge there. Later, the newly freed colored men streamed into Indianapolis, as it was one of the first Northern cities of any size on their trek away from the South. In Public School 34, the fact that there was a Negro question first came sharply into my childish thoughts. Because of my Catholic background, and what my father had told me of the Negro people, I could see no essential difference between my white and colored schoolmates. It was as startling as a dash of cold water in my face when some of the white pupils let me know that I was "queer," because of this attitude. How could I think otherwise when Christian doctrine told me of the Church Universal, with St. Benedict the Moor honored on its altars as well as men and women of all other races? How could my seven-year-old mind accept any other view when the dignity of every human soul before God was taught in the very definition of the word "Catholic"?

How could it be otherwise, finally, when one of my father's close associates at work was John, the mulatto porter at the bank? When I would wait in the bank until my father was ready to bring me home, there was nothing more attractive than the last hour behind the closed doors of that institution. It was then that John and my father, at that time the chief paying teller, put the money away in the vaults. And there was something touching, which even I grasped then, in the way the two men enjoyed those moments in the discussion of literature, music and art, which their daily pursuits denied them. As we went home together, my father frequently recalled that John was a college graduate, that he was a man of culture and that had he not been a Negro he would be in an entirely different position in life. The sin of segregation was thus marked, so early in my recollections, as something repulsive to a Catholic from the very fundamentals of his beliefs.

Attendance at only one convention of the United Mine Workers in those days would have been sufficient reminder that there was a Socialist movement in America. For years there was a strong Socialist representation among the delegates. Adolph Germer was one of the followers of Marx who was regularly elected to American Federation of Labor conventions for the U.M.W. I was struck by his conspicuous position in the delegation led by Mitchell to the Philadelphia A. F. of L. meeting in 1913, which I attended as a delegate. Resolutions pledging the coal diggers to a class political party of labor in the Socialist sense and to "a co-operative society" were a frequent occurrence. Oratory which hailed the coming "common ownership of the means of production and distribution" rang out in many such assemblies.

A native Hoosier had many more reminders of the existence of the Socialist party. Ours was the state of Eugene Victor Debs, as his disciples averred because of his birthplace in Terre Haute. It was not unusual to run into a "Debs Socialist," but except for the fact that he called himself a Marxist on occasions, it was quite difficult to tell him from a Brvan Populist. But every Socialist, whether he was a Debs man or a more orthodox follower of Victor Berger or a radical supporter of Bill Haywood, chanted "class struggle" and "state ownership." That was something which had to be answered with a yes or no.

There were those who said that this doctrine was impossible and would be unworkable. From the start it did not appeal to me. The ups and downs of history caution us that many things are workable in the sense that they can be established. The great query is: Will they tend to benefit mankind? It did not seem to me that Socialism as it was proposed could do this. Almost inevitably its imposition would involve mankind in chains. "The Servile State" predictions of Hilaire Belloc seemed to have a sound foundation. No matter how certain extremists of the Daniel DeLeon type of Marxist might criticize "bourgeois freedom," there was much good in the clash that could take place in the press, in the freedom I had to go to Mass, even though the majority of my fellow citizens did not as yet do so, and in the ability to assemble in order to present grievances. The almighty State, which under Socialism would be both buyer and seller, sole employer and sole master of the people's fate, was something that man had been striving to get away from for centuries. So far, only on a small portion of the earth was it acknowledged that men had the rights which went with the term "self-government."

This tyranny of the State was linked in the Socialist slogans and objectives with an inherent enmity to religion. Within the philosophy of Socialism was the permanent pledge to obliterate all worship of a Supreme Being. Materialism was as much a foundation stone of Marxist doctrines as collectivism. The "why" of this puzzled me for a time, but eventually it made itself clear. There are several "whys," and one of them is that the almighty State which Socialism would create cannot brook the existence of God or any higher moral authority. No matter in what period statism imposes itself on mankind, such is its fruit. In the case of the Roman Empire, it produced a God-Emperor. Under Louis XIV, where it could not go so far because of the profound Catholicism of France, it sought to subvert the universal Church with Gallicanism. Socialism is compelled to impose a discipline of blood and iron, which must of its very nature do away with any rival morality in the person of the Divine.

But Socialism's atheistic view arises, too, from the "liberalism" of which it is the heir and at the same time the proposed executioner. That extreme individualism which permitted children of seven years of age to work in the mines of England and for so long made a merit of exploiting the workers, did so because it put Mammon in the place of God. Socialism accepts the same view of life, but puts its trust in the Moloch of the all-powerful State. The power of the Socialist Servile State rested on its claim to sole proprietorship and its abolition of private property and, inevitably, of all private choice. The more I thought of it, the more convinced I became that the right of private property was one of the natural rights of man, and that, under control, it was conducive to the general welfare. In the words of Leo XIII: "The right to possess private property is from nature, not from man; and the State has only the right to regulate its use in the interest of the common good, but by no means to abolish it altogether."

Such materialism as Socialism taught was ruled out of bounds by my faith and reason. The existence of God was proved by the necessity of a first cause, the hand of providence in nature and its laws, and the striving of the world for a perfection which it always failed to attain. The song of Daniel, "All ye works of the Lord, Praise Ye the Lord, Bless the Lord," was also to me an argument for the necessity of the Lord, their Creator. As Chateaubriand had said in his *Genius of Christianity*, a book which I soon purchased for my personal library: "There is a God. The plants of the valley and the cedars of the mountain bless His name; the insects hum His praise; the elephant salutes Him with the rising day; the bird glorifies Him among the foliage; the lightning bespeaks His power; and the ocean declares His immensity."

Equally strong was my conviction that God's work for the redemption of man—the urgency for which was evident all around me—was carried forward by Christ the crucified and the visible Church He had established. One could look back to the days of the Apostles to witness the beginning of the Church's labors from the See of Rome. There was a peculiar sense of joy in knowing that at the turn of the first century, the Church was already hailed as "Catholic," by St. Ignatius, Bishop of Antioch. There was a warm satisfaction in the fact that an unbeliever such as Walter Pater could acknowledge the apostolic origins of the Mass, and praise its beauty. It was good to remember, in confirmation of what that great English stylist wrote in *Marius, the Epicurean*, that as early as the year 198 A.D. Justin Martyr described this service of sacrifice in the general form in which it has been preserved for more than nineteen hundred years. The very words of transubstantiation which I heard with bowed head in the early morning at St. Patrick's were the words uttered in the catacombs.

This faith had inspired the fealty of such noble personalities as St. Thomas More—who had aroused the wonder of Macaulay a century later. That More, a Lord Chancellor of England, the author of *Utopia*, and a genius, could give up his life rather than deny the presence of Christ in the Blessed Sacrament was more than the British essayist could fathom. A test of that kind, he agreed, pointed to faith extraordinary. The communion of saints, in the long line of men and women who had lived and died that God might receive thanksgiving and praise, mankind peace and love, was the sign of the holiness of the Catholic Church, that stood out as the world's hope. The more books I read with testimony of this character on the grandeur of the Church, the more I thirsted to make such wonders known to other men.

Such convictions spurred me to become part of the Lay Aspostolate, that zealous group of American laymen who through pen and platform strive to defend and advance the Church, in order the better to serve America. The simple slogan, *"Pro Deo, Pro Patria,"* gave expression to the guiding thoughts and inspiration for such labors. In August, 1913, I had the privilege to serve as special correspondent for the *Indianapolis News* to the convention of the American Federation of Catholic Societies at Milwaukee and there heard and reported the stirring address by majestic, white-haired Archbishop John Ireland of St. Paul, on "Catholicism and Americanism." Replying directly to those who sought to find discord between the Catholic's creed and his country's, the great prelate said: "Those who so speak misunderstand either my creed or my country; they belie either the one or the other." And then, proceeding to show the supernational as well as supernatural character of the Church, the Archbishop declared: "And this, the beauty, this, the grandeur of the Catholic Church—that it is Catholic, as the eternal God is Catholic, as the salvation given by Jesus Christ is Catholic. Narrowness, provincialism in religion, in faith and morals, on the first face of things, is a perversion of God's eternal law, and of the revelation given to men, nineteen hundred years ago. The days of tribal religions are past; they must not be revived in America." This theme accorded with all my thoughts and was the *raison d'être* of the activities on which I was launched.

I knew that during the recent past, and particularly throughout the nineteenth century, more and more laymen had begun to speak out on behalf of the Church's claims to the consciences of men. From the professor's chair, the journalist's sanctum and the orator's rostrum, they had taken up intellectual sword and lance in the name of Catholicism. Conspicuous among them was Frederick Ozanam, professor at the Sorbonne and founder of the St. Vincent de Paul Society. One hundred years ago, in the late 1840s, his Christian plea for an equitable solution of the social question was heard along with that of Bishop Von Kettler of Mainz. What he, and others like him showed, was that well-equipped Catholic laymen, understanding history and their nation, could perform a special duty to their age by combating the abuses of extreme individualism and the threatened slavery of collectivism. If this could be done in Paris or in Dublin, I reasoned, why not in Indiana?

To any such ambition there was plenty of discouragement in the Hoosier scene, as elsewhere in the nation in the Nineties and the early 1900s. Secularism was creating havoc with the home, and that was accompanied by a growing neurosis of fear and boredom among the people. There were boys and girls in the public schools—friends of mine in our neighborhood—who said, in unguarded moments, that their parents didn't think living was worth while. New hope had to be given them and the proclamation of the blessings of the Sacraments would help many a fainting soul. Here was work for a lay apostolate. Then, there were those who had been poisoned by the *Menace* and like publications, caricaturing and assailing the Church and denouncing all religion. They had to be combatted, and so it was but natural that in a few years after my departure from Indianapolis for St. Louis, that should become no small part of my aims and activities. The more the Catholic Church grew in the fertile soil of America—as I was sure it would grow—the greater would be the need for defense against such vile misrepresentation.

To spread enlightenment about the Church was the first responsibility of the sincere and patriotic Catholic; that seemed clear even then, in the early 1900s. In a negative way, this would hinder or halt the rise of another A.P.A. or Know-Nothing movement which had spread persecution through this republic. That anti-Catholic raging such as the *Menace* could be inspired in our country, pledged to the right of religious worship, was intolerable. America's salvation lay in the spread of the Catholic worship and the Catholic world view. Our country needed to heed the proclamations of the Popes on divorce and the labor question and the studies of the Schoolmen.

On all sides, too, we heard the word "progress." Editors and educators vied in uttering it. My grandmother, Julia Budenz, made up a whole new world ahead of us, under its banner, in which men would fly in the air and follow Jules Verne under the sea, in addition to their adventures in the oncoming horseless carriage. Our family physician, by whom my parents swore, aged veteran of the Civil War, made a brave try at bootlegging Herbert Spencer, the "prophet of progress," to me when I went to his office for vaccination. "You are a smart boy and should know what Spencer said. I don't know what your father would think of that," he added by way of precaution, "but you'll find that science is the basis of life." Well meant as this counsel was, there was a subversion of the truth in it that I vaguely sensed at the time, and that I know and recognize today, fully forty years later.

All this talk of progress, I came to learn even then, was against the synthesis of true progress for mankind. The advance of intellectual acumen which comes from science has to march hand in hand with a greater spiritualization of the people. With science as "the basis of life," the resultant materialism would spell "progress" only in terms of the progressive wiping out of mankind through more and more earth-shaking missiles of destruction. (We did not know of the horrors of Hiroshima then but that prospect was envisaged in this thought.) Under such materialism, in the name of winning "common wealth," Commonweal would be obliterated. The very battle cry "freedom" would be perverted to bring about the absolutism of the communistic state, in which man would be denied the use of his intellectual powers, refused a free press, cut off from free worship, and prohibited freedom of association.

The key to the world's progress, as Professor C. S. Devas of Stoneyhurst in England reminded my youthful mind, lay in the magnificent *Via Media* under which the wisdom of the Church restrained the extremes of every age and the alleged "advances" by men. The future of our country, and the future of humanity, rested on the harmony of science and religion—such a harmony as only the Catholic Church could create.

There were many incidents, of course, which intruded themselves—sometimes pleasantly, sometimes challengingly—into such considerations and conclusions. When I was twelve years old, one day around noon I ran into James Whitcomb Riley, the Hoosier poet, while he was buying an early edition of the *Indianapolis News*. With an unusual boldness I went up to him and gaspingly introduced myself. Quickly he put me at ease, patting me on the head as "Mamie Sullivan's son." My mother had often told me how he had stood back of the stove at L. S. Ayres store—now the great department store in central Indianapolis—and jested with her on "the beauty of her eyes" as she waited on counter there. He repeated that phrase to me, gallantly.

Then, in my public-school days, the sedate, black-dressed Miss Ellen Skillen had rubbed my zeal the wrong way by reciting the Lord's Prayer every morning in the King James version. But she had spurred me on to read widely, had skipped me through several grades and had taught a doctrine of "tolerance" concerning my religion—a doctrine which to me represented America.

Again, every New Year's Day my father would conduct his sons—stiffly dressed up—on "calls" upon several old friends. One of these, the most popular, was "Yawkob" Lizius, a well-known architect who had married my father's cousin. He was a merry-faced and merry-voiced German from the Rhineland, who had all sorts of Christmas cookies for us, baked by his own hand. He was a freethinker, to my childish amazement, and his brother was the Theodore Lizius who in earlier days had edited the German anarchist paper in Indianapolis which had preached such violent doctrines. This latter fact I was to learn by a sort of "underground" information channel such as youth always has at its disposal.

My father's mother—who lived until my tenth year—also brought before my imagination a strange heritage from her Lutheran father and her merry Catholic mother. Every evening I read the daily papers to her, after I had learned to do so, and she in turn would present her own versions of history, including laudation for the French Revolution and the French nation. She recounted, too, at certain infrequent moments the story of her husband, Henry Joseph Budenz's, coming to America from Hesse-Cassel during the Revolution of 1848 and how the German tailors had been active in that attempted upheaval. But when I had listened to all these conjectures and had mulled over all these incidents I builded still more strongly on my Catholic foundations, since to my mind they created the synthesis of the best from all these conflicting views.

My grandmother now lies buried in beautiful Crown Hill Cemetery in Indianapolis alongside her pioneering parents a stone's throw away from the novelist Booth Tarkington. My father, her son, is interred across the city in Holy Cross Cemetery, testimony to his Catholic faith. Miss Skillen's name is engraved in stone over the school which is now Public School Number 34. They each made their contribution to my early development, and all they said led inevitably to the warm acceptance of the Catholic viewpoint which colored my youthful days.

For the salvation of nations, I was convinced, no less than for the salvation of each individual soul a great return to the Catholic tradition was necessary. The more extensive and enthusiastic the movement to the faith of our fathers, the better grounded would America be for the expansion which we could feel was to take place in the several decades before us. The year 1900 opened with a burst of optimism in the material developments promised by the machine; in that expectation there was concealed a dread lest this good fortune lead to such tragic letdown as was then, unjustly of course, associated with the name of Grover Cleveland.

Along with such high hopes there was also an uneasy

recognition by many that there was no such equitable distribution of our material well-being as the ethical counsels of Leo had deemed essential. This was the time when *How the Other Half Lives* and *The Stranger at Our Gates* were being read; these were the years when muckraking was giving way to a more serious and studious indictment of some of the gaps in American social justice. We of a rising generation were being influenced by the "Pittsburgh Survey," that unique bird's-eye view of the heart of the steel industry. Whenever, after examining its books, I passed through that area of skies flaming from the blast furnaces and the endless smoke, I recalled the urgency for unionization. But there was no gesture toward Socialism in my thoughts; there was, rather, a burning belief in the promise of the Catholic doctrine of just relationships in the labor field, based on the rights of private property and of a just wage to the workingman.

This, then, was the answer: the Church, the strengthening of American liberties, and the advance of social justice—including the organization of the working people. Such was the objective of the American patriot, laboring in the Lay Apostolate. It warranted the sympathy and support of the seers and saints of the twentieth century. It could arouse the zeal of many much less favored by Divine grace, those who had the zeal of the crusader to apply to humbler zones.

One could not be content that there were but eighteen million Catholics in our United States in 1912. High on the shelves of my father's library the blue-bound books of the Oxford Tracts told everyone who glanced at them that men of great intellect and good will could be won to the cause of the Cross. The outpourings of John Henry Newman and his allies welled up like new springs out of the soil of modern times, reasserting the holiness of the Church led by the Roman See. Health in our national life required something more, too, than the small percentages of organization that existed among the workers. The American Federation of Catholic Societies, which rose to a membership of many millions in those days, agreed that Christian principles eagerly demanded a growth in the union ranks. And the National Catholic Welfare Conference, which succeeded the Federation, took a similar and even stronger view. The subsequent declaration of the Bishops of the United States held forth the grave necessity for social legislation and coupled it with the recognition of the value of workers' association. These attitudes had a profound and favorable effect on labor organization's advance.

It seemed to me that the concord of Catholic views on political life and our American liberties was also possible to bring forward successfully before our fellow citizens. My native state had erected a high-towering monument in the center of its capital city to those who had died in the good cause of freedom. Well would it be if we could erect a living memorial to those who had devotion to Catholicism and love for liberty. There had been many such, and Indiana had furnished her quota to this galaxy of gallantry and courage. Did we not cherish the memory of Father Gibault, the patriot priest of the Northwest who helped save the prairie country for the Republic by his aid to the Lewis and Clark expedition? Were we not alternately stirred and rendered spellbound by the account of Father William Corby of the Holy Cross order at Notre Dame, who gave fire and fury to the Irish regiment that had saved the day at Gettysburg? What these heroes of holiness had done for their country could be repeated in a new way in this new day. Every time I crossed the circle around the Soldiers' and Sailors' Monument, I thought these thoughts and dreamed these dreams.

Such were the drives which led me to become the national

organizer of the Catholic Young Men's Institute, while still studying law, traveling from St. Paul to Savannah. The fervid addresses which I then made in behalf of the alliance of Catholicism, Americanism, and the right of association won me the distinction of being asked to act as editor of *The Carpenter*, the official organ of the United Brotherhood of Carpenters and Joiners, and at that time the largest organization in the American Federation of Labor. Into my office there, on the second floor of the Carpenters' Building, came Samuel Gompers on at least three occasions, with his inevitable cigar and his oracular conversation. Labor was then markedly on the defensive, and the discussions with Gompers impressed upon me the cold reality that "to agitate, educate and organize"—terms which he always used—would not be easy. The extension of the Catholic viewpoint into the camps of both employers and employed was beyond any doubt what America required. With that in mind, the next year I went to St. Louis to be associated with the Central Bureau of the Catholic Central Verein, that agency of the German-American Catholic Societies which had performed such distinguished service for the Catholic viewpoint and social legislation.

That was 1913, the last year of the reign of the tenth Pius, the humble Giuseppe Sarto. This man of lowly origin and great zeal had been instrumental in giving to our Catholic generation a new spiritual source of strength. In my twelfth year, he had become Pope, even though his famous two-way ticket was in his hand. That same year I received my First Communion, and the two events are coupled in the cherished remembrance that Pius X was to become known as the Pope of the Blessed Sacrament. All Catholics are aware that, among the many Church reforms to which he lent his name and authority was the renewed practice of early and frequent communion, which had been the custom in the catacombs. To be worthy of receiving the Holy Eucharist frequently had been the yearning of hundreds of young men and women, lay persons as well as candidates for the convent and priesthood. The gift of Pius X to them was to have a profound effect in stimulating Catholic zeal; it was to influence deeply a Communist editor more than three decades afterward.

But the young man of twenty-two who bade farewell to the stream that ran through his father's place, to the luscious grape arbors, to the huge willow trees and the precious library—as he left for St. Louis—knew nothing of thirty years hence. He was intent on the work of his apostolate; on forwarding the cause of social justice and the Church of which Pius was the head.

TWO

Birthright Lost

THREE BLOCKS back from the water front of the sluggish, muddy Mississippi, stand the old cathedral and the old courthouse in St. Louis. The cathedral under the patronage of the French king, whose saintly name the city bears, became a testimonial to the pioneering Catholic missionaries, who followed the footsteps of Marquette. The courthouse achieved a degree of fame in being the scene of the slave sale in the American Winston Churchill's novel *The Crisis*.

In that quaint neighborhood were to be found the Central Bureau of the Catholic Central Verein, the headquarters of the publishing house of B. Herder; the office of the noted Catholic intellectual, Arthur Preuss; and the editorial offices of the German-American daily paper *Amerika*. It was a center of Catholic cultural activity, directed by the organized German Catholics in this country.

Within the shadow of the courthouse, nestled several exceptionally fascinating secondhand bookstores. It was high adventure to pass the noon hour there, selecting volume after volume for some vaguely planned future purchase which seldom came off. But upon occasion, unable to contain the desire any longer, one would get a book quickly and be off lest the temptation to buy another became too great. I can remember the high spirits with which I bore off to my room in South St. Louis a copy of Alan Pinkerton's alleged account of the unearthing and undoing of the Molly Maguires. It was a rare find and F. P. Kenkel, director of the Central Bureau, and I had discovered it at the same time, but he graciously permitted it to become my trophy.

I have met few men so widely equipped in literature, history, and the arts as Kenkel. He was a walking encyclopedia of European culture, American history and Catholic philosophy. He was representative of the rich contribution which so many of German birth or ancestry have made to Catholic thought. Under his direction, we at the Central Bureau were laying the foundations for nation-wide Catholic action on the social question.

In this congenial atmosphere, pamphlets, studies and articles poured off the press—rebuffing those who poisoned the waters against the Church and upholding a Christian view of labor legislation. One of the popular tracts thus co-operatively edited was "The Slime of the Serpent," which forcefully refuted the falsehoods promulgated by the *Menace* about the Catholic priesthood. It established the true zeal and devotion of the overwhelming majority of the priesthood through the testimony of such non-Catholic authorities as Alexander Humboldt, the German naturalist and traveler; George Borrow, the Protestant author and agent of the Bible Society; and Robert Louis Stevenson, who wrote the fiery apologia for Father Damien. This pamphlet received wide distribution and, at the time, did much in winning the battle against bigotry.

In the field of labor-management relationships, one of the first pieces of research in the use of strong-arm men and labor spies entitled "The Employer's Tactics in the Industrial Struggle," was issued under my name. It was an extensive résumé of what actually occurred on the industrial battlefield, and it aroused far-flung interest. Its various installments were even reprinted by the *Socialist Call*, the New York daily newspaper, up to the final section which

combined the sharp condemnation of the extreme individualism of economic liberalism with a condemnation of
collectivism. This the *Call* could neither appreciate nor print.

We extended, too, the campaigns already begun for more
adequate workmen's compensation laws. As a representative
of the Central Bureau, I prepared some liberalizing amendments to the Missouri and Illinois statutes on compensation
which became part of these laws. The pride of creation is
great in every man, and there was more than satisfaction in
examining the newly printed statutes and being able to say,
"This is my handiwork." There was great pleasure in the
realization that the several trips to Springfield and Jefferson
City and the addresses before the legislative committees
had not been in vain.

It seems another age, indeed, when one had to struggle
to assure the passage of workable workmen's compensation
laws. Perhaps it was no more strange than that the scene to
which I had been born was without automobiles, airplanes
and radios, and to which even the promise of the submarine
would have been incredible. The expanding factory system,
by creating more laborers, was making the word "labor"
loom larger in American life. That seemed to confirm the idea
that ethical counsels to economic activity, such as produced
labor legislation, were highly essential. Was it not only the
year before that I had listened with deep attention to a
speech by one Daniel Tobin of Boston before an Indiana
legislative committee for compensation action? The progress
of protection afforded to the workers by our statutes is
scarcely greater than the tremendous growth of the labor
movement out of the weak federation the stocky, sandy-
haired Tobin then represented. At the same time, the Team-
sters' Union, of which he had been elected president in 1911,
was composed of only 90,000 men, whereas in 1946 it numbered nearly 600,000.

Representing the Catholic Societies at civic functions, we of the Central Bureau reached out still further. The Catholics did not remain aloof or work alone for moral principles. Whenever possible, we joined hands with progressive and Protestant groups in forwarding many phases of community welfare. In St. Louis alone, such an attitude brought about Catholic association for social welfare with the League of Women Voters, under the presidency of Mrs. George Gellhorn, with the Federal Council of Churches, in which Dr. W. C. Bittner, the well-known Baptist minister, was a leading figure, and with the local Council of Social Agencies, in which Roger N. Baldwin, then secretary of the St. Louis Civic League, was so prominent. Thus began a new phase in the exercise of Catholic social responsibility—not in the isolation of an ivory tower, but in co-operation with all good-will groups in the community.

If anyone were to inquire what inspired the Central Bureau, the reply could readily be made: "Christian Solidarism." That was the theme most frequently discussed in the pages of its organ, *Central Blatt and Social Justice.* It was the organized expression of the papal encyclical on the "Condition of Labor," as brought forward particularly by the Jesuit Fathers, Heinrich Pesch and Victor Catrein. Though the Pope had nowhere employed this term, "Solidarism," it was adopted as the best formulation of the proposals he had outlined. It contemplated the exercise of state power; but in a discreet and restrained manner. Its goal was a united society, to be established not through a totalitarian state but through the invigoration of all associations within the commonwealth, working together.

Solidarism looked upon itself as the middle road, designating the extreme individualistic spirit as "the root of all evil" and rejecting statism as a menace to the very class it claimed to protect. Profit sharing, if accompanied by union organization, was considered one co-operative bond that could help restore a proper social balance and order. This aim to curb rampant individualism and to control statism by stressing co-operative relationships between labor and capital would, its advocates contended, give renewed life to the promises of the Declaration of Independence and the purposes of the Constitution.

That American ingenuity and energy could rise to new heights of popular welfare, if it avoided extremes, was, it seemed, foretold by the historical monuments around St. Louis. The saga of the colonies and the Republic was written in the Indian mounds across the Mississippi, in the ruins of the Mormons' migration in near-by Nauvoo, in the memorial shaft to the Abolitionist, Lovejoy, overlooking the river at Alton, and the records of how St. Louis was saved for the Union by the Germans. The Merchants' Exchange, still the "trading post" for the dealers in fur though the hunting fields had moved far away, was a reminder of the French *voyageurs'* conquest of the Mississippi-Missouri country—and what a long, long time had passed since then.

In the midst of my St. Louis activities, I suddenly left the Catholic ranks. Rather, by an act of disobedience I was thrust out of the Catholic community.

After all the justified indictments I had penned against divorce and the evils it caused, I presumed to marry— civilly—a divorced woman. This antisocial deed was one more homage to the anarchy in marital relations which was furthering moral chaos in America.

There has been some gracious effort to explain away my act, to give some partial excuse for it on the ground that I was not fully informed of what was involved. This is a kind gesture, dictated by Christian charity. It is not deserved. As an educated Catholic, I understood that marriage under these circumstances was a negation of marriage in the

eyes of the Church. I was fully aware of what the fragmenta-
tion of the family meant.

Not long before, I had gone over the whole subject with
my good friend back home, Father Raymond R. Noll—now
Monsignor Noll, pastor of the Cathedral in Indianapolis—
our discussion had arisen over a novel by Frank Spearman, a
convert to Catholicism. *Robert Kimberly* as this piece of
fiction was titled, was no masterpiece of craftsmanship, but
it did contain an idea of some significance. Briefly put, it
dealt with the difficulties of a non-Catholic man of substance
who had fallen in love with a married Catholic woman who
was abused by her husband. In the conclusion, the non-
Catholic admitted the correctness of the Church's stand on
divorce, embraced Catholicism and became a ministrant at a
leper colony in the South Seas. Thus, the tale tended to
perpetuate the absurd illusion that men and women rush into
Catholic service because of some rebuff or failure in romance.
But it did reinforce, in a popular way, the indictments of
the evil of divorce.

Perhaps here, since Father Noll was mentioned, he should
be referred to in another respect. The incident is in itself of
small consequence, but it is valuable as an example of the
Catholic view as expressed in public life. At this moment,
when such loud libels are uttered about the political influence
of the Church in America, this incident is worth recalling,
because I have seen it duplicated a thousand times in one way
or another. When I was nineteen, an Indiana Congressman
requested that I become his secretary and at the same time
go to Georgetown University to complete my law schooling.
Father Noll and I talked it over and we agreed that I should
tell the gentleman that I could not be beholden to the political machine he represented. It took me a full hour before
the interview to screw up my courage to say it, but I finally
did so. The officeholder was gracious, as most politicians are,

expressed his understanding of my position and asked me to give his best wishes to my "good father." Please note that the priest in this case could have curried favor politically by aiding in my journey to Washington and in soft-soaping the public official, had he followed the course which some of the political caricatures of Catholicism indicate.

My revolt against the wisdom of the Church had flowed not only from the weakness of my heart, but also from a rising impatience with the slowness of reform. I had made several surveys of housing in the United States, and the slum conditions under which human beings were obliged to live in many sections of our rich country offended my sense of justice. The low degree of labor organization was another grievance. When I think of the injustices to which I finally consented in the name of justice— the scattering of hundreds of thousands of innocent human beings across the face of Europe under the lash of the Red Army—I have reason to repent this rashness by recounting such thoughts as Cardinal Newman's on "The Patient Church" in his poem of that name. But that impatience with the progress of reform, plus indignation at the approach of World War I to which I was bitterly opposed, brought about an accumulation of anger that obscured my vision. This furnished an alibi, so I thought, for a break with the Church.

Do you recall the case of Felix, the Roman governor, who came to St. Paul, eager to believe? When the Apostle told him of the Christian life he must lead, Felix was alarmed and said: "For this time, go thy way; but when I have a convenient time I will send for thee." This drama in the Acts of the Apostles occurred for only one reason: Felix had enticed his wife, Drusilla, away from her lawful husband and could not give up the life he was leading. Those who break with the Church do so in passion but seek to rationalize their departure as "intellectual" and the fruit of reason.

My revolt, for instance, was accompanied by a thought-less disturbance over the condemnation by Pius X of *le Sillon*, "the furrow," the social movement in France. Marc Sangnier, the founder of the movement, made his immediate submission to the ruling of Rome and thereby continued his good work. He was one of the forerunners of Catholic Action on the one hand and among the first of the Catholic stream into the newly formed M.R.P.—the Popular Republican Movement— on the other. The organization of young Catholic intellectuals under the symbol of the furrow was part of that ferment in many lands which worked toward the establishment of something like Guild Socialism. I chose to call it Catholic syndicalism–a very maladroit expression. The aim of many of these groups and discussions was the restoration to the worker of the tools which had been his in medieval times. When it came to a consideration of how the tools were to be restored, these groups inclined too much toward the general-strike methods of the Syndicalists, though rejecting their materialistic philosophy.

In those days we read with much interest, though with some sharp criticism, the *International Socialist Review*, which was graphically attractive and which largely expressed the Bill Haywood, I.W.W., viewpoint. Although a little later I was to write an extensive article for the magazine section of the St. Louis *Post-Dispatch* criticizing the Syndicalists, at the time of my exile from the Church I inclined more and more in their direction. Could I have foreseen how in the future this exaggerated antistate attitude which led me to Syndicalism would bring me along the road to Communism, the last word in the deification of the State, the irony of the political circuit would have been overwhelming. That very demonstration of the way in which extremes meet was a positive confirmation of the Church's conclusions.

However, it cannot be denied that the influence of the

Guild Socialists—who were not out and out Syndicalists, but who sought to modify the extreme state worship of the orthodox Socialist movement—was considerable. In some measure the writings of A. R. Orage and G. D. H. Cole, at his youthful best, prevented the British Labor party from becoming a strictly Marxist political agency. To the extent that I spread the Guild Socialist idea in America—and I read their publications avidly as they came from across the seas—I helped to spread sane ideas in the "progressive" labor movement.

Since these particular radical theories no longer redden the political skies, it would be well to redefine them briefly. "Syndicalism" sought to abolish the wage system and to establish common ownership—not through the state apparatus but through revolutionary industrial unions. The general strike was the means by which it fervidly expected to shatter the state machine and put the workers in control of the nation. It scorned the reliance on the state which characterized the Socialists' beliefs.

There were many variations of Syndicalism, and "Guild Socialism" may be regarded, in part, as one of them. It aimed to set up workers' control through strong unions, but did not reject the State entirely. It can be readily understood that anyone inbued with the Catholic opposition to Statism would turn first to Syndicalism and to Guild Socialism, if he turned "radical."

Such was my course. When the Shop-Stewards' movement in England at the close of World War I seemed about to sweep that country, through the impetus of Guild Socialism, I rejoiced. The slogan of "workers' control," taken from the Guild Socialists, was heard all over the British Isles, and we who held similar views here were enthusiastic. Even after the uproar subsided, we held to our convictions. That was one reason why I never joined the Socialist party, though I often worked with Socialists for some immediate ends.

Even as the clouds of the oncoming World War I were gathering, some of the bastions that had to be strengthened in the American republic were laid bare by my labors in a new post. This was the secretaryship of the Civic League, an organization for municipal reform. In it I succeeded Roger Baldwin, who had left for the East to found the American Civil Liberties Union. When I took up my new duties, the first thing I recognized was that the status of the utilities, and particularly the transportation system, was a key to the city's political life. So I looked up the franchise of the Street Railway Company, but found that it still had twenty years to run. This indicated that any change in the franchise, which I knew to be antiquated and inadequate, would be a matter for the dim distant future. To my surprise, two days later, an attorney for minority stockholders appeared in my office with the startling information that the franchise was under a cloud and that the company was about to make a big move for a new charter, continuing on a watered stock basis. Immediately, I persuaded the Civic League to create a special committee on this subject composed of five eminent former city councilors. Among these distinguished lawyers were Charles Bates, who had long been noted locally as an authority on city affairs; William Woerner, a well-known liberal; Lambert Walther, an honest though conservative attorney; and J. P. Hornsby, a respected Catholic member of the bar. After an extensive investigation they condemned the proposed new franchise. This roused the St. Louis *Post-Dispatch*, whose managing editor, O.K. Bovard, was the last of the great managing editors who derived from the school of Bennett and the elder Pulitzer. And at the same time, through the activities of Stephen H. Butler, a versatile organizer, the Central Trades and Labor Council took its stand against the franchise.

The battle precipitated then lasted for almost five years.

It was to feature the passage of the franchise by the Board of Aldermen, despite tremendous opposition, the beginning of a referendum for the defeat of the Board's action, and the theft of the referendum petitions by an agent for the Street Railway Company, who subsequently burned them in the basement of the company's barns in Milwaukee. This led to the withdrawal of the franchise and a new round in the fight. Whatever the merits or demerits of the controversy, Mayor Henry W. Kiel brought on this new round by giving legal life to the rejected franchise through the withdrawal of certain suits against the old franchise, on condition of its amendment. The attempt to recall Mayor Kiel was then begun by the Civic League and Central Labor Union. Although thousands of petitions were obtained, the referendum provision in the St. Louis city charter proved to be unworkable, since it required that a certain percentage of the petitions be obtained in each one of the city's wards.

These dramatic events are recorded in several articles which I wrote at that time for the *National Municipal Review*, of which the present president of Princeton, Dr. Harold W. Dodds, was then editor. These articles summed up the attitude of most civic reformers of the period. They advocated theories of valuation and antimonopolistic regulation leading to public ownership. Even though cautiously stated, these observations represent quite a contrast to the present trend of regulation, which in our current railroad legislation goes to the extent of encouraging combination.

Because of them Lincoln Steffens looked me up in New York after I arrived there in 1920, to urge me to prepare a supplementary volume to his *Shame of the Cities*. We had a pleasant afternoon in the garden of the old Civic Club, discussing his theory, with which I did not fully agree, that no progress whatsoever had been made against corruption in our municipalities. The former muckraker was lost in admiration of the Russian Revolution, which he considered the "diagram of the future," and was correspondingly negative about all American institutions and their prospects. "You are writing too soon the obituary of capitalism in America," was my comment, "and in the cities, too, there is still the chance for large-scale reform." We laughed at our differences and let it go at that, but Steffens typified that branch of the liberals that was to look with awe upon everything connected with the Soviet Union as all-perfect.

To the Street Railway battle there was to be a unique denouement. Certain financial interests did not like the fact that the St. Louis *Post-Dispatch* was carrying out the Pulitzer tradition of going after the Street Railway interests. Somehow they persuaded the department stores to refuse to advertise in that large and influential daily. For some days the *Post-Dispatch* looked like a country weekly, being completely innocent of large-scale advertising. The labor and "progressive" groups retaliated by calling one of the first department store strikes in the United States—a further objective being organization and better wages. Four thousand girls walked out and marched down the center of St. Louis every day to let the city know that they had taken this daring step. Within a brief period, the ads went back in the *Post-Dispatch*, and we sighed with relief, feeling we had saved an ally.

The department store walkout did not fare so well. It was not viewed with much enthusiasm by a number of the craft unions—technically it was under the auspices of the retail clerks' organization which belonged to the American Federation of Labor. And many craft union officials were thoroughly persuaded that workers such as those in department stores could not be organized and that the sooner the wasteful plans for their unionization were abandoned, the better. Thus the shadow of opposition to wider mass organization still darkened the labor scene and continued to do so until the San Francisco Convention of 1934. Then, the colorful John L. Lewis, from the United Mine Workers, was to challenge that attitude on the floor of the American Federation of Labor's national gathering.

But the 1914 department store strike was settled in an unsatisfactory manner—partly as a consequence of this indifference on the part of some of the better entrenched unions—although it did promote better wages and conditions in the retail clerk field. In the meantime, all the public controversy over the Street Railway franchise had stirred the streetcar men to organize, strike, and win recognition as a local of the Amalgamated Association of Street and Electric Railway Employees, another A. F. of L. affiliate.

Some of us who participated in these drives to bring the workers under the union banner felt that in this general fight we had found new evidences against capitalism, and so became more confirmed in our "radical" stand. Looking back upon that day, I confess that we did not realize then that the abuses which aroused our ire could be corrected more readily than we admitted, and that we were actually demonstrating the possibilities of correction. However, difficulties with some of the craft union leaders convinced me that in the future labor agitation would have to be carried forward with the co-operation of the American Federation of Labor affiliates. The big responsibility of those who wanted to make labor grow was to urge organization of *all* the unorganized upon the unions and leaders of the A. F. of L. Those Syndicalists led by the fanatical Daniel De Leon, who were engaged in setting up rival organizations to the A. F. of L., were on the wrong track, and would end in a blind alley. There were many more thoughtful people who had been stirred by the dynamic and dramatic struggles of the Industrial Workers of the World—at Lawrence and in the copper country—but who were convinced, nonetheless, that permanent labor progress lay through work for the Federation, which had been in existence since 1883. It was the first national alliance of the workers to stay on the scene for such a length of time, and this was in itself no small recommendation.

The shot at Sarajevo had finally brought the great war upon us and those of a radical bent experienced, by and large, an evolution in their thinking on the matter which is not without interest. Among these in St. Louis, for instance, was Kate Richards O'Hara who was the author of the anti-war resolution of the St. Louis national convention of the Socialist party. We of the "Nut Table" at the City Club—of that aggregation I shall presently say more—had bade her farewell just before her departure for the prison at Jefferson City, where she was confined for her activities against the war. Avidly we read the letters which she wrote from her cell and which were conscientiously mimeographed and distributed by her husband. They told of her work among the women there, of her Socialist-molded views of prison reform, and served to keep alive her spirit of protest against World War I.

Three years later, when she had been released from prison, we met again, and by then her attitude had shifted considerably. While highly critical of the Treaty of Versailles—and we must never forget what a disillusionment was caused by that document—she had been softened by Woodrow Wilson's pleas for industrial democracy and looked on the world in a new light. Hers was approximately the gamut of my own feelings. Though bitterly regretful over the failure of the Allies to deal justly with their conquered foe, I was also certain that ·the Wilsonian school in our political life had brought in something new and good in the "New Freedom" legislation.

It was symptomatic of the two-mindedness of the liberals and progressives immediately after World War I that the "Nut Table" split into opposing camps over the proposed League of Nations. This group was composed of a small number of publicists, professional men and preachers, and they represented the most liberal tendencies in the organizations, churches and neighborhoods to which they belonged. In the endless discussions that went on at the luncheon table they too reflected many of the current lights and shades in liberal thought throughout the nation. In this gathering I met that charming conversationalist, William Marion Reedy, who was then being so highly praised for having published Edgar Lee Master's *Spoon River Anthology*. Unfortunately, so it seemed to me, fine as this piece of writing was, it had much of that sense of futility that I later discovered pervaded the outlook of so many of our "liberal" writers.

Reedy took me aback by laughingly declaring that he had judged from my writing that I was most Germanic in appearance and had a flowing blond beard. On the basis of that mistake we became friends. It was a delight to listen to his comments on American literature, and in them my conscience often detected an affection for the Catholic Church which he never acknowledged. It was no surprise to me to learn that on his deathbed he returned to the religion of his youth and was buried from the Jesuit Church. With his sprightly comments on passing events in his weekly *Reedy's Mirror*, this versatile journalist was a predecessor of the newspaper columnists, particularly those few of the liberal tradition. He was a sort of forerunner to Heywood Broun and the broad similarity between the two men, despite marked detailed differences, serve to map out a stream in journalism which still flows on—now fortunately, I hope, with the current turning toward the Catholic tradition.

When the League of Nations covenant was presented to the country as something to which it must say yea or nay—and with little in-between ground to stand on, the liberals in St. Louis and throughout the nation were far from happy. Their division on the proposal was sharp, but no one was pleased that it was so. The more radical, and I among them, were against the League because we considered it founded on a falsehood, the unjust Treaty of Versailles. But we did not enjoy the predicament in which this stand placed us, for it tended to divorce us from the labor movement which on the whole stood close to Wilson, and it also cut us off from any organic connection with the Wilsonian reforms. All of us were of the opinion that the opposition of Henry Cabot Lodge was based not even on genuine isolationism but rather on a super-imperialistic thirst. And yet, we could not stomach the Treaty nor the heavy burdens it placed upon the German people. That the *Nation*, then one of the oracles of the liberals, would be anti-Treaty and anti-Wilson was more or less taken for granted. But the desertion of the Wilsonian camp by the *New Republic*, which had been one of the President's stanchest supporters in the war years, gave us the glowing—though sometimes half-guilty—feeling that we were right in our stand.

When, in August, 1919, the anticipated announcement came that the Champion of the Covenant would take his case to the country, everywhere in the liberal camp there was an alert. There was a sudden sweep of sympathy for the President and a desire to hear what he had to say, as he carried his message from the Potomac to the Pacific.

The local Democratic committee of the League of Nations Association, or some such group, provided seating capacity in the Stadium for the Wilson rally in St. Louis on the night of September 5.

Well do I remember that evening. An atmosphere of

doom hung over the assemblage, and the President's defeat
was forecast in the tone of despair with which he addressed
the boys who had fought in France and Flanders. "Boys,"
he said, "I told you before you went overseas that this was a
war against wars, and I did my best to fulfill the promise,
but I am obliged to come before you in mortification and
shame and say that I have not been able to fulfill the promise.
You are betrayed, you fought for something that you did
not get."

We all went away from that sad spectacle assured that,
just as Senator Jim Reed, with his bitter barbs, had taken
Missouri away from Wilson and the League, so had gone
the whole country. In the local labor movement—and this
reflected what was happening among the workers everywhere—the concern over postwar wages and the possibility
of an all-out assault upon the new "war baby" unions, over-
shadowed all other issues. The League of Nations, for which
labor originally stood, became more and more a misty,
faraway matter. There were more precious and immediate
things to fight for.

The "deportation delirium," as Assistant Secretary of
Labor Post dubbed Attorney General A. Mitchell Palmer's
savage assault on aliens, was now thrust upon us. The sensational raids upon private homes and the holding incommunicado of persons who had committed no offense
other than to be born abroad aroused the entire liberal-
radical camp as nothing else could have done. We were aware
that the whole "scare" was worked up to further Palmer's
presidential aspirations and suspected that the uproar was
not unconnected with preparations to declare war on the
legitimate trade unions.

Reedy and I were conspicuous in our concern about these
abuses and became conspicuously busy in opposing them.
We wrote letters to Congressmen, got others to do so and

prepared wider appeals to the public conscience. We were aware that the Bolshevik revolution in Russia had led the foreign-language federations in the Socialist party and other groups of recent immigrants to turn Communist, and we knew that they were committed to unrest and upheaval. We had heard even in St. Louis of large sums of money being bootlegged into America to promote dissension here. We watched the air of mystery in which the "Soviet Ambassador," Martens, operated, which made still more unintelligible to the mass of Americans what the intent of the Soviet agitation in our midst really was. These gestures we regarded as fantastic; they definitely did not justify in our opinion the violations of civil liberty Palmer unleashed. In this connection I wrote a letter to the St. Louis *Star-Times* comparing the Palmer raids with the persecution of the Abolitionists before the Civil War, and recounting the mob scenes and arrests launched against the enemies of chattel slavery. In referring to that letter, I characterized its appeal for the first time as the "American approach"—a term which deeply affected my subsequent years and was heard more than once in the labor movement.

During the fever of war St. Louis and vicinity had had more than its share of ugly episodes, and we didn't want them to be revived. A German-American doctor whom I knew well had been yanked out of bed in the middle of the night, hustled to jail and held incommunicado. Other citizens had been terrorized in a similar fashion, and the German-descended section of the community had been effectually cowed. Only a few weeks before writing the letter to the *Star-Times*, on a smiling midsummer day, I had hiked to Collinsville, Illinois, and was reminded that only a year before Robert Prager had there been strung up by a mob until he was dead—for no better reason than that he was of German birth and not ashamed of it. There were uneasy signs that the Palmer madness might arouse new mobs and resurrect a new atmosphere of oppression.

One morning in December this shadow fell close to my own front door. Scarcely had I arrived at my office than two men rushed in, each asking to see me on private and urgent business. Although they were not acquainted with each other, they had the same message and it was a rather startling one.

"Aren't you connected with the Committee of 48?" breathlessly asked the first, a lieutenant in the war and previously associated with me at the Civic League. He was now active in the American Legion and that was the cause of his visit.

When my reply was "Yes, I have been acting as local secretary of a welcoming committee," he reported: "Well, the local Legion plans to break up any gathering they arrange here and has served notice on the Hotel Statler to that effect."

"And the Statler?"

"It plans to cancel the contract and tell the Committee of 48 to meet elsewhere." So likewise stated the second man, a labor official also just returned from the war zone. At that moment Reedy rang up with confirmation of the incredible news. "The local Legion leaders are rollicking in reaction" was the way he put it. "The Committee is lashed as the spawn of the Bolsheviks."

Such an opinion of the comfortable, well-fed men who were even then descending upon St. Louis seemed freakish and fantastic. The Committee of 48's leading members were the cream of culture and affluence among the liberals. They came from prosperous offices and comfortable homes. Their chairman, J. A. H. Hopkins, a distinguished white-haired Wall Street broker, had been treasurer of the Theodore Roosevelt Bull Moose excursion into national political life. The aim of the Committee was a new political deal to head

off the depression, which they wisely foresaw, and to establish such reforms as would move America forward at a
decent rate of progress. The present head of the American
Legion, having a progressive slant from his office holding as
lieutenant governor and then governor of Illinois, is much
closer today to the Committee of 48 than the Committee was
then to the Bolsheviki.

The substantial character of the Committee's members
assured a victory within a few hours. And Arthur Garfield
Hays, counsel for the American Civil Liberties Union,
obtained an injunction to prevent the Statler or anyone
else from interfering with the national conclave of the
Forty-eighters. But the few hours of uncertainty were tense,
nonetheless, and reflected the uneasy state of civil liberties.

This group and its subsequent convention were extremely
educational to me, and apparently to many others. There
was something disconnected about its debates and discussions. The many talks I had with its leading liberal
members reinforced my conviction of the chaos and confusion
of their aims. They had ideas that sounded realistic but
were nowhere connected organizationally with reality. They
did not share the optimistic outlook of those who predicted
perpetual prosperity; neither did they know how to attract
labor and the farmers into a coherent camp to halt the
joy-riding catastrophe they foresaw. My belief became
stronger than ever that the continued organization of the
unions and the winning of civil rights to permit that organization were the real goals of immediate progressive action.

From the coal fields and the steel communities, two large-
scale events added their weight to this belief. Through the
spring and summer we had watched the gathering campaign
for the enrollment of the steelmakers in the American
Federation of Labor. Everyone knew that any walkout would
be fought savagely, and Judge Gary, head of the United

States Steel Corporation, had boldly announced that "our corporations and subsidiaries" refuse even to talk with the unions. When the down-tools movement came on September 22, the more than three hundred thousand men who struck found that the state constabulary and other police forces were employed 100 per cent against them. The killing of the Irish-American organizer, Fanny Sellins—nee Mooney, was dramatic proof of this tragic reality, tragic to the thousands of men who were still laboring at the twelve-hour day under nonunion conditions. In sorrow we saw the strike crushed and drew the lesson that full industrial unionism—of one union in steel—was the only method which would establish the right of association for the workers in that industry. The rising towers of steel trustification made that a "must" on America's economic-political diary.

The injunction initiated by Palmer in the miners' strike in November was event Number Two in our education—certainly in mine. With the war at an end, the price restrictions on the coal operators had been lifted. The coal diggers were of the opinion that they should catch up with the high cost of living and made stiff demands. Before they could leave the pits on November 1, the date for the strike, the government, through the Attorney General, obtained a drastic injunction forbidding any such action. The officers of the union were ordered not to counsel or advise or abet the miners in any way. Five hundred thousand men followed the original walkout order just the same; but President John L. Lewis made his famous declaration, "We cannot fight the Government," and the walkout faded finally into thin air and the strike was officially called off. Savage criticism was leveled at Lewis, particularly by the Communist-tinged left wing because of what they dubbed his "betrayal." On the other hand, those who defended what Lewis had done pointed out that the very foundation of the union and all its funds might have been dissipated in a struggle in such an unsatisfactory political landscape.

For those of us who had been active in organizing in connection with the St. Louis Central Trades and Labor Union the vital concern in this contest was the issuance of the Palmer injunction. Whatever one's view of the miners' aims, we argued, the prohibition of the right to strike, when no other recourse was left open, constituted a gravely undesirable state of affairs for the country. We directed this argument to the business community as well as to the rest of the people, and with some effect. It was an opinion beginning to be shared by many, and ten years later, after many more tussles, was to be the recorded judgment of the American nation in the Norris-LaGuardia Act.

As a result, out of the St. Louis incidents, I adopted another tenet of the political faith of the groping progressives of that time—the public ownership of many utilities. This had led me to persuade the *Post-Dispatch* to employ Dr. Delos F. Wilcox to write a series of articles assailing the proposed streetcar franchise some years back. Wilcox, a chubby man, full of chuckles, was the leading exponent of the theory of public ownership among electric-railway experts. The reasoning processes that led to our conclusions need not be imposed upon you now. They have been expounded at length and can be found in any library. They were simply a protest against the venality and bad administration which marked so many American cities and which we felt were direct results of the unholy alliance of public utility corporation and political machine. Our beliefs were echoed by Tom Johnson in Cleveland, Brand Whitlock in Toledo, Mark Fagan in Jersey City and Freemont Older in San Francisco. The Hydro-Electric Development in the Province of Ontario, Canada, was one of the stock exhibits of the Public Ownership League and other zealous foes of the utilities, and we can point to the Tennessee Valley Authority and its kindred projects as fruits of this agitation in the long run of political history.

Having reached this particular stage in my thinking, I accepted with warmth the offer by Roger Baldwin to go East as publicity director of the American Civil Liberties Union, with the added chance to work with Dr. Wilcox for the Federal Electric Railways Commission. There were some good, ultraconservative members of the Civic League who thought I had worn out my welcome with these anti-injunction, pro-civil liberty and public ownership "fantasies." The president of the League, a progressive manufacturer and civic reformer, ventured to discuss this conservative criticism with me one day. We were riding in an automobile, when he turned to me and said: "Budenz, some people think you are sometimes pretty radical; and then, you are very young." This was when I was twenty-six, and therefore eager to make reply. "Pitt was chided with being too young for high political office," I retorted, "but he replied that the crime in statesmanship was not in being young but in being wrong." The League's president laughed heartily at this. Perhaps some of the boldness of my reply was due to my knowledge that intellectually he agreed with me but had become a cautious man by instinct. It was he, though, who had stressed to me that it was the duty of businessmen to recognize unions, holding that there was no other way to establish stable conditions in a democracy.

There were many good friends who regretted my leaving St. Louis and I on my part regretted the loss of the fellowship of many able local members of the fourth estate. The ideas which ruled the progressive camp then and which were to make their mark in national history a dozen years later were given much impetus, I felt, by the support of such papers as the St. Louis *Post-Dispatch* and the St. Louis *Star-Times*.

The proposals with which I left St. Louis had little speaking acquaintance with fundamental Marxism. They were not founded on class struggle. They were not the inevitable forerunners of an omnipotent, ominipresent state. They were much more akin to the Catholic conception of social relationships. Many friends of various shades of socialistic association criticized my attachment to municipal public ownership and my reluctance to abandon the word "Syndicalist." Some went so far as to intimate that this "contradiction" arose from a desire to keep in line with Catholic caution against "state worship." There may have been some truth to this amiable "accusation." It's a fact, just the same, that many Americans of many religious backgrounds were subject to the same general "confusion"; that was characteristic of the ranks of the movement gradually calling itself "Progressive." Could it be that these thousands were seeking and searching for the *Via Media* view which I had held and was to hold again?

Though I had worked with Socialists, left and right wing, as well as with liberals, I was never one of them. In one sense only was I an incipient Marxist at the end of the St. Louis period. I recognized there was something wrong with capitalism and that if it could not right the wrong it would have to pass out of history. The connection of the utilities in that day with the worst elements in the political machines and the refusal of the right of association to the workers were blights that would have to be removed. The entire winter of 1914 I had studied Marxist literature in a special study course conducted voluntarily by two left-wing Socialists in the settlement, Neighborhood House. While Lewis Morgan's theories did not register with me at all, and Marxism in general was not accepted, I did "leave my mind open" on the matter. Life was to provide the answer, and upon its course would rest any decision on my part.

To Kate Richards O'Hare, while she was in prison at Jefferson City, I had written: "There is too much of conjecture in Morgan's conclusions on primitive society. As to the materialist conception of history, as expressed by Marx, that is something else again. I shall look into it thoroughly and study it over with care."

That letter was an omen as to what the future held in store. The materialist conception of history—under which mankind has supposedly proceeded from primitive communism to slavery to the feudal system to capitalism, through class struggle—was to captivate my mind and imagination for some years. It was the road that led me to the Communist camp. It armed my revolt against the Church with an "intellectual" artillery. Its promise of the inevitability of Socialism long haunted me, as it does Communists everywhere, and furnished as much of a "conscience" as those who reject all spiritual ties can have. Only God's grace and the recognition of the debacle that denial of the spiritual and moral law was bringing into the world could, after many years, make me appreciate its bankruptcy.

There was one immediate check in St. Louis on any temptation to an out-and-out entry into the Marxist camp. That was the memory—Catholic-learned—of the unhappy experiences of Lammenais, Lacordiare and Montalambert in tending to rush into extremes for liberalism eighty years before. The latter two—the Dominican and the layman—had learned the wisdom of restraint whereas Lammenais had petered out into nothingness by wanting too much.

Unfortunately, such memories did not signify that I was still guided in my spiritual life by the signposts of the Church. These were days of drifting away from the Church. They were like the seeds thrown among thistles in the Quinquagesima Sunday gospel, with the everyday deeds eating up all religious impulses. "For a vain matter and slight promise men fear not to toil day and night," wrote the wise Thomas à Kempis four hundred years ago, "but alas, for an unchangeable good, they grudge even the least fatigue." In the quest for the public good the young man from Indiana was forgetting his own good, injuring his own integrity. And the tragedy of it was that this need not have been. He could best have served the good of the people by advancing his own religious welfare. So the sequel was to show.

A cloud of sorrow fell over my family at my anti-Catholic act. We were always kind to each other when we met and I visited them as much as I could. But there was a veil between us, we were careful how we spoke. When I told my father what had occurred, he said quietly, with a look of pain in his light blue eyes, "You have sold your birthright. . . . " That was all that ever passed between us on the matter; thereafter my parents' petitions were addressed to heaven in the form of prayer.

There were well-meaning souls, among them a woman high in public esteem, who sought privately to induce me to join the Episcopal Church. They presented a picture of a comfortable, flabby code in which one might hold almost any sort of doctrine. These offers were rejected with a touch of kindly scorn. "You would have me accept a religion that puts one on soft cushions, whereas the merit of Catholicism is that it says without equivocation that if you wish to rise you must first take to your knees. If one is to accept religion, this is it. The golden core of Catholicism is its insistence upon conformity; your thought that there can be religion and nonconformity to that religion's tenets is a huge contradiction. And then, I know well that these sects all sprang from the attempt to make the State the source of grace and the king the head of the Church of Christ." That ended the chapter for good. Now I began to call myself a rationalist, though in a minor key. But there was a constant bitterness in my religious life, or lack of it, as though I always had a bad taste in may mouth. The "De Profundis" came sometimes to my lips.

Part of the pleasure in being New York-bound on that February day in 1920 was the opportunity it gave me to get away from the vacuum created by the absence of religious worship. The excitement of Gotham would do away with the tedium which often threatened to set in. From my earliest boyhood, the city on New York Bay had been a magnet, and was the goal for me, just as Paris was for many other people. It would be a national sounding board for public reform. These were the hopes and aims with which I, like a lot of other Midwesterners, crossed the railroad bridge over the Mississippi, looked down with some temporary nostalgia on the poverty-cursed mud flats of the river bottoms, and left the "forty-ninth State" for good.

THREE

Hounded by Heaven

GOTHAM'S SIXTH Avenue in the Twenties was not the handsome boulevard it is today. The "EL" switched over from the narrow neck of downtown Manhattan, just below Fourteenth Street, and gave the street a secretive and shut-in air. There was something half-in-hiding about it, like a poor relation. No one then would have predicted that in time it would blossom forth as the Avenue of the Americas.

To the Midwesterner in love with O. Henry's Bagdad, this very quality of the street in those days gave it a rare attraction. For him the "EL" was its charm. There was something about its jingle and jangle, its lights and shadows that made a hike to the Pennsylvania Station from the Union Square area an ever-new marvel. In the heat of the summer, the wooden ramparts afforded shade; in the fall or winter, they were an unbrella for the rain or snow. The foghorns along the river and the music of the "EL" are blended in my memory into a kind of "Gotham rhapsody."

The street's asset was that it gave a man a chance to think. That's what I was doing then, very strenuously— thinking of a publication which could express that burning mission with which I had left the Middle West. Those in the labor movement who stood for the organization of the unorganized seemed to be separated from each other. It would be a "mighty national service"—those were my own words to myself—to create a mouthpiece which would bring them together—at least in discussion.

Many a sunny Saturday noon or a late night in an almost empty street, the steel girders of the "EL" were the confidants of my schemes to bring the needle-trades unions, and the miners and machinists closer together. The publication was the thing. The office of the American Civil Liberties Union, in which I was then publicity director, was located in an old brownstone house down on Thirteenth Street. The *Dial* magazine was down the street and the *Masses*, under the editorship of the Eastmans, was next door. In leisure moments I poked around, picking up information about running a monthly on an independent basis. The headaches would be many compared to an organ like *The Carpenter*, which was subscribed to automatically and in which the "reader appeal" question was not too important. Crystal Eastman, tall and gracious, was all kindness in devoting some time from a number of busy days to giving me the "inside information" on managing such a magazine. In her good will there was also a touch of amusement at the eagerness of the young man from the West.

This was 1921, and the American Federation of Labor had already begun to stumble down from its pinnacle of progress during the war years. The 1920 all-high membership of more than four million was slipping. Company unions were no longer confined to the Rocky Mountain Fuel Company and such centers as Bethlehem Steel; they were sneaking into many hitherto organized plants and places. The Achilles heel of the A. F. of L.'s position was, according to many of us, its failure to take up industrial unionism of the basic industries and to follow some coherent form of political activity. That's what would have to be said, speedily and strongly, from a national platform, to all the unions. "Normalcy"—which was to win in the November national elections—and the smashing of the shop-crafts unions the next year, were in the air. That trend had to be halted, and a common meeting ground for "progressive" unions and unionists would help.

If this had become a grand passion with me—and it now occupied all my otherwise unoccupied moments—it was also near the hearts of other people. During the campaign for civil liberty in Logan County, West Virginia, which was then surrounded by a huge Chinese wall of anti-unionism, I had met Arthur Gleason of the *Nation*, author of *What the Workers Want*. He told me about his work with the Intercollegiate Socialist Society, and now he persuaded its officers to change their *Review* to the magazine *Labor Age*, to be labor-led. The Socialist-tinged leaders of the needle-trades unions and certain mine union officers like John Brophy, then president of District 2, would be represented on its board. That was just down my alley, we both agreed.

Then, in the same week, along came Prince Hopkins, heir to the Hopkins of Southern Pacific fame with a proposal for a monthly that would further general humanitarian and labor aims. Roger Baldwin, ever ready to help a friend along with an idea, had introduced him to me and recommended that we get together. The merger of Hopkins' subsidized embryonic paper, tentatively called *Humanity*, with *Labor Age* —under the latter name—was my achievement. It took some weeks of patient planning and conferring to bring it about, and on the day of its conclusion I was in holiday spirits. *Labor Age* was definitely the forerunner of that alliance of unions which was to form the Congress of Industrial Organizations—though that had not been its purpose at its birth.

In the course of the negotiations one humorous and notable incident occurred. I insisted, to the point of stubbornness, that the declaration of principles of the publication contain a phrase pledging it to oppose "state worship." Some of the Socialists spluttered and stormed, but I stood firm. Since I

was actually creating a trade-union voice, the trade unionists among them gradually came over to my side, and the
phrase stayed in. With rare satisfaction, I was able to quote
to the Socialists one of their own prophets, Frederick Engels.
His book, *Socialism, Utopian and Scientific*, with its promise
of "the withering away of the state" almost immediately
after the social revolution, had been a favorite in my later
St. Louis study days. I used it frequently in arguing for the
Syndicalist stand, and still referred to it after my Communist
affiliation, even though by then the almighty state of the
Soviet Union had completely negated Engels' prophecies.
To refute the Socialists, I drew up a whole thesis, based on
Engels, so that the condemnation of "state worship" could
be included in our *Labor Age* program. This determination
shows how completely the Catholic stand against statism,
the Syndicalist preachments and the words of Engels were
blended in my convictions. I would have scrapped the whole
magazine business rather than surrender this position against
a superstate.

A man with a mission has few idle moments and the birth
and infancy of *Labor Age* were absorbing times. The only
leisure they allowed were some hikes around Rahway, New
Jersey, where I then lived, and a jog around Union Square
almost every morning at eleven—either with Art Young, the
genial artist, or with Eugene Wood, the poet and father of
Peggy Wood. The magazine's office was in the Hartford
Building, on Union Square. That was the beginning of a
quarter of a century for me around that center. Young's
studio was across the way on Seventeenth Street, and since
he often worked at night, he would be ending his labors
shortly after I was starting mine. When we met in the Square,
he would often tell me about his long and somewhat strange
friendship with Arthur Brisbane, the noted columnist, and
about the days when he worked for the "capitalist" press.

Labor Age had come upon the national scene at the right time. My work for the Civil Liberties Union in assailing the policy of Palmer, in working for the release of the war prisoners, and in the free-speech drive in West Virginia, had been stimulating and significant. And the editorial and expert franchise labors with Dr. Wilcox over the report for the Federal Electric Railways Commission and over his book on the street railways had been in a good cause. But the rallying of labor to defend its trenches by renewing its inner strength was, I thought, far more vital. It was "nearer the grass roots" of every community and was something that had to be done if there was to be a healthy balance in our democracy. Labor's banners were now in full retreat.

Our magazine had scarcely been started when it was entreated to aid the striking railroad shopmen. Their "war baby" unions were under deadly fire and were likely to go down under the fusillade. We did all we could, and among other articles, launched an all-around assault upon the Pennsylvania Railroad, which at that time was especially stubborn in its antiunion stand. But the company-union cloud had spread over the entire economic horizon. In the giant electric industry the arrangements had been made during the latter days of the war. Labor was angry because W. Jett Lauck, whom it had considered its friend, had okayed these company-controlled groups. And they were rapidly reducing the membership of the A. F. of L. affiliates. When the miners tried to reply to this offensive, they were met by the armed forces and President Harding's show of the flag at the mine mouths. In many places the coal diggers went out and saluted the flag, but they refused to work. They were not completely defeated, but it was a dark day for them and for all the unions. The sale of stock to the workers—on the condition that they keep clear of the trade unions—rose to new heights.

To anyone who believed in the right of association as a

foundation stone of good national life, this period was tragic. To insist upon the organization of the unorganized, when many felt the effort was in vain, and to write burning words was not enough. It was essential that *Labor Age* go out and "spread the word." The campaign began in the Greater City and was to extend through many states, notably the "keystone commonwealth" of Pennsylvania.

Three or four nights in one week would find me in odd and obscure sections of New York, climbing ill-smelling stairs and waiting until local union business permitted my speaking. (Those bodies were not always so well quartered as they are in 1946.) In another week I would be in Philadelphia insisting to the battered textile unions that general labor recognition of industrial unionism such as they had in their own union would make for success. Swinging deeper into the country, I would later invade the hard coal areas or go into "soft coal." Nanticoke and Clearfield became as familiar to me as New York and Chicago.

James H. Maurer, Socialist and trade unionist, was president of the Pennsylvania Federation of Labor and president of the first corporation that issued *Labor Age*. His Federation was the first of the state bodies to endorse our publication, and this open door was one reason for our preoccupation with Pennsylvania. The other reason was that state's prominence in the national industrial picture, particularly at that time.

These visitations were ostensibly for the purpose of obtaining subscriptions to the magazine, which were frequently voted by the union. In Local 1 of the American Federation of Full-fashioned Hosiery Workers, in North Philadelphia, I would get as many as two hundred subs in one night. Beyond that, I would be accorded an enthusiastic reception. This message of the possibility of organizing the unorganized was what the young, vigorous hosiery workers wanted to hear. And that was the chief reason for these rounds of the unions.

Many of the subs could easily have been obtained through the executive boards without the personal appearance, but much in the way of education would have been lost. No other method would have conveyed either the information or the crusading spirit so successfully. In every local union visited, *Labor Age* was hammering home the idea that organizational activities could beat back the open-shop onslaught and that industrial unionism would do the trick. To many trade unionists it seemed to be a flash of light in the darkness. In every town there were grins of welcome and hearty handclasps on my arrival. Through the half-darkness of heavy weather and a smoke-filled room, the sun would suddenly seem to shine in some semisecret meeting in Altoona or Johnstown. If you have ever come upon the grim gray valley in the latter city on a bitter-cold winter morning and then through the soot suddenly beheld the face of a friend, you will understand the zest of those experiences. "My return performance always seemed to combine the appearance of a missionary to a forest community after months of absence and the return of the rambling Parson Weems, with his pack of books, to some settlement in the early American Republic," I reported to the *Labor Age* board back in New York.

To be a Democrat openly was to risk social ostracism in what is now Democratic-dominated Pittsburgh. And in Middletown, that nom de plume for Muncie in my native state, the Lynds found the unions and union men buried deep under community indifference or disapproval. But those social surveyors were not to have the privilege of unearthing the new men of labor who would be heard from later; that was my privilege as "the best known man in the labor movement," as some people began to call me. Those new men were there, in almost every community, and many a local union secretary of the Twenties was later to become an international union official. The first beginnings of a renewed labor movement were visible then in the shadow of the fortresslike textile mills of Fall River, and under the flaming night skies of Gary and Youngstown and in the byways of Buffalo.

In the doings of these local labor leaders, whether they were to remain obscure or to become famous, *Labor Age* foresaw the "day after tomorrow" in America's history. As the giant combinations of industry continued to multiply, large associations of workers would become inevitable—one union for each of the big industries. The forward march of this industrial unionism was, then, a patriotic "must," and in stressing such a proposal *Labor Age* considered that it was zealously serving the American nation.

Others were aware of the same possibilities but were employing the propaganda in a different direction. Using the prestige of his big part in the steel strike, William Z. Foster had recently started the Trade Union Educational League for the advancement of industrial unionism. In Chicago he and his associates had launched the *Labor Herald* as their organ, with Earl Browder as editor. Ever eager to build and not to tear down, I suggested the possibility of merging their magazine with our own. Such a move would gather together rather than scatter those standing for similar goals. "One of the occupational diseases of the labor progressives has been flying first at each other's throats and then flying apart," said I by way of persuasion. "We must get beyond the days of Daniel De Leon, when every man who disagreed with that Marxian prophet was a scalawag and a scavenger."

One fine morning early in 1922, a young man of my own age—we had both just turned thirty—came into the Hartford Building office. It was Browder, come to talk over the merger proposition. A slim, quiet, inconspicuous-looking fellow with a sandy mustache, there was about him no sign of the fire-eater. When we got down to "brass tacks"—a favorite *Labor Age* phrase—we learned that we did not see eye to eye after all. The T.U.E.L. group would have nothing to do with anyone who favored or winked at "class collaboration," their representative advised me. This touched a tender spot in the *Labor Age* attitude; we thought that the phrase was thoroughly overdone, that it was uttered too loosely and could have a number of definitions. At all odds, we would not imperil our association with the trade-union movement by a pledge to "fight it in all its aspects." Continued connection with the trade unions came first and would be maintained by us at all costs. So I told Browder. Years later he reminded me of this conference and said that I had impressed him as one "mistaken at that time but with a lot of good sense."

Not long afterward another visitor arrived. This time it was Foster, en route to Moscow. With a childish candor that I was to laugh at later, I counseled against his affiliation with the Communist International. "We can aid the newly born Soviet Republics and be loyal to the American nation. However, the Communists are Soviet Russian patriots and are not of the American soil," was my theme. "The American labor movement must be American led, associated with the American nation and not with another power no matter how beneficent its objectives."

Foster was patient during my assertions, but constantly diverted the discussion to an assault upon Samuel Gompers. "I will make no peace with the Gompers bureaucrats and their corruption," he stated over and over again during the course of the talk. It was plain that he was evading the subject of Moscow allegiance. It did not dawn upon me until sometime afterward that he had already agreed to become a member of the Communist movement, but was to camouflage his colors as long as he could. This was my first conscious experience with concealed Communists and it was not a pleasant one. The deceit in that relationship is as unfair as that which any *agent provocateur* practises on one he enmeshes.

A dozen years after this conversation by a formula worked out with Foster—I was to contend, as a Communist, that concealment of Communist membership was no different from the denial of union membership in an antiunion shop or factory. That contention does not hold up. The union man's act is in his own defense, with no ulterior aim other than the prevention of discrimination. The Communist, whether he knows it fully or not, is employing his concealment to turn others against their own country. What is worse, they are innocently engaging in these Fifth Column deeds on behalf of a foreign power hostile to the American nation.

During the Twenties, the Communists were ardently pledging eternal enmity to the American republic. That has been no more clearly stated than by Robert Minor, the former cartoonist and now an almost ex-leader of the Communist party here. Minor has a pleasant personality, a charming home in Westchester County and a nostalgia for the French villa that was formerly his. He has an overweening ambition to be a Marxist "theoretician"—but is only a wheel horse. His theoretical inventions such as "political McClellanism" are looked upon by the conspiratorial bosses of the party as so much nonsense. In the summer of 1929, however, when he prophesied imminent war against the Soviet Union, to be waged by the "imperialist" United States, he was speaking officially for the C.I., the Communist International. In such an event, while the Red Army was firing on American boys, what were the American workers to be doing? "The interest of the workers in the United States," Minor advised, "is to defend the Socialist republic and to make war upon their 'own' capitalist government." They should, he continued, "transform the imperialist war into a revolutionary civil war," waging "universal class war against all enemies of the Soviet Union." What is more, according to Minor, "the Red Army is the advance guard of the working class of the world." Behind its banners, then, the workers should fall in line, doing any and all subversive acts that will hasten the triumph of the Red Army over any opponent, including the American Army. This was published for the whole world to see in the official *International Press Correspondence of the Communist International* of July 26, 1929 (Vol. 9, No. 36).

To win a free hand in molding the workers into camp followers of the Red Army, the Communists were everywhere striving to break up the regular trade unions. The affiliates of the American Federation of Labor were loudly branded as "social fascists and fascist unions." And any progressive who refused to swear fealty to the Comintern and its Red trade unions was likely to be blasted in the same terms of scorn. The speedy extinction of the American Federation of Labor was predicted, and any near-Communist who doubted it was assailed as a "renegade." At first under cover, and then openly, Foster, unfortunately, was to participate in this tragic burlesque. "Industrial Unionism" and a "Labor Party," which were favorite slogans, were purely propaganda props to Soviet foreign policy maneuvers. Some years later, in an incident which will presently be recounted more fully, Browder startled me with the unqualified assertion that this manipulation for Moscow's interest was the Communist view of the Labor party's function.

As Harding's regime came to a close, the Teapot Dome scandal gave warning that all was not well in Washington. The big bid for the Presidency on a progressive ticket by the elder Senator Robert M. La Follette got under way. With enthusiasm, *Labor Age* became one of the first and most earnest cheer leaders for the Wisconsin Senator. While some railroad union leaders were talking about Senator Borah as an opponent to Coolidge, *Labor Age* forced the issue. With a big picture of La Follette on its front page, it dedicated an entire number to his support. At last, we submitted, labor could align itself with the farmers and the small businessmen to introduce a "new deal" politically. When the representatives of many unions, and notably Sidney Hillman's Amalgamated Clothing Workers, assembled in Cleveland under the banner of the Congress for Progressive Political Action, I was one of the delegates from New Jersey. And when that gathering, which crowded the commodious Municipal Auditorium, officially called upon La Follette to run, we were all moved deeply. Hope ran high.

How those hopes were dashed is now part of American history. The five million votes registered for La Follette throughout the nation were not enough to build a permanent party. The campaign, nonetheless, was not without value. There were quite a few folks who could draw a number of lessons from what they had observed around America during this "crusade." In acting as campaign manager for the La Follette-Wheeler ticket in New Jersey, I had made my own observations and reached certain conclusions. On the whole, they agreed with those of many other "Progressives." What they were can best be illustrated by recalling several dramatic events that occurred in the years immediately following.

These are episodes from my own life, but they are also pages from the history of the American labor movement. The two went together. At first these scenes may seem detached from each other; they will soon be seen as parts of the whole. The battle against the company union, the yellow-dog contract, the injunction, and the labor racketeering, all belong to the campaign for wider organization of the unorganized. Since La Follette's defeat was a political rebuff to labor and its allies, it must acquire greater industrial strength. That was the moral for me, and that was the incentive to the following organizing activities.

SCENE I. **A gray street in Lackawanna, N. Y., leading to the Bethlehem Steel mill.** Two years had passed since the La Follette campaign, and it was 1926. I moved from "soft drink" parlor to "soft drink" parlor, all of them selling wares that were hard in fact and harder to drink. The stale smell of beer and whisky filled the air of the barrooms where the steelworkers gathered. From their front doors you looked out on a scene of desolation, tin cans and decay. Men in broken English, the men—most of them Poles—spoke their indictment of the company union, so highly tooted by Eugene Grace as the choicest gift to the workingman.

From Lackawanna I went into New England, with its white-columned houses and its textile-bred poverty to search out the ways and wiles of the company-controlled labor organization. In a quiet corner of West Lynn, I heard the whole fantastic tale of the pressure brought to bear upon the delegates to make them forget hours and wages and think only of banquets and good times. At that time, apparently, General Electric's method was to inveigle the workers into exchanging their birthright of free association for a mess of hot dogs and cheap beer. So went the whispered stories, in one form or another in workers' homes near the Lawrence Leather Company at Peabody, Mass. and around the Real Silk Mills at Indianapolis, and in sight of the Standard Oil tanks at Bayonne on the Kill van Kull. In these journeys I was rediscovering America, and marveling at the ingenuity and efficiency with which its citadels of production were being built and maintained. Almost before my eyes—it seemed—between visits to Bethlehem, I saw the creation of mighty blast furnaces for tons of additional steel. And in the "heart of the anthracite" I watched the building of the

mechanical breaker which all but abolished human labor.
It was like a seven-day wonder. Coal and slate, which had
been separated by the tired hands of wan breaker boys, were
now quietly divided by a chemical process as they tumbled
down the chute. For all who still had to labor at such tasks
with bleeding hands and hearts in other parts of the earth,
it was a source of wonder and hope.

"Our U.S.A. was a wonder-land in the making of things;
could it continue to be a Land of Promise in the just, democratic division of the things it made?" The company union
was an obstacle to such justice and democracy, said *Labor Age*,
and buttressed its position by printing the evidence accumu-
lated on my journeys. By blocking the over-all consideration
of higher wages and shorter hours, the corporations were
damming up the sources of America's prosperity and inviting
depression. That was another *Labor Age* contention, and it
was stated with warmth. In that connection we cited the
findings of the Commissions on Unemployment appointed by
Presidents Harding and Hoover. I had consulted Dr. Wesley
C. Mitchell of Columbia University, a prominent member
of both commissions. While, of course, saying nothing about
the company-union dispute, in a short time he had enlight-
ened me immensely on the depression dangers inherent in the
inadequate purchasing power of the people. The works of
Foster, the economist, and Catchings, the professor, now
almost forgotten, were also valuable sources of enlightenment. The debacle of 1929 did not catch *Labor Age* napping.

Human dignity was affronted by the company union, we
also contended, and that was one of its worst offenses. While
walking knee-deep in Maine snow, after learning the story of
the unorganized Pepperell sheet manufactory, or trudging
up and down in the hot summer before the Hudson plant in
Detroit, I worked out those ideas which were later so successful in bringing men into the unions. Chief among them was

the loss of human dignity which accompanied the denial of the right to free association. The strong man made craven by job fear, the thoughtful man rendered silent by concern about discrimination, the man of deep faith able to worship God only indifferently because of long hours of labor—these were robbed of the attributes which distinguished human beings from animals. The most shocking information learned later from Communist sources about the Soviet Union was the grave extent to which human dignity is suborned by the fear-producing, ferret-fostering dictatorship. To be sure, the right to think and speak one's mind was to be used with restraint and responsibility; to deny that was, in its turn, to be irresponsible and anarchic.

This pioneering in exposing the company unions resulted from the first of the conclusions I reached during the La Follette campaign. Labor would not be able to influence the country politically until it was more powerfully organized. That would have to come first. Of course, labor had often followed a pendulumlike course of "now political and now industrial" action. Nonetheless, organization now had greater chances of success than it had had for a long time. This was fully apparent only to those who had the opportunity to look below the surface and note the fervid desire for unionism that I had witnessed. As we rode across Jersey night after night in the La Follette campaign and told our story in some town like Dover or Phillipsburg, the eager faces of the people and their talk after the meetings had been confirmation enough.

SCENE II. **Military Park in central Newark on a sunny Saturday afternoon.** It was still 1926. A meeting of the committee for Sacco-Vanzetti, which was Communist controlled, had been announced. I had been invited to speak and accepted. However, Lieutenant of Police Emil Schmidt had other instuctions, and broke up the meeting. After some verbal fencing we came to an agreement—which became the pattern for many other similar tests—that he would arrest me after I had read the first amendment to the Constitution, which guarantees the rights of speech, press and assemblage. This he did and I was trundled off in the patrol wagon. The business ended in my acquittal.

This Essex County arrest, which attracted considerable attention in the labor movement, was part of a series of activities on behalf of the "united front" with the Communists which I had initiated. During the discussions which led up to the nomination of La Follette, the maneuvers of the Communists were enough to make anyone dizzy. Taking advantage of the close relations between Foster and President John Fitzpatrick of the Chicago Federation of Labor, because of the steel and packing house organization efforts, the Reds had seized control of the current Farmer-Labor party development. Then they proceeded to scuttle the shell of the organization they had captured.

Though this "sectarian" debacle was followed by self-criticism and many *mea culpas*, in the form of self-criticism which I read in the *Daily Worker* with amazement, it didn't make sense. Perhaps, I argued, co-operation in the united front would convince the Communists that in their relations with others they had to act with more honesty and also with more intelligence. I only half-realized then that each of these turns and twists was directed by Moscow. It took many years and many buffetings in "united fronts" and C. P. membership actually to convince me. The record is so plain for all to see that my blindness is something to wonder at. But my desire for unity, for peace with Soviet Russia and for working relations with the Communists was so great as to cover a multitude of obvious Communist sins against all these objectives.

And so it was that in 1926 I spoke in the united front rally against Queen Marie of Romania—which inspired big headlines in the tabloids—and then addressed the concluding open-air mass meeting under the Communist-controlled Sacco-Vanzetti committee. Hugh Frayne, the American Federation of Labor's representative in New York, was disturbed because of such activities and inquired concerning me. *Labor Age* was at that time receiving free rent in the national office of the International Ladies' Garment Workers' Union and the chief member of the committee making the inquiry was David Dubinsky, then manager of Local 10. To all queries I replied that I would join with any group fighting for social justice and civil liberties and that the Communists had afforded such an opportunity. Thereupon, as a test, the Socialists invited me to address their Sacco-Vanzetti meeting to be held in a hall near Union Square on the very same day as the Communists' open-air meeting. I accepted this invitation and so had the unique distinction of speaking for both groups within the space of a few minutes.

Neither the I.L.G.W.U. nor the A. F. of L. harassed me further—a manifestation of considerable tolerance when one recalls the manner in which the "Red trade unions" were striving to tear the needle-trades union to pieces. It was only when *Labor Age* decided upon active organizational work that we realized that the Communists, under this "Red trade union" policy, would tear down any effort to build up the legitimate unions. Then we were the ones who were the butt of their sneers and smears.

SCENE III. **A workman's apartment in Hudson County, New Jersey, with curtains drawn.**

In this secretive atmosphere, where breaths were baited and words were uttered in whispers, two members of the Ironworkers' Union and I made plans to dislodge Czar

Ted Brandle from the dictatorship of that union. Though this was 1926, the sequel was not to be written until four years later. Brandle was then in the unique position of occupying key places in both the union movement of New Jersey and in its employers' association. At one and the same time he was head of the Building Trades Council of the state and director-general of the employers' Iron League. Even so, these were only part of his business enterprises. In banking, bonding, and the extensive sale of gravel and other materials he also prospered. Within his union and several others he ruled with a rod of iron—having an efficient strong-arm squad to impress his mandates on the membership. Close at his right hand was the former bartender from upstate New York, the notorious Joe Fay, now reposing in Sing Sing for extortion. Fay acquired national ill fame in his own right, after he struck David Dubinsky at the 1940 New Orleans A. F. of L. convention for advocating a resolution against racketeers and racketeering.

In the La Follette campaign, Brandle had become notorious by the rough-and-tumble manner in which he had taken over the New Jersey State Federation of Labor convention of 1924. That body was prepared to support La Follette, consonant with the decision of the national executive council of the A. F. of L. With his customary crude methods, however, at the last minute, Brandle packed the convention with "delegates" under his control and compelled the assemblage to vote an endorsement of John W. Davis for President. Even at that, the vote was exceedingly close. I will never forget the sight of white-haired Henry F. Hilfers, the honest-minded secretary of the State Federation, as he stood in the La Follette state headquarters and with bowed head reported on Brandle's bludgeoning of the convention. Such a man as Brandle was a corrupting influence in the labor movement; he had to be removed if organization was to go forward. His activities merely provided weapons for the enemies who were opposing the organization of the low-paid textile workers in Paterson and Passaic. He was a deficit all around.

Racketeering and related evils hobbled the organization of the unorganized. They were enemies to the unions' purposes, and should therefore be treated like traitors to any cause or country. In alliance with the Scripps-Howard press and such papers as the *Newark Evening News*, *Labor Age* began to level its guns at the racketeers. In Brandle's case, the contest was desperate and, for a long time, doubtful. His downfall finally came in 1930. As a consequence of the depression there was wide revolt among those of his union's members who during more prosperious days had either been cowed or merely acquiescent. Mayor Frank Hague of Jersey City publicly abandoned Brandle just as the latter was compelled to bow himself off the labor stage. It was a Humpty Dumpty fall, for good and all. His demise, held in an atmosphere of job fear, had been prepared in those curtained conferences which *Labor Age* had initiated so many years before when he was a political power and an industrial czar in New Jersey. The cleansing of labor's ranks, even though too slowly, made possible the performance of the new responsibilities that were to be thrust upon the labor movement.

SCENE IV. **Mass picket line before the Allen-A mill in Kenosha, Wisconsin on a snowy mid-February morning. Year: 1928.**

The scene was a strange one for that time. The injunction had been mowing down any and every incipient inauguration of unionism. The yellow-dog contract—in which the workers bound themselves not to become members of a union—was made the ground for many a court order prohibiting almost any form of workers' action. The yellow dog existed at Allen-A, and was introduced by a man named A. R. MacDonald, who specialized in this form of union-busting. The unions dubbed it "labor spy" work.

The company had erected a new high wire fence in anticipation of "some trouble"; it never anticipated the strong singing line of pickets that actually materialized. MacDonald had assured the officials that only a few agitators, if anyone, would walk out and that those few troublemakers would be quickly squelched. He regularly ran around from employer to employer with a copy of the Hitchman Case—decided by the United States Supreme Court—in his hands, saying: "See here! If you have a contract against union membership, the courts will grant a sweeping injunction." His face was as white as the snow around us as he looked out through the wire fence on that February morning and heard the chant of hundreds of voices.

What had happened was this: On February 12, I had received word at Buffalo to report at once to Kenosha to try to arouse the public—through a ministers' committee, if possible—to prevent any discharge of the workers. The union did not want a fight, but neither could it surrender to the contract that was obliterating it. When I arrived on the thirteenth the atmosphere was tense. The entire working force met that night, and I appealed to one and all to stand up for their right of association. The argument for the dignity of man was cheered to the echo, and four hundred girls who were auxiliary workers joined the union as one group. This took the company by surprise. It responded by announcing a lockout for all who would not agree without equivocation to the yellow-dog arrangement. That was late at night. In the morning the mill had slowed down to a snail's pace, as the long picket line stamped through the brisk, bright winter day.

The curtain had gone up on one of the most colorful dramas of that period. An entire community went on the march in favor of the locked-out workers in one mill, and on more than one occasion, tens of thousands of people assembled in the public park to back the union. There was violence such as was seldom seen in labor disputes at that time, though the union maintained that labor spies and the six private detective agencies involved were to blame. Acid was thrown under my door at the Hotel Dayton, and when the man who did it was caught, he confessed that he was employed by the Railway Audit Bureau and had intended the acid for my face. Finally, a long cavalcade of automobiles wound across Wisconsin to lay a wreath on the grave of the elder La Follette as a reminder to the state that its late leader had been "an outstanding opponent of injunctions."

The climax came in the inevitable injunction trial held in the Federal Court in Milwaukee. I and twenty-seven leading union men were tried—I alone was on the stand for two days—and all the defendants were acquitted. Judge Joseph Padway, now counsel for the American Federation of Labor, told me at the last A. F. of L. convention that he would include me in his memoirs because of "the brilliant testimony in the Kenosha trial." He was our attorney in that case and contributed much to our victory—a victory that paved the way for the coming Norris-LaGuardia Act against all such injunctions. But from the very moment of the Kenosha battle, the injunction was no longer the weapon against labor that it had been before. Some may not think this a good thing; it belongs, nonetheless, in any record of the fight for freedom, and is a milestone in this story of a man's pilgrimage toward the truth.

Since *Labor Age* had decided that in order to set a good example it should itself plunge into the organization work, we had accordingly written to five unions offering my services as organizer. Of the three who accepted, we selected the American Federation of Full-Fashioned Hosiery Workers. After Kenosha, the little Pennsylvania-Dutch town of

Nazareth, in the pocket above Easton, was to witness the struggle of the hosiery makers against MacDonald and his yellow-dog arrangements. The Kramer Hosiery Company was here involved.

In all these campaigns the "American approach" was employed in a big way with particular reference to the words and works of Thomas Jefferson and American liberties. But it was in Nazareth that it scored its most pronounced moral victory. In the injunction case there, Mr. Justice Maxey— now Chief Justice of the Pennsylvania Supreme Court—acclaimed my views as those of a "patriot" in his opinion, upholding my fight against the yellow-dog contract. You may read his warm appraisal of my campaign in the Pennsylvania Supreme Court Reports, in the case of the American Federation of Hosiery Workers vs. Kramer Hosiery Company.

Though the two Thomases of the American Revolution— Jefferson and Paine—held a high place in my current considerations, the three Thomases of Catholicism were not entirely absent. Aquinas, à Kempis and the martyred More no longer figured in my public utterances, but I had not forgotten them. Secularism and its urge to be busy about many minor matters crowded my mind and hollowed my heart, and though Heaven kept knocking at the door, I was too preoccupied with "the people's problems" to give proper heed. In my secret thoughts, nevertheless, I was the pursued by that Hound of Heaven of which the sweet-voiced Francis Thompson tells. *I fled Him, down the nights and down the days, I bled him, down the arches of the years.*

In every book I read, and they were many, He walked into my meditations. If I picked up Oscar Wilde, where you would not expect Him, in the preservation of the Greek chorus I found the charm of the Catholic Mass exalted. If I turned to the classic pen of Walter Pater, his description of the early Mass of the catacombs filled me with the beauty of the service and the wonder of the sacrifice. In *Marius the Epicurean*, where least we might expect it, Pater wrote, "The Mass, indeed, would appear to have been said continuously from the Apostolic age. Its details, as one by one they became visible in later history, have already the character of what is ancient and venerable." And again, in describing through the eyes of Marius, the devotion of the early Christians to the Holy Eucharist, he said: "What Saint Louis of France discerned, and found so irresistibly touching, across the dimness of many centuries, as a painful thing done for love of him by one he had never seen, was to them almost as a thing of yesterday; and their hearts were whole with it."

Perhaps in the gilt-edged collection of Bryon, that singer so like to Shakespeare, I might not find Him, or, as Thompson says, "feel the gust of his approach." But when I took that volume from the shelf, therein "Childe Harold" was the burst of praise and prayer to "Christ's mighty shrine above his martyr's tomb." And to St. Peter's the errant and erring poet cries,

> But thou, of temples old or altars new,
> Standest alone, with nothing like to thee—
> Worthiest of God, the holy and the true.

Examine closely Byron's chant to *this eternal art of worship undefiled* and there is a perception much deeper than artistic appreciation of a magnificent triumph in architecture. In that "Holy of Holies" there was visible to the poet the accumulation of all the religious aspirations of man. What pagans had sought in "Diana's marvel," and the schismatics had searched for under "Sophia's bright roofs," the hunger and hope of what was now "Zion's desolation," were all in the divine promise of the Church. Who would look for such perception in the works of one whose restless spirit strained in vain for peace?

Such musings were the companions of my steps along Sixth Avenue, as the Twenties began to melt away into history. So engrossing did such meditations become that on several nights, New Jersey-bound after late meetings, around some corner I would bump into a rambling drunk and have to apologize for what he claimed was my own "drunkenness."

Poets and poetic minds could not escape the charm of Catholic culture, the inspiration of Dante and Michelangelo. What many of them revered as artistic or aesthetic excellence had for me a religious beauty that flowered from the countenance of God. Did not Chateaubriand show that, while scorning the Church, even Voltaire and Rousseau had felt impelled to pay warm tribute to the efficacy of Confession and the Holy Communion? Did not both of them draw from Catholic imagery? Still, they persisted in their unbelief. Indeed, Chateaubriand had noted: "A religion which furnished its enemy with such beauties deserves at least to be heard before it is condemned." Why then, did I, who was harassed by a power in the Church far deeper and more divine than these men had felt, act in accordance with their credo?

The vanity of disbelief numbered my will into substituting a multitude of activities and "accomplishments" for religion. As the Twenties faded into the Thirties, I had parted from the companion of my St. Louis and New Jersey days. For her, too, those fifteen years had been painful, since she likewise had a Catholic conscience. Technical grounds no longer shut me off from the communion of the Church. I was afflicted, however, with what men of the world call "an honest doubt" and say they admire; the Catholic conscience terms it something else and is not so complacent in its judgment.

Two avenues of speculation had been constantly in my mind. While recognizing the glory of the Church, I likewise had an understanding of the coming collapse in the economic setup. With scorn I had derided Professor Thomas Carver of Harvard for prophesying "eternal prosperity" for the United States, "because it followed the Kingdom of God and His righteousness."

Every analysis that *Labor Age* had made proved Carver wrong and showed the imminence of another depression. Since "the higher they go, the harder they fall," this fall would be harder than the Long Depression of the Seventies. *Labor Age* said this in various ways and I stressed it in all my speeches. As a result, I began a new and intense study of economics, in which Marx loomed large. On trains or in automobiles, hurrying to strike meetings, I reread *Capital* and Lenin's *Imperialism*. A paper-covered copy of the latter was almost always either in my pocket or in my traveling bag. The half-truths contained in these studies had a profound effect on my thinking. Had the Communist tactics not appeared so bizarre and even barren, I might even have drawn closer to them as 1929 began to dawn.

What *Labor Age* and I did take up, without equivocation from this "Soviet slant," was a campaign for friendship with the Soviet Republics and recognition of the U.S.S.R. For years, the foreign comment section of the magazine was given over to that theme. Since the publication was distributed to more than two thousand libraries, including colleges, it was no small factor in building public opinion. Furthermore, at all state federation and international union conventions, I always framed or forwarded resolutions for Soviet recognition. So much was this the case that in 1932, when the Roosevelt Administration was preparing to take the step, advocates of the idea came to me to compile the various resolutions to that effect that had been adopted by labor organizations.

For the high crime of organizing the unorganized, the Communists denounced me at this period as a "social fascist." But because of my stand on recognition of the U.S.S.R. they looked upon me, privately, as one to whom they could turn in a pinch, one of their favorite "innocents," as the Social Democrats labeled such people. If that had to be, it was all right with me. The Soviet Union, even though not consistently, was a weight in the international balance against the Treaty of Versailles, which in my lexicon was a crime against the German people and against the peace of the world. Besides, I argued, the existence of the U.S.S.R. was something that could not be denied.

My growing preoccupation with this theme led James O'Neal, then one of the chiefs of the Socialist party, to prophecy that I would soon be a member of the Communist organization. Others said the same thing. And to several friends who told me these rumors I replied sardonically, "My history will be entitled, 'From Rome to Moscow and Return.'" They had a good laugh at that. It was considered a rare joke.

FOUR

Meeting the "Revolution"

Back in 1921 the Communist party had introduced itself to me officially. That spring and summer, the national executive board of the American Civil Liberties Union met for luncheon once a week in the back yard of the Civic Club. There were a few sad trees there and little chairs and tables—some bright red, some green—were scattered about in their shade. I have always wondered whether these attempts at countryside scenes in New York are an imitation of Paris or merely the Midwesterner's yearning for that landscape in which the barefoot boy forever saunters down a dusty road in spring.

As publicity director I was in attendance at these committee meetings, to which guests would come to present civil liberties cases and appeal for aid. One bright day a pair of guests—Jim Cannon and Mother Ella Reeve Bloor—asked me to linger behind with them for a chat. The garden was a pleasant place, they explained, to talk over what they had in mind. They were chummy together then, and neither they nor I could guess that in a few short years they would be castigating each other as the spawn of Hell, or its equivalent in Communist jargon. When Reds fall out, throttles are wide open on expletives and execrations. Cannon was to become the leader of the Trotskyites in America, while for years Mother Bloor continued to be the always-present speaker on "the women's question" at all Stalinite Communist rallies.

They were in a good mood, even the secretive Cannon, for they were there to ask me to join the Party. They had been watching my methods for some time, they explained, and a young man of my caliber was just what the organization wanted and needed. This was a surprise, for the Communists then were all "underground" and I did not recall knowing any of them well enough to have been under observation. The winter before I had stayed for a while at the apartment of Bob Dunn—Robert W. Dunn, the writer on economic topics, and now director of the Labor Research Association—and had there read several of Lenin's works including, specifically, *State and Revolution*. The book had impressed me by the skillful manner in which it spoke to the Anarcho-Syndicalists and pledged the withering away of the State at the end of its usefulness as an instrument of revolution.

The underground aspect of the Party was repulsive to me as being entirely out of character in free America. Even if dictated by the Palmer raids, that hidden atmosphere merely added more zest to the events. "Most of the members are foreign-born, fully 80 per cent, and they require protection" was another argument for the underground setup. But I felt that its continuance would merely perpetuate the preponderence of foreign-born membership, since Americans would shy away from such a patently conspiratorial outfit.

That is what I told the Red duo, with much earnestness, after they had explained the Party structure more fully. At that time the new Party member joined a group of ten led by a captain. That captain was, in turn, one of ten whose representative belonged to a still higher decemvirate—and so on to the top Central Committee. The only ones of the Party the new member actually knew, then, were the other nine in his "phalanx." Any such arrangement in America was asinine and "an open invitation to the *provocatuer*." Blindly, to follow orders from someone I did not know would be worse than hara-kiri, I maintained. For a good part of the afternoon we discussed this pro and con. They argued that

I could come in and help change that condition if it was no good and I held that the member was powerless to change any condition if he could function only in a group of ten. Later on the extraconspiratorial setup did lead to the arrests in the Michigan woods at Bridgeman, and a number of years afterward when I again met Cannon I embarrassed him no end by saying, "Oh, yes, this is the man who tried to get me framed at Bridgeman."

If there was any shrewdness in my argument dictated by a sense of freedom, there was also an immense infantilism. I was talking as though we were considering an American organization, whereas the reality was the fact that the Communist party was not a party at all but an extension of the Soviet Foreign Office, and it was taking on this conspiratorial appearance simply because other "parties" in other places were doing the same. A discovery I was to make later, from a startling experience, was that the Communist setup had always remained conspiratorial, even when it appeared to be "out in the open." The real rulers of the organization were layers deep below the surface of public examination, in close connection with the Soviet agents and under strict Soviet supervision.

The rigid Moscow control is so patent—so grossly in violation of the pledge of the Soviet Union to the United States in the recognition agreement—that a man almost apologizes for mentioning it once more. And yet, there are a host of "liberals" and others who so often look the other way when this is pointed out that it has to be said all over again. After all, this narrator was deceived more than once, and in succession, before he woke up, so that his story should be of value to some other folks, who may be a little too softheaded and softhearted.

The first Congress of the Communist International to which I devoted full-dressed study—the Sixth, held in

Moscow in 1928—pledged itself to "struggle for the world dictatorship of the proletariat." That is, it committed its associates and affiliates to setting up the world dictatorship of Stalin who was hailed as "the leader of the proletariat." This was as much a promise to act as a fifth column for the Soviet government as any Nazi agent ever made to Herr Hitler. And yet, at that Congress, William Z. Foster, the present chief of the American Communists, begged to be recognized as the leader of this program in America. In the yellowed pages of the proceedings, which were available then and which I have kept through the years, is the acknowledgment of Moscow dictatorship over the American party from Foster's own lips. Said he:

On May 16, the C.I.—Communist International—sent a letter to the American Party. This corrected half a dozen serious mistakes of the C.E.C. (American Central Executive Committee). All these mistakes were to the Right. That letter proves conclusively that the Lovestone majority are following a line definitely to the Right.—*International Press Correspondence*, August 18, 1928; speech delivered at Thirteenth Session of Sixth World Congress of Communist International.

The "Lovestone majority" referred to here was that majority of the Communist party in the United States which backed Jay Lovestone, then General Secretary of the American Red organization. Lovestone had graduated from City College, or New York University, into the Communist leadership, but was to be ousted, in time, by Stalin. Then Moscow was actually to declare the "majority" wrong and decide for the "minority"—which furnished a crude but dramatic illustration of the iron control of the Soviet dictatorship over the American group.

I read this confession of complete subservience to Stalin with pertubation. These Reds were using the same slogans that I used—"organization of the unorganized," and "industrial unionism in the basic industries." But they also said, unequivocally, in order to build up internal agencies that they were taking this stand for the benefit of a foreign power. That kept me from affiliation with them.

Since I was opposed to sending American troops to Nicaragua in the Twenties, I had become interested in the Anti-Imperialist League. In amazement, I heard the Communists urging American marines to desert and munition workers to refuse to make weapons for the American Army. Then they tried to commit the League to the same subversion. Then editor of the *Daily Worker*, the late J. Louis Engdahl proudly reported these plots to Moscow in print, in order to create dissension in the armed forces.

Moscow, in turn, brazenly published the Engdahl reports in the *Inprecor* and other papers, and told how faithfully the American Communists were spreading sedition in the American Army. Though on a longer time basis, that same purpose still exists, as I was to learn later.

Regretfully and reluctantly, I had to reconcile myself to the impossibility of co-operating with the Communists— "regretfully and reluctantly" because they frequently associated themselves with proposals that seemed desirable. This is one of the direct products of Communist deceit: it helps label as subversive many movements which have no such tendencies. My hope then—the hope of so many other innocents—was that co-operation with the Communists would tend to change the course of their organization. It took a long time to realize fully that the only change that the foreign-controlled agency will make is one dictated from the Kremlin. In the course of 1928 the Communists themselves convinced me by their activities that one could not work with them and that their object was the destruction of all who did not make Moscow their Mecca.

The first rude awakening was at Kenosha. In the midst of that heated battle, a representative of the Young Communist League arrived. Still hoping for the united front, I welcomed him and introduced him to the members of the strike committee. He was permitted to sit in at our committee meetings, and to distribute copies of the *Daily Worker* to the locked-out workers. What was my surprise when, at a critical stage of the strike, I discovered that he was trying to spread discontent among the strikers and split their ranks. Copies of the *Daily Worker* blossomed forth with stories— you can read them in the 1928 issues—in which it was said that I rode around in luxurious limousines while the strikers starved. The truth was that I had no car and was actually using cars furnished by certain locked-out workers—members of the highly paid hosiery industry. The manufacturers were making enormous profits at that time, and the workers had been well paid. It was only the company's effort to break down that pay which we were opposing.

Another of these fabrications, published in the *Daily Worker*, stated that 1 was the favorite after-dinner speaker of the local Rotary Club—and at a time when some of its influential members were trying to jail me at the behest of the company! To crown all this, a Communist leaflet comparing me to the McNamaras was widely distributed when it should have been obvious to anyone that the violence in Kenosha was labor-spy induced. The corporation eagerly reprinted this Communist sheet and made it an open invitation to imprison me. Fortunately, the people of Kenosha rebuffed such schemes. Well could I say a short while later, "There are two *provocateur* sources we have to watch for in strikes—the labor-spy agencies and the Communists. It's a tossup which is worse and to be the more feared."

The Kenosha strike committee was indignant at these Communist-concocted falsehoods and refused to let the representative attend any more meetings or distribute any more copies of the *Daily Worker*. But I did not really believe that the strike sabotage could meet with the official approval of the Party, with which as I have said I had co-operated in the Sacco-Vanzetti campaign. With the agreement of the Hosiery Workers' officials, therefore, I made a special trip to New York to bring the matter before Jay Lovestone, then General Secretary of the Party. He received me graciously, since the introduction came from Bob Dunn, and told me, in effect, that the central organization could do nothing about the business. I saw that "a line" was being carried out, and that Lovestone himself was probably powerless to amend it. In the proceedings of the Sixth World Congress, which Lovestone attended that year, I was to read in the final address of the chairman, Nicholas Bukharin, that the united front must be conducted only *from below*. It was a counsel of strike-breaking and disruption, internationally planned. Bukharin is now dead—shot by Stalin—but he was the big bug for Stalin at the 1928 Congress. That whole gathering, incidentally, becomes a congress of ghosts, as we read its roster of delegates now. Name after name, starting with Bukharin and Rykoff, Tomsky and Béla Kun, have been liquidated by Stalin—a far greater number than ever fell victims to the black- or brown-shirted Fascists.

The following year, after I had left Kenosha, the young Communist who had engaged in such offensive work was involved in a free-speech fight with the local police. His colleagues sent Frank Palmer, then taking up "civil liberties" fights for the Reds, to see me about helping him out. They wanted the recent leaders of the strikers to come to the rescue. Since free speech was so close to my heart, I agreed to do my best to help them. At first, the boys out in Kenosha absolutely refused to act. Lovers of free speech that they were, they said they could not lift a finger for a man like the one involved. But after I had made it a personal request, they acceded and held a special meeting for his right of free speech.

My motive was not to curry favor with the Communists, but I did have hopes that it would evoke some decency in their future strike tactics. It all turned out quite to the contrary. In the Nazareth strike, which followed in 1929 and 1930, they sent a woman to subvert the strikers from the union, but without success. She entered the strike hall and tried to create disorder—an old Communist trick—by hurling offensive phrases at me, such as "tool of the bosses," "seller-out," and the like. The women strikers were so angry, that they actually wanted to beat her up. Counseling restraint, I asked two of them to escort her quietly to the door and out into the street. And that was that. Later on when I was in the Communist party, I had occasion to meet this woman in a friendly way. She was then an official of the International Workers' Order, the refuge for retired Communist organizers.

When the Paterson general walkout in silk was being proposed with the American Federation of Labor, Communist conduct was even more reprehensible. Hearing of the organization drive, they immediately started one of their own to try to offset the A. F. of L.'s activities. Their excuse was their alleged "Red trade unions." Since The Red Trade Union International was functioning from Moscow, they had to create the same dual movement over here. Beaten at every point in Paterson, they finally resorted to the subterfuge of sending in an alleged "strikers' committee" from Allentown, where they were also fighting the A. F. of L. and its strike. Their committee of about twenty was admitted to a hall packed with nearly two thousand strikers. They immediately set about creating a panic by shouts and imprecations and attempts to take the platform by force.

Hysteria was on the verge of breaking out, when I quietly moved to halt it. "Regretfully," I announced, "we will have to teach these men a lesson. The picket captains will do their duty." So the picket captains, in good order, quickly escorted them out of the hall and down the long flight of stairs, and the meeting continued without any further difficulty.

Even after the complete defeat of the Communists in Paterson, I offered their group of strikers united picket lines. Ex-Communist Benjamin Gitlow, who was looking in on the Paterson situation, cautioned me against such a move. But, in the hope of winning them over, I was eager to get the few remaining and badly defeated "Red trade union" members back under the protection of the A. F. of L. organization. On the whole, the plan was a success. My weakness was in not remembering, later, that a Communist organization does not change its stripes, even though it changes its name to "People's Front," or anything else that sounds pleasant and popular. As an agency of dictatorship, it remains inherently inimical to democratic processes except where they can be used to defend its own life.

During the Paterson affair, and others like it, Communists heaped billingsgate on my head in pages of the *Daily Worker*. Was there not a peculiar perversity in this? They hurled scorn at those whom they charged would not organize the unorganized. Yet, when someone like myself—and this applied to several others—actually did organize the plants, the Reds sought to blacken their names, too. This was not perversity or madness at all, as I should have known. It was the product of a set purpose to obliterate—"liquidate" is the word—all individuals and institutions standing in the way of the destruction of the American nation. This will become even more obvious later in these pages. For the present record it is enough to quote the words of eventual damnation for the United States and other democratic nations that D. Z. Manuilsky was there delivering to the E.C.C.I. (Executive Committee of the Communist International):

"The set tasks lie on the line of revolutionary upsurge, on the line of struggle of the working class, not in words but in deeds, for the overthrow of capitalism and the establishment of the proletarian dictatorship. To carry out these tasks means to work for proletarian revolution and its victory. It means to set up the enormously broad front, to draw in the backward elements, to keep the advance guard together, to consolidate the rear, to mobilize the giant army of the toilers of the whole world for the decisive struggle. And only on such conditions will the general staffs of the revolutionary world movement—the Communist Parties—be able to say firmly and calmly at a decisive historical turn of events, the date of which cannot be predicted by us: 'We are prepared!'"

In, 1946 Manuilsky is still pushing this "revolutionary" warfare against the United States as an alleged representative of the Ukrainian S.S.R. in the United Nations. Among "the tasks" to which he referred in his 1930 exhortation was the fight against "left social fascism," which, of course, meant calling off any honest-minded group which sought to organize workers in a progressive way independent of the Communist machine. Manuilsky was then presiding over the political execution of Bukharin, Ryhoff and Tomsky— the men who had been so prominent in the Sixth Congress of the Communist International in 1928 and had also supervised the political demise of the Trotksyites on the one hand, and of Gregory Zinoviev and Leon Kameneff on the other.

Hitler's ambition—world domination—was acknowledged by Manuilsky to be Soviet Russia's aim also. The German elections of 1930, in which the Communists had forged ahead, made him "dizzy with success" and he showed Russia's fangs to the world. Two years later he expounded the same theme at the Twelfth Plenum of the E.C.C.I., and boldly urged the "proletariat" to disrupt and destroy their own governments on behalf of the Soviet state. Even in 1934, when he had to acknowledge that the capitalist collapse in the United States was not so complete as he had hoped, Manuilsky was still stressing world domination when he declared, amid thunderous applause, at the Seventeenth Congress of the Communist Party of the Soviet Union: "Lenin led the toilers in Russia to October. Stalin, following Lenin's path, is leading them to victory throughout the whole world." The planned use of the various "proletarian" groups as a fifth column throughout the world, under Stalin's leadership, could not be more clearly stated. These subversive statements can all be read in the pages of the *International Press Correspondence* for 1930 to 1934; the last mentioned in the issue of February 26, 1934. Similar declarations of perfidy to the United States can be read in the *Daily Workers* of that period. That paper obediently followed every pronouncement of Manuilsky, as Secretary of the Communist International, and in every way conformed to the Soviet plans of the time. To read these would be to appreciate even more intensely the coming account of how Manuilsky secretly sent disciplinary orders to the Party here at the time of the San Francisco meeting of the United Nations.

Those in the American labor movement who would not agree to this fifth column role were to be hit hard and harassed at every step, particularly if they were militant or progressive. The war against the "social fascists" was to be intensified, said Manuilsky in his orders to the Red puppets in America and elsewhere. The impact of these orders was felt almost immediately in the Toledo Auto-Lite strike where the Red tactics nearly robbed the workers of the victory we had gained.

In labor history the name "Toledo" signifies the beginning of successful permanent union organization in the auto-mobile industry. It is the real birthplace of the United Automobile Workers' Union, although it was a local A. F. of L. federal local union that was involved in the Auto-Lite dispute. I am justly proud of the contribution I made there toward turning a lost strike into a tremendous victory, with union recognition established as the foundation for future labor-management relations. The right of association was there made a living thing.

In the second edition of his book, *Dynamite*, in which he refers to me as "one of the leading strike strategists in America," Louis Adamic has outlined at some length the events of May, 1934, in Toledo. The *New Republic* has like-wise vividly detailed the affair. From these accounts you will·learn that the company had gone back on its promise given to the workers earlier in the year, and that the strike of some months back had again broken out in April. The mill was rapidly manned with strikebreakers from near-by towns.

Called into Toledo by the unemployed leagues, which were then in opposition to the Communist-controlled unemployed councils, I began to speak in front of the plant on Monday, May 21, to a crowd that in three days grew from one thou-sand to fifteen thousand people. The burden of my talk, delivered from the front porch of a house across from the plant, was that a cut in wages would make the depression worse. I referred fervidly to the N.R.A. and its promise of unionism. This struggle was the people's struggle—that of all Toledo.

Alarmed at the growing number of persons sympathetic to the pickets, the company had me arrested and launched a gas attack against the pickets and the populace. The big battle that ensued is now history. Toledo became thoroughly incensed at the company and within a few days there was a settlement of the strike with union recognition.

The Communists, who had made no contribution to this victory, rushed in from Detroit, Cleveland and other places to stir up a general strike and general confusion. They almost achieved the latter—which would have turned public sentiment against the union and lost what had been gained. Fortunately, the Communist schemes were squelched. Never was there demonstrated more brazenly how willingly the Reds would break the workers' spirit and blast their cause to advance certain "political objectives." The *Daily Worker*, it need hardly be said, poured vials of rhetorical acid upon my head—for having planted the union banner in the automobile industry! Their accounts were completely distorted. Hitlerism may have boasted coarsely about the big lie, but it was the Communists everywhere who invented it.

The reason given for these concoctions was that I was associated with the Conference for Progressive Labor Action. I was then national secretary, and A. J. Muste of Brookwood Labor College was chairman. The organization sought to develop the "American approach," which I had brought to the fore again in 1928 in a series of lectures at Brookwood. At first, Muste had been wary of the idea but later on had accepted it. As I saw it, it was more than an "approach." It was the use of American traditions. It had, too, peculiarly American features—such as my suggestion that Socialism be introduced by an amendment to the Constitution just as chattel slavery had been abolished! Whatever the weaknesses of such a view, it did not make a man or movement the tool of Russia's foreign policy, and that offended the Communists exceedingly.

The Communists were aware that with them I was a champion of the united front and that I was under fire from the Trotskyites within the unemployed leagues for being too friendly with the "Stalinists." They knew of my repeated and patient proposals for our working together. In the unemployed movement, they had witnessed my part in stopping three thousand evictions in the city of Columbus, Ohio. They were aware that in the summer of 1933 I had spoken to seven thousand people before the state capitol in that city and had won higher relief for the whole state. They had been present, in the persons of many of their leading representatives, at the National Unemployed League convention at the State Fairgrounds in Columbus, at which the united front with the unemployed leagues had been adopted through my persistent efforts. It puzzled me that they really should continue to abuse me. Only when I was within the Party did I learn that it was Manuilsky's Moscow-gram of orders, through the E.C.C.I., which had made them act in that manner.

Why, after so many rebuffs, did I persist in finding ways and means to work with the Communists? There was, of course, the desire for unity behind such proposals as industrial unionism. There was the desire not to be a "Red baiter," that ridiculously fictitious label applied by the Communists to everybody who is not wholly with them. Then, there was the constant breast-beating of the Reds, which took me in pretty badly. They were always "self-criticizing" and explaining that they had had the right line but had applied it wrongly. This gave me high hopes of showing them the light, and how to do things in an American way. Men like J. B. S. Hardman, then editor of the Amalgamated Clothing Workers' paper, *Advance*, but formerly associated with the old Communist Workers Party, unconsciously helped perpetuate these fictions for me by saying that the Communist movement was all right in the Soviet Union but no good here.

How was I to know, then, that the very malice and mal-practice of the "line" was molded in Moscow? Ah, but there were those who did!

There were some experiences, pretty vital ones, which tended to make me overlook Communist chicanery. The C.P.L.A. had been founded to defend Brookwood Labor College when that institution was charged by the A. F. of L. executive council with harboring Communists—an accusation not entirely incorrect, as things turned out. Those who composed the original Conference ranged from old-line Socialists to near-Reds. It gradually assumed the attributes of a proponent of the "American approach," antithetical to the Communists both in that instance and in its insistence on working within the American Federation of Labor. It was the C.P.L.A., in co-operation with the A. F. of L. United Textile Workers Union, which prepared and launched the Paterson organizing strike of 1930–1931.

The Trotskyites, having no base from which to operate, began to "colonize" the C.P.L.A. with a view to agitating for union with them. To this I was utterly unsympathetic. In the Trotskyites I saw crudely expressed those evils which only later I discovered were also present in the Stalinists. When, at a Pittsburgh convention in late 1933, the C.P.L.A. formed the American Workers Party—an abortive arrangement for which I confess myself responsible—that group was definitely committed not to affiliate or merge with "any of the splinter groups from the C.P." That resolution, aimed at the Trotskyites, was my handiwork, together with Hardman. Scarcely was the convention over, however, when several of the executive committee members of the new "Party" collaborated with the Trotskyite colonists to work for unity with the Trotsky camp. And the proposal went through, after painful parleys, over my unreserved and unrelenting opposition.

The more I recoiled from the Trotskyites, and in this connection I met and disagreed with Cannon again, the more I inclined toward conciliation with the Communists. My first attitude, as the months after Toledo edged toward 1935, was: "a plague on both your houses." This was expressed in an article that appeared in the January, 1935, issue of the *Modern Monthly*, edited by V. F. Calverton. I castigated both Stalinists and Trotskyites for their lack of Americanism. It was then that I proposed the constitutional-amendment method for meeting our "Socialist" problems here. This article attracted wide attention, and in countries other than the United States. John Middleton Murray, Katherine Mansfield's husband, recommended it to English audiences.

Calverton was enthusiastic about the reception given the piece and invited me to expand these views further at a dinner-meeting for his magazine at which Max Eastman and Harold Laski were also to speak. Here it was that I ran afoul of Laski's anti-American animus of which I had hitherto been unaware. In explaining America's lack of sympathy for Communism or even for a national Labor party, I reasoned that the early absence of feudalism here had helped keep down class-consciousness. In England, I stated, there had been a peculiar intermarriage of the City and the nobility which had developed along unique lines while on the continent the trend had been more toward "class versus class," Laski didn't like this at all and angrily "defended Britain." by accusing America of its own form of feudalism—industrial feudalism—"worse than that which Europe had ever had." I have understood Laski's tart observations about the United States much better ever since: he is inherently pro-Soviet and anti-American and considers America's existence a sort of personal affront!

Communist contempt for things American had long puzzled me; it had stood out boldly in the early numbers of the *Daily Worker*, and continued even into the late Thirties. Out in Columbus I had prepared a replica of the old "Don't Tread on Me" flag of the American Revolution for use in the eviction contests. It was a great help later in the Toledo picketings. Israel Amter, a leading Communist, who is always spoken of with reverence among the comrades, was passing through Columbus and looked me up. Noting the flag, he condemned it completely. It might become "a form of fascism," he averred—and that was the Communist view at the time. The traditions of freedom became "fascist" in their hands. It was Russian chauvinism to which they were devoted and are devoted—as abjectly as the Nazi Bund was to Hitler.

After the "People's Front" was adopted, there was a twisting and turning on this matter. Browder even went so far as to proclaim: "Communism is Twentieth-Century Americanism." A huge sign to that effect floated over a number of mass rallies at Madison Square Garden and other places. Every Communist speaker made it his theme, and it was prominently displayed at the national headquarters of the Party. Then one fine day, Browder suddenly announced that this slogan was wrong and that the Communists had been mistaken in following it. It tended to undermine the Russian chauvinism on which service to the Party is based, and so it had to be "corrected."

In my early reading of the *Daily Worker*, there were a number of other items that struck me as totally lacking in sense. "THERE IS NO GOD—BIMBA" was one of these. That huge headline appeared across the *Daily Worker*, over a lurid account of the trial of Anthony Bimba, a prominent member of the Party. To the delight of the editors of the Party's official organ, he had made this raw declaration of atheism at his court hearing. He was also the author of the standard Red *History of the American Labor Movement*, which, in effect, denounced Abraham Lincoln as an enemy of mankind and taught subversion and scorn for all our national heroes. The Bimba headline later became a laughing matter among the comrades, because it had exposed their views so crudely. Their concern was not the insult to all believers, but the cross giveaway of the atheistic views they really held.

Equally difficult for me to understand was Foster's declaration, made before a congressional committee in Washington, that he was "proud to take orders from Moscow." And he hailed the Red flag of the Soviet dictatorship as the flag of all "advanced workers," including himself. He declared the Soviet Union to be the land to which he and his colleagues were loyal, and proclaimed the abolition of religion to be one of their chief objectives. This whole treasonous harangue was a grave violation of American citizenship. But Foster's leftism—which once put him in the company of the Trotskyite group in the C.P., led by Cannon—might lead him to say anything, however anti-American if Moscow but gave the nod. The intermittent factional quarrels of the first Communist party days confounded me, too, as I diligently read the *Daily Worker* and tried to understand them. Every organization is likely to have disturbances of this sort in its early history, but there was an element of hoodlumism about these differences that was disconcerting. The quarrels went on without end— Foster against Charles Ruthenburg, who died early enough to become "the American Lenin," Jay Lovestone and Benjamin Gitlow against Foster and, in between, many other combinations and shifts from group to group. All of a sudden a Lore-Poyntz group appeared and I read its declaration with interest, but without understanding. It soon disappeared. Ludwig Lore was quickly to be labeled a "renegade" and "Trotskyite" and Julia Stuart Poyntz, an

American schoolteacher, was to step right off the face of the globe one day while working for the Soviet conspiratorial apparatus. Supposedly, she had been about to double-cross it. Of her we shall hear more.

The quarrels went on until Stalin ruled Lovestone and Gitlow out of the Party, bitterly reprimanded Foster, and put Earl Browder of Kansas, who had been in Moscow for several years, in command. This was quite a blow to Foster and his prestige, since it put Browder, upon whom he had long looked as his assistant, in the superior position. This offense of Browder's was never forgiven or forgotten.

What was the common thread beneath all these charges and countercharges, admissions of subversion and chants of superpatriotism? Even before my entry into the Party I had pieced it together to a considerable extent. It was my experiences within the Red organization, though, that supplied the final key. The American Party apparatus reflected the state of affairs in the Soviet Union with the sensitiveness of a seismograph to an earthquake. The history of Soviet Russia is written in the gyrations of the Communist movement in the United States. The bitter contests here were essentially contests to determine who would be the highest servants of Moscow. But behind them, always, were considerations and speculations based on the course of the Soviet Union in world affairs.

When in 1930 the Communist party here was hell-bent on separate Red unions and the defamation of anyone not in complete accord with that aim, they were reflecting the optimism of the Soviet high command. As chief of the Soviet agents in other countries, Manuilsky based his calculations on the Red successes in the German elections and the prospect of sweeping into that country and shaking "world capitalism." In 1928 the speculation had been that the United States, the arch-capitalist country, as V. M. Molotov

then called it in some derision, was about to experience a
complete collapse. Our country was held to be at "the apex
of its power." The expectation of a depression was justified,
as 1929 proved, but the rosy prospect of a general debacle
in the U.S.A. faded out, despite the predictions of Stalin
and Manuilsky. In 1933 there was more caution because the
Hitlerites had come into power in Germany, though the
Soviet leaders still banked on a setback for the Nazi economy
that did not come. They believed that Hitler would not last
long and continued to talk of their "world revolution" in
imminent terms. It was not until 1935 that their tune was
temporarily changed.

Fear of the Axis and its efficiency, which was justified by
the rapid German advance across Soviet Russia in 1941 and
1942, caused them to talk nice to the democracies at the
Seventh Congress that year. But, as the documents of that
People's Front Congress will show, this was only a temporary
device to fend off Hitler's shadow. That the destruction of
the "bourgeois democracies" was to be accomplished later
is evident in those proceedings.

During the greater part of this time, the Soviet leaders
were confidently prophesying war between the United States
and Great Britain. They formulated their instructions to
their agents everywhere on that premise. Similar chatter was
echoed here in the Communist press. In his report to the
Enlarged Presidium of the E.C.C.I. in 1930, Manuilsky
stated without any ifs or buts: "The developing world
economic crisis is greatly accelerating the approach of
imperialist war between Great Britian and the United
States." They contemplated, then, the possibility of turning
this imperialist war into a civil war, and they foresaw the
Communist party here as a mass party within a short time.
(*International Press Correspondence*, April 23, 30, 1930.)

In that very year Stalin was obliged to caution the Party

workers in the Soviet Union against "becoming dizzy with success." That was a result of trying to push industrialization too far and too fast. A similar warning to the leaders of the Soviet Union and the Communist International on world affairs would have been in keeping. They made fools of many of their puppets in this and other countries, as the comrades shamefacedly confessed to me after my entrance into the Party during the "People's Front" era. Again, in 1946 the warning may not be amiss, when Soviet Russia is pushing forward like a gangster with its guns aimed at the United States. That may also be the result of dizziness.

Fifteen years ago the Soviet Union was functioning in a nonfriendly world. The United States had not even recognized the regime there, and I was strongly committed to recognition in order to "assure peace and concord." "Defend the Soviet Union" was then repeated like a litany in all Communist and fellow-traveling publications, and I was dead set against any new intervention against "the Land of Socialism." It was baffling, then, to be treated to these pronunciamentos of the C.I.'s boasting of coming world domination, counseling sabotage and subversion in the big democratic countries, and anticipating the impossible "war between the United States and Great Britain." All of them were partly the product of wishful thinking, I was to find out later, and partly to fill the need to present the U.S.S.R. as a more tremendous success than it actually was. Many a day I scratched my head over the braggadocio in the *Daily Worker* and the *Inprecor*—the popular name for the *International Press Correspondence*—, not aware that such a simple explanation as Moscow's own needs could account for such inconsistency.

If I went to the Communists for some unscrambling of this political potpourri, they would repeat by rote the same stuff I had read. Even in the days when they were assailing me for forming unions, there were several with whom I kept in touch. One of these was Herbert Benjamin, then of the Workers' Alliance, and later to become nationally known as secretary of the National Unemployed Councils. I met Benjamin soon after I moved to the East, and he was active in Pennsylvania during some of my own visits there. "When are you going to join the Party?" was his question whenever we met and always asked with a smile of welcome. When I raised the difficulties I had in grasping the "world domination" slant of the C.I. pronouncements, he would give me the same stale and stilted rejoinders that the other Reds had given.

Their whole thinking was Moscow-made. Even in those meritorious causes that they espoused, the inception was due to the masterful Manuilsky. To the Sixteenth Party Congress of the Communist party of the Soviet Union, held in 1930, he declared: "In the United States, for instance, the Communists must launch a powerful movement for social insurance. They must place themselves at the head of this movement and lead it to victory." And launch the social insurance movement they immediately did. The purpose of this campaign in the U.S.A. was to "strengthen the sections of the Comintern organization," as Manuilsky expalined. It was to do what V. M. Molotoff, now Soviet Foreign Minister, had recommended in his main report to that Sixteenth Congress: "Under Lenin's banner of the Comintern the million masses of the workers and toilers are rallying in closed ranks to the revolutionary struggle against the bourgeoisie, for the victory of the proletarian revolution." (These proceedings can be read in the *Inprecor*, July 25, 1930, Vol. 10, No. 34.)

Although the Communist objectives seemed pretty thick to me, still I jumped into the national campaign for social security and the organization of the unemployed. I had long had such a campaign in mind, and had raised the matter with Muste from the organizing field at Nazareth before the big trembler struck Wall Street. The gradual drop in the number of employed was visible in cities like Easton and Philadelphia early in 1929, and railroad men began to tell me of layoffs as I traveled to and from Nazareth. The organization of the jobless seemed a good way to win relief for them and still nurse along the trade-union movement. This judgment led to the start of what later became the National Unemployed League, a rival but a co-operator with the Unemployed Councils.

This formation of the Leagues and the preparation of our own social insurance legislative proposals should be recorded among recent historic acts in America. Our proposed law was much more realistic than the first suggestions of the Unemployment Councils, for they felt uneasy as social reformers and tried to reach for the moon. The Leagues brought the whole matter down to earth. They did more; they made Americans appreciate that good could come out of their own people, their own soil, and that not everything "progressive" was hatched by a foreign government and its satellites.

There are some who do not appreciate how vital such a way of doing things is to our country. As soon as they—let us say, hypothetical Congressman XYZ or Colonel ZYX—hear that the Communists have endorsed any measure, they are against it. They label it "Red," no matter how desirable it may be. Such conduct is difficult to understand, for it does just what the Communists frequently want done. It tends to make them appear the sole custodians of a worth-while proposal. They are, as a matter of record, the very opposite; for their championship of a needed reform often delays its adoption an inordinately long time.

I pursued the Communists about their practice of deceit and falsification wherever I ran into one among them of any consequence. After a conference at Corliss Lamont's house on the possibility of establishing the *People's Press*—that was in 1935—or in a restaurant near Union Square or on the street of a Pennsylvania town, I would ask how these falsehoods could be justified. The reply was invariably the same: there is objective and subjective truth. To serve the "real truth" you have to represent a person as he is politically, whether you give the exact facts about him or not. It was a rather fragile moral concept. It seemed closely akin to Hitlerism.

To anyone looking over the labor scene of 1935 the Communists seemed to stand out favorably in one respect. That was in the alleged "monolithic" character of their membership, which they frequently and fulsomely stressed in press and on platform. True, leading representatives were expelled from time to time; indeed, the list of expulsions of those who once held leading positions would be a long and imposing one. But the organization itself stayed constantly and actively before the public. That commended it to many people who were looking for some continuing form of radical political expression. To anyone looking in from the outside, of course, it was not apparent that this "monolithic" quality was artificial and forced. They could not be fully aware that it was enforced by the iron hand of an absolutely antidemocratic setup under which a man would be politically, and even sometimes physically, shanghaied if he became troublesome in disagreement. They were not informed of the agents of the Communist International, and therefore of the Soviet Government, who functioned in the Communist party apparatus and directed it. They did not know that the only privilege even a leading member had was to get up and hurrah for the line sent down from the Kremlin. With this hardhanded, undemocratic rule, a show of "unity" could readily be maintained.

The Social Democrats looked quite different. Always uncertain where they were going or how to proceed, they were split into widely different camps. The Norman Thomas Socialists were moving toward the extreme Left, which embraces a sort of pacifism. The Social Democratic Federation, more realistic and serviceable to labor—although more set in its methods—had abandoned independent political expression as a party. The Debs Socialists, who were ever inclined to their own peculiar "American" way of talking and acting, were moving into the Democratic party.

This came to my attention quite sharply when my old friend, former Socialist Mayor James B. Furber of Rahway, New Jersey, was elected Mayor of Linden on the Democratic ticket in 1932. Unfortunately, he died from a heart attack just as he was taking his new office, or he probably would have been heard of again, nationally. Around 1925 he and I had aroused the interest of the nation's press, and of many people everywhere, by the installation of the municipal sales of potatoes, milk and other products in the city of Rahway. This was reputed to be a reply to the high cost of living and several journals picked it up as "an experiment in Socialism." It proved to be neither the one nor the other. There was, of course, nothing inherently Socialistic about it. Under certain circumstances it could just as well have been initiated by an adherent to Catholic social views. Furthermore, the experiment was conducted on too small a scale to have any effect on the cost of living, and had so many free contributions in the form of management, store space and the like, that it was in no sense truly competitive with private business. The most that it did was momentarily to attract national attention to rising costs and the inflationary bubble that was threatening to explode—as it did three years later.

A native of Michigan, Furber had all the go-gettiveness of a Midwesterner who knew his way around the East, and he was an excellent executive. However, he had too much contempt for political ingratiation so that when he offended the volunteer firemen by introducing a professional fire-fighting nucleus, thereby reducing fire-insurance rates locally, he was defeated. On that occasion, the enmity of certain local interests was so great that an organized mob paraded through the streets all night, even beating on my own front door and vowing to toss me into the Rahway River. That was a long time ago, in 1926, but I remember vividly how cold-sweatedly disturbed I was, and how I resolved that thereafter in any crisis I would "be at the head of the crowd, not ahead of it." And a profitable resolution this was, for it led me to inaugurate the weekly papers during the labor disputes at Kenoska, Nazareth and other places, and won the communities' good will toward the labor cause.

I became even better acquainted with the Social Democrats when they co-operated in the strike at Kenosha. Leo Krzycki, of the Amalgamated Clothing Workers, often came down to help me by speaking to the locked-out workers. He had been assistant sheriff in Milwaukee during the Socialist regime. Social Democracy appeared to be afflicted with the "two souls" of which Goethe speaks, pulling it in different directions. It seemed to aim at a totalitarian state, so far as anyone could make out, but it also wanted to hold on to democracy. This made it highly indeterminate and, in the opinion of many, highly inadequate.

The Trotskyites also wooed our Conference of Progressive Labor Action group, but they, too, were woefully wanting. They had a hatred for religion—"bourgeois morality"—and everything currently in existence. It is no wonder that, according to a recent article by Rebecca West, Hitler used German Trotskyites as guards and encouraged them to persecute Catholics of the resistance movement. That is the Trotskyite style. A good while afterward I was to learn that they represent "Stalinism out in the cold," but that essentially the two Communist camps are the same.

When the Trotskyites succeeded in taking the C.P.L.A. group into their camp, through the amazing weakness of certain of its leading members, my refusal to go along started a weird campaign of falsification against me. The Trotskyites took advantage of my severe illness at the moment to send out information that "the pain" was making me "slightly irresponsible." Having got the super-clever falsehood off their chests, the Trotskyites then represented me as really being with them. I immediately sent letters to the *New Republic* and *Nation* stating that I "had never been a Trotskyite" and wanted to have nothing to do with them.

The *Daily Worker* ran an editorial commending my action but still phrasing the statement as though I were a Trotskyite. To this I wrote an objection, again declaring that I had never had any sympathy with the Trotskyite movement and that I had always stood by the "American approach." I then referred to my long sympathy for the Soviet Union, "the Land of Socialism," and added that the various defects still existing there were comparable to Charles Dickens' criticism of the American republic upon his first visit here. While this was markedly different from the hosannas of perfection to the U.S.S.R. which streamed from the Communist press every night and morning, the *Daily Worker* printed the letter.

Reading it in Moscow, leading C.P. members, at the Seventh Congress sessions, said: "Something is happening over there." It encouraged them to continue the People's Front policy which Dimitrov was introducing at the Congress of the Comintern. That's what they said, at any rate, when I saw them.

Even then, Communism had not won me over to the extent that some suspected; there were still plenty of reservations in my mind. It would take a big demonstration of good faith and a changed policy to make me fall in with that movement. Too well did I recall what Browder had said at a critical point in the united front between the Communists and the C.P.L.A. in 1933. At that same time, with the unemployed movement at a high peak, we considered the formation of a labor party. The League had tried the idea out in a local election in Allentown, Pennsylvania, with some success. So we met with a special committee of Communist leaders to discuss the whole subject. While our committee was outlining the possibilities of such a party, Browder interrupted to declare, "We will enter a labor party in order to disrupt it." That was too much for me. "This is a policy of guile and deception," I spluttered, "it is a gospel of futility." We parted in friendly fashion but with mutual mistrust. Actually, Browder had not appeared enthusiastic about his own stand. And Stachel told me later that it had simply been forced upon him and he had had no choice but to repeat it, parrotlike.

One major reason for my constant attempts to co-operate with the Communist party was the gathering clouds of another war that darkened the world's horizon. It was all too visible to me, though many others did not seem to see it. The approaching Axis alliance against the democratic nations was, to me, a foregone conclusion. In the fall of 1934 I wrote a letter to the *New York Sun*, commenting on one of that paper's editorials, and I forecast the line-up in World War II just as it eventually occurred. Roughly, I said, there would be the United States, Great Britain, France and the Soviet Union against the Axis nations. The one thing impeding the alliance against the Axis, said I, is the "vacillation of Great Britain." This letter reflected so much of my thinking and sheds such light on the events of that day that I venture to reprint a large part of it. Referring to the *Sun's* editorial on the Franco-Russian pact, the letter stated:

International circles are not merely discussing this particular accord; they are equally concerned with the Franco-Russian-American grouping, as it is coming to be called. Common political and economic needs are throwing these strange bedfellows into each other's arms. If France and Soviet Russia feel that they face "a growing menace" in a re-armed Germany, the United States and Russia no less find themselves confronted with an aggressive, militaristic Japan.

Over against this grouping there stand the powers which suffer from nationally inferiority complexes: Nippon, Germany and Italy. The Asiatic Monroe Doctrine, the yoke of Versailles and the glory of the Caesars draw these lands together in something like a common interest. "A holy war against Fascism" on the one hand and "a crusade for a place in the sun" on the other, are therefore in the making. The lineup would be more complete were it not for the vacillation of Great Britain, which cannot decide whether British destiny lies in continental or colonial expansion.

Economic nationalism—with its reflex in the Soviet Union itself in the doctrine of "socialism in one country"—is preparing for another inevitable world war. At a time when the world is drawn physically closer together, the nations have embarked upon the suicidal policy of economic self-sufficiency. Failing at rationalization along that line, they turn to military conflict.

Despite the interpretation of certain radical and liberal journals, the Franco-Russian pact is not a pact for peace. It is an alliance for war. The Frency military mission, recently returned from Moscow, reports that the Russian airfleet can bomb Berlin on the one hand and the Japanese cities on the other. It is an alliance for a world war, which other foreign offices know is hastening toward us.

That was a much sounder view, incidentally, than the one I adopted eight months later in joining the Communist party. It will be understood, though, how much I hoped to aid in averting or ameliorating such a catastrophe and how I rejoiced when the Communists adopted, or pretended to adopt, the "People's Front policy." It was a pretense and a deceit, for the Trojan Horse tactic of which George Dimitrov, the hero of that Congress, boasted, was to win out in the end so far as Soviet aims were concerned.

These thoughts lay heavy on my mind, and I spoke them to everyone I could reach. The radical editor of a large union paper pooh-poohed these ideas. "For one thing," he said, "there, is no reason for Japan to war upon the United States." To that I replied that Japan was aware that the American Open Door policy in China would interfere with her Asiatic empire ambitions and that the defense at Guam and Hawaii was not to her liking. Finally I stressed the Tanaka memorandum, in which plans were proposed for assaults upon our Pacific possessions and our West Coast. Also, the marching men in Hitler's Reich were more of a menace than many would admit. The Germany of 1934 to 1935 was rapidly growing into a mammoth war machine. The German food supplies service was already included in the military machine's vast plans. And the "National Socialist Service for Covering Requirements" had placed all raw materials, canning plants and the distribution of agricultural products in the hands of the military chieftains.

Whether or not the American Communists were quisling agents of Moscow—a question that I tried to evade for years—they were solidly committed to "Soviet-American understanding." I reasoned that the Soviet Union, with its "withering away" tendencies, would become a democratic ally, and that the Communists would help to bring it about.

Would I not discover later that the Soviet Government was also engaged in a war economy which it would never give up? Would I not see the Soviet state continuing the same military economy in postwar 1946 that Hitler imposed on the German people? But in 1934 and 1935, I would have declared hotly that any such prediction was "an unjustified reflection upon the Soviet Republics."

These years of the early Thirties represent the lowest ebb in my religious life. The altar at St. Patrick's was a vague, misty memory. Some would call what had come over me a spiritual numbness. I was sufficiently impregnated with Marxism so that I now thought almost exclusively in terms of production—which eventually destroys all moral values. While reading with the same voraciousness of my earlier years, my present calendar of books indicated my exile from Catholicism. Shakespeare was always near at hand, and Gissing gave me many moments of pleasure in spite of his antisocial animus. The same feeling for a book that he had, that desire to touch it and hold it, was also mine. And Lenin's works were read from start to finish all over again. There were excursions, too, into American history, and Stephen Vincent Benét's *John Brown's Body*, in partic- ular, made me feel the exultation of being an American. The conversion of Willa Cather and Sigrid Undset to the Church sent momentary pricks of pain into my conscience, but it was pretty deeply buried now.

It was at that time that I met Margaret and we became husband and wife. Little did we suspect then, when our views of life and morals almost mocked at Catholicism, that her understanding and intelligence would help us back to Bethlehem and Rome. A Unitarian, educated on a Godless philosophy at the University of Pittsburgh and in the Freudian psychoanalytic school for social work, Margaret had no knowledge of Catholic history or philosophy. But hers was a warm heart, and a long-suffering patience. It was on the very day that I was arrested at Toledo in the Auto-Lite strike that our first daughter, Julia, was born prematurely in New York. After her came Josephine and then Justine. They were not reared in the knowledge of the Church and God, but had a respect for the beliefs of their neighbors that testified to an effort at education of the heart.

When we visited Indianapolis, which we could do only rarely, my parents treated us with Christian love. Never did they mention the state of sin in which we lived, and everything was as it always had been. Every evening, though, they prayed the rosary, and we were high in their intentions. Heaven was stormed for thirty years on their son's behalf. If prayer could change the heart of man, it was powerfully at work. Mary the Immaculate, who had exclaimed, "He has filled the hungry with good things," was besought to aid this man who had succumbed to the vanity of the world.

Thirty years is long, is it not, to wait and hope? Great is the faith that can put such trust in the Mother of God.

FIVE

In the Party of Stalin

ELEVEN YEARS ago—on the hot morning of August 3, 1935—I left the apartment building on Montrose Ave., Williamsburg, with my year-old daughter and walked to the near-by newsstand under the "El." We had been doing that every morning for months. I invariably purchased two papers, the *New York Times* and the *Daily Worker* and then went across the street to the abandoned platform of a boarded-up warehouse. I read while the baby played.

I was convalescing from a stubborn illness, and we had moved into this gaunt Brooklyn district to be nearer my wife's place of work as a social worker. The heat that morning drove up from the sidewalks and put to flight the faint damp of the earlier hours of dawn. Assorted slum smells began to burden the air. Everything seemed the same as it always had near the foot of the Williamsburg Bridge. That wasn't true, though, so far as I was concerned. It was to be a memorable day; it was to make me "a leading American Communist" for the next ten years.

I picked up the *Daily Worker* and stopped dead in my tracks. Across its front page was a large picture of George Dimitrov, known as the man who had "told off" Goering at the Leipzig trial. The headlines and the columns beneath them proclaimed a sweeping change in the Communist line and Red adherence to the People's Front. I halted at the near-by subway station and sat on the fourth step up, the baby by my side. She could amuse herself by watching the passers-by while I read avidly what Dimitrov had said in Moscow at the Seventh Congress of the Communist International the day before. The columns were still couched in Communist lingo, but they said something far different from what the Reds recently had been saying.

First, the address called for a "united proletarian front— no longer "the united front from below" which had been the occasion for so much mischief and Red strike-breaking. Those who had been blistered as "social fascists" were to be grasped by the hand all over the world. And beyond that united front, there was to be something else even greater. Said Dimitrov:

> In the mobilization of the toiling masses for the struggle against fascism, the formation of a broad anti-fascist people's front on the basis of the proletarian united front is a particularly important task. The success of the entire struggle of the proletariat is closely connected with the establishment of a fighting alliance between the proletariat on the one hand and the toiling peasantry, and the basic mass of the urban petty bourgeoisie constituting a majority of the population of even industrially developed countries, on the other.

That declaration was made, it is true, in the colossal and clouded language that Communists so frequently used to cloak their real purposes. But it did mean something—or at least I thought so. Hitler firmly fixed in power in the Reich, contrary to former Communist expectations, the Reds had to find a new set of friends. They were to be sought, first, among those whom they had formerly vilified as "social fascists." They were then to be discovered among those "broad" political groups which the Communists had once viewed with contempt. Their new scheme envisaged a plan to work with the older political parties in most countries. Indeed, resorting to figures of speech that had become peculiarly Russian, Dimitrov went on to state:

You see consequently that in this field we must put an end all along the line to what frequently occurs in practical work—the ignoring of, or contemptuous attitude toward the various organizations and parties of the peasants, artisans and urban petty-bourgeois masses.

That was soft and silken language—almost incongruously so compared with what had been heard from Communist organs and organizations only a few weeks before. Was this not the big change in the Communist movement which would weld all "forward-looking groups" together against fascism? To me, as I read more of Dimitrov's address the reply seemed to be emphatically in the affirmative.

Coming out flatly for use of national traditions—at which the Communists had hooted in the past—he quoted from Lenin's article "On the National Pride of the Great Russians," written in 1914. My quotation of this very article at a meeting held in Baltimore the preceding year had caused pandemonium among the Communists. For a moment, they had even threatened to resort to their well-known hoodlumism, at this "desecration" of Lenin's writings. They wouldn't believe he had written any such thing as this praise of national pride in the "great examples of the struggle for freedom" among the Great Russian people.

Dimitrov not only quoted these words of Lenin at the Seventh Congress, but was warmly applauded for doing so. He was applauded again when he went on to refer to his own use of Bulgarian patriotic expressions at the Leipzig trial. "Nor was I wrong," said he to further applause, "in declaring that I had no cause to be ashamed of being a Bulgarian." We are advised of the repeated applause, since it is recorded in the proceedings as published by *Inprecor*, August 20, 1935, which issue also ran the whole address.

What a turn-about this represented—at least so far as words went! And I was prepared to accept those words as genuine, in view of the mighty crisis which I saw about to grip the world. I was no longer in any doubt about the advent of World War II. Although the German Communist, Wilhelm Pieck, had, only a few months before, made a bombastic report in which he had prophesied the forceful overthrow of Hitler from within Germany, there was nothing to back up the boast. Nazism was steadily gaining in strength. It was building great military roads and in 1934 had increased the production of steel from the preceding year by 60 per cent, crude steel by 50 per cent, and rolling mill products by 40 per cent. The German Communist Party, under Comintern direction, had aided Hitler's progress by appealing to the German people on May 7, 1934, to turn to Communism rather than to democracy in the battle against Nazism. The response had been nil. It had, unfortunately, merely split the anti-Hitler camp at a critical hour. The vote in the Saar, too, had registered 476,089 for a return to Germany, with Hitler in control, only 46,613 for the international control hitherto exercised, and a mere handful for union with France. That was an ominous opening for the year 1935, in that the Nazis had acquired additional prestige for their war program. The scowls of the Fuehrer, be it remembered, were directed against the democratic as well as the Bolshevik camp, against the "pluto-democracies" as well as the "Jewish-spawned Marxists." The shadow of the Axis alliance was getting longer over the international scene. It reached from North China, where Japan was pushing its aggressive war, to Ethiopia, where Mussolini was instituting his invasion, and then across Europe, where German compulsory military service had been resumed.

Dimitrov's address did not go so far as had my letter to the Sun the year before. It still had the flavor of such observations as the British Communist, R. Palme Dutt, made in September, 1934, when he called the United States the fore-

most imperialist power." The forecast of a working arrangement between the United States and the Soviet Union against
the Axis was conspicuously missing from the report for peace
made at the Seventh Congress by M. Ercoli, now known as
Palmiri Togliatti of Italy. In the war that was to come he
apparently looked for a general "imperialist" war against
the Soviet Union and for the "turning of the imperialist war
into a civil war." To applause Ercoli-Togliatti said: "We
shall [then] fight for revolution and the conquest of power."
The hope for world Soviet domination still haunted even the
Seventh Congress.

All this was largely lost on me, who saw the "new features" perhaps too vividly. The working together of the
United States and the Soviet Union "against fascism"
would emerge from the People's Front policy, I reasoned.
That thought tended to blind me to all the ironic phases of
the Dimitrov speech. He thundered against the "fascists'
denial of the right to strike," and yet the Soviet Union
has put an iron fist to any strike and has, in grim effect,
completely suppressed that right. He caustically referred
to the Catholic Church as the "stronghold of reaction" and
thereby tipped off the Red faithful to the hypocrisy of
Communist "concern" for the Catholic martyrs of brown
fascism. He again reminded Communists that they could
act as a "Trojan horse" within "fascist" organizations.
And while he made this comment specifically in connection
with the "fascists," the "bourgeois imperialists" were so much
under Communist fire and their democratic nations so
despised, that the allusion seemed to be intended for them as
well. Over the immediately preceding months, the term
"fascist" had been applied to President Roosevelt, to President William Green of the American Federation of Labor
and to many other heads of democratic organizations. It was
taken for granted within Communist circles that the phrase

was elastic and could be aimed at anyone not in step with current Stalinist objectives. Now, in 1946, it is again being applied to anyone who expresses doubts or proves difficult about Soviet expansion and aggression. In any case, the "Trojan horse" metaphor was so vivid a reminder of the way the Communists had acted with all groups with whom they had been allied that it tended to arouse suspicions. In the long run, those suspicions were justified. Liberal and "social democratic" organizations continued to be treated just like the fascist groups when it suited Communist purposes to disrupt or deceive them. However, had anyone mentioned any such possibility to me in 1935, my indignation would have been aroused. To me, the words of Dimitrov, asserting a change away from "sectarianism" and toward fair play, were magic pledges of a renovation and revamping of Communist thought and activity.

The Communists had always talked much of "democratic centralism" in the government of their Parties and the formation of their policies. With this People's Front declaration, the "democratic" portion of that phrase seemed to come to the fore. With the eventual removal of Hitlerism and its threats, this tendency would grow in the Soviet Union and in the Communist movements throughout the world. So I argued, and Dimitrov, himself, gave food to such argument by stressing the democratic aspects of "democratic centralism." The tremendous and bitter irony actually contained in that phrase I was to learn only after the Bolshevik strait jacket was fastened around me. No one could say nay or yea—or even sneeze should that be considered important—without the consent of the puppets of still other puppets responsible directly to Moscow.

For anyone not blinded by exaggerated hopes in an "anti-fascist front," the resolutions and "reports" of the Seventh Congress again affirmed that world domination was as much the Stalinite objective as it was Hitler's. Every speech ended with ejaculations similar to those of Ercoli-Togliatti, who concluded: "The world party of the Bolsheviks and of Stalin is a guarantee of our victory on a world scale." The insatiable Manuilsky, who came close to aping Goebbels in his adulation of Hitler as world Fuehrer, exclaimed amid loud cheers: "The exploited and oppressed of all the world regard . . . our Stalin as the great, wise and beloved leader of the whole of toiling humanity." The resolution then adopted by the delegates unanimously hailed Stalin, the actual head of the Soviet state, as the world's leader. Those were blind indeed—and I was one of them—who could not see that this was as inimicable to democratic nations as it was Hitlerism; that it was still Soviet totalitarianism merely stating its imperialist ambitions under a world-saving guise.

Men like myself were so busy rejoicing over what Dimitrov said about the People's Front that we did not study sufficiently what William Pieck, the German Communist wheelhorse, said as the "official reporter" on the Communist International. His was a continuous call for "attack" within non-Soviet nations. "The need of the hour," said he, "is to strengthen the Communist parties as leaders in the struggle for Soviet power. . . . Our main slogan is: 'Struggle for Soviet Power.' Our leader is Stalin."

But he was a happy man who studied the Dimitrov words on the station steps that morning. As I concluded my first reading—for there were many additional ones—and walked back to the Montrose Avenue apartment, everything seemed to be fitting into a magnificent mosaic. For almost a year I had been too ill to work and during that period had done much thinking. It all led to the urgency for closer relations between the United States and the Soviet Union. One would mellow and mold the other, was my idea—similar to the hope later expressed by Henry A. Wallace to a Madison Square Garden Soviet-American Friendship meeting during the war.

Certainly the lively hope for a democratic-minded anti-Axis coalition led to self-deception on my part, so far as the expressions of the Seventh Congress went. But that was not all there was to it. The Communists had, superficially at least, come closer to the "American approach" which I held paramount; but I, too, had come much nearer the Communists than ever before in my life. Lenin's writings had done their work. The vision of "imperialist" governments walking the gangplank of history in the wake of victorious Socialism was not a mirage for me then.

The catch was that I envisaged something other than the adoption of the Hitlerite methods by the "Socialist state" that finally developed out of its world-domination ambitions. The word "revolution," which I uttered so readily, was different in content from the way the Communists understood it. With them it proved to be synonymous with devotion to the totalitarian state, to the denial of free press, free speech and free assembly, merely dressed in the domino of "Socialist democracy." They would follow it, even if it meant the imposition of Communism as a tyranny over reluctant and even resistant peoples. I thought of it as something which welled up from the people, as had our own American Revolution and the fight against chattel slavery. But in 1935, I failed to see the difference in our definitions.

It was with no reservations, then, that I read these words of Ercoli in his summation to the Congress:

In this fighting front for peace we can include also the masses of the social democratic toilers, the broad masses of the pacifists, Catholics, the women, the youth, the endangered national minorities and their organizations. We can even include those bourgeois governments which at the moment at least, are interested in the preservation of peace.

Fine phrases indeed, which fear of the efficient Hitlerite war machine had put into the mouths of Communist leadership. They effectively obscured these concluding proclamations of Dimitrov:

The present rulers of the capitalist world are temporary rulers. With Stalin at the head, our political army of millions can and must overcome all difficulties, rise above all obstacles and storm the fortress of capitalism to win the victory for socialism throughout the whole world.

Although draped in "Socialist" verbiage, this grim vow to bring the world in bondage to the feet of the monolithic Soviet state was very similar to that uttered on behalf of the "National Socialist" state by the "Sieg heils" at Nuremburg. That fact I overlooked.

When Margaret arrived home that evening I had the paper ready for her, marked in many places, and with annotations in the margins. "This is a sign of the vitality of the revolutionary movement," said I enthusiastically—believing that the decision at Moscow was related to such discussions as I had carried on here. My profound belief then was that the entry upon the People's Front had created an entirely new outlook for the Communist movement, both with regard to America and to religion. While the latter was no longer my prized possession, I considered it of the utmost importance that the anti-fascists keep their cause clean of antireligious persecution. To fight for freedom while denying the freedom of worship was completely contradictory. That the Soviet Union had offended seriously in this respect I knew well, but that had been laid to the "excesses of revolutionary moments." And now the prospect of a change was warmly welcome.

Just in this month of August, the doctor stated that I was much improved and he permitted me to wander farther afield than the highways and byways of Williamsburg. I immediately headed for membership in the Communist party, and began to frequent those places in Manhattan where Communists I knew would most likely be found. Having heard that I was improving in health, several unions and newspapers had invited me to join their staffs. But I put off any such decision until, as I told them, "I can find my political foundations." Once or twice I did wince at the galling yoke that Communist membership would impose; after all, I had witnessed it in action, to a degree. But that was quickly dismissed by my devotion to the anti-Axis cause, and the conviction that Communists could now champion democracy and serve the American people faithfully.

Within a few days I had run into an outstanding Party member whom I had known in the unemployed movement. He took me to Herbert Benjamin who, in turn, escorted me to Clarence Hathaway over at the *Daily Worker*. Hathaway and I had become quite friendly at the Continental Congress, which had been called in Washington by the Socialists in 1933. At that gathering I had introduced a resolution to include the Communists in "a broad united front." But now we talked over my present position and Hathaway suggested I apply for membership in the "Party of Stalin." The card was signed and for ten years thereafter, night and day, I worked for that party and its purposes as I saw them.

I was not openly announced as a Party acquisition until October 2, 1935, when a photograph and story appeared in the *Daily Worker*. That was exactly a decade prior to my departure. The weeks from late August to October had been devoted by the leading "comrades" to consideration of where I could best function. They were also waiting for the return of Earl Browder, Jack Stachel and others from the Moscow Congress, since those men would have to participate in any decision. We then agreed, upon my suggestion, that I would become an "open Communist," after a brief trip to the Middle West to visit some of those associates who were tending toward the Trotskyite movement.

That trip, though not immediately fruitful, eventually brought a number of active people into the Communist party. The biggest game on my expedition was Arnold Johnson, National Secretary of the National Unemployed Leagues and a disciple of Sherwood Eddy, whom I had induced to join the C.P.L.A. Johnson postponed all final consideration of the matter, pleading his responsibilities to the Leagues. It was evident that a temporary attachment to Trotskyism caused his indecision. "Give me a few weeks of constant, quiet conversations with him," I reported to the comrades back in New York, "and he will come around." That proved to be the case; he is now District Organizer of the Party in Ohio.

If you skim through the *Daily Worker* files of 1934 you will run across my statement upon joining the Party, acclaiming the leadership of Browder and Stalin. It was written with wide-open eyes, for it affirms "the road of the revolutionist" to be "the path of the Comintern." Although I would then have heatedly denied any such accusation, it did present a blank check to whoever led the Communist movement. That it would enmesh me in a thought-controlled world almost as tight as the Japanese system—beyond the comprehension or experience of the average American—was something I did not dream. I was still thinking in an atmosphere of freedom, where men need not dread political or physical assassination for deviation or differences from the "powers that be." The mental imprisonment that exists in the Communist camp was beyond even my more or less sophisticated speculations. But as I discovered with bitterness, when a man enters there he signs his death warrant as a free agent in thought or word or deed.

The possibility of advancing the "American approach" was the excuse I furnished myself for joining the Party. Soon the opportunity to apply that "approach" presented itself. Following my admission at Browder's request, I was assigned to cover the first "enlarged session of the Central Committee." It was staged in New York at some such hall as the Fraternal Clubhouse in the Forties—one of the favorite rentals of the Communists.

Everything about the assemblage was secretive. Admission cards were given to all those invited, and carefully checked at the door. There was no public mention of the place of the meeting, or even that it was to be held, and the notice of the address was given only at the last minute, the evening before the meeting. I was called to "the ninth floor" and told the place.

The term "ninth floor," which will appear frequently in this narrative, designated the top story of the building at Fifty East Thirteenth Street, in New York City, which was owned by the Communist party and housed many of its immediate Party agencies. The ninth floor was the national headquarters of the Red organization. To that center every day came hundreds of reports from all over the country, as to the temper of the workers, the thoughts of big and little politicians in both "old parties," the condition of production and many other vital subjects. Some of these reports came directly from their source through the United States mails, and were addressed to the East Thirteenth Street headquarters or to Thirty-five East Twelveth Street, which was its other entrance. But many were brought to the ninth floor by hand, having first been sent to the home of some comrade unsuspected by the FBI or other government agencies. A number of these secret, conspiratorial mail drops, such as the home address of a secretarial worker, were always maintained.

Notices of private, semi-conspiratorial meetings of various national committees were also given out quietly by the ninth-floor staff. These notices were always delivered by hand with instructions to destroy the information as soon as examined. Sometimes the specific place of meeting of national committees would be announced in advance in the *Daily Worker*, but often no one knew of them—including the daily press—until Communist headquarters issued a statement that they had been held. The Reds demonstrated their contempt for "freedom of the press" right here in America.

Such precautions were held to be necessary so that under-cover Communists—those functioning in mass movements as non-Communists—could attend without press or police molestation. That explanation might seem to have some validity; it was not, however, the sole reason for the secretiveness. Another very important one was to permit the presence—almost always in excessive incognito—of a few of the shadowy figures or their go-betweens to whom the reader will shortly be introduced. These were the men of many aliases who directly represented the interests of the Soviet state, frequently as agents of the Communist International.

Like a new spring, the American language blossomed forth in wonderful profusion at this Central Committee session. There were references to things American, at Dimitrov's bidding, that would have been the objects of scorn a few months before. This impressed me as a good omen. Indeed, it inspired me to produce an article of no mean merit, comparing those Communists present to the Abolitionists. It was an old theme, of course, with me. But the introduction of Browder's "Kansas twang" was a new human touch and a daring departure from the humdrum chant in his praise that had hitherto appeared in the paper. The piece was warmly received among the comrades and was even noted in Moscow, where the representatives of the C.I. began to follow my writings with approval. Sam Darcy, famous for his super-revolutionary and anti-American expressions at Moscow, told me on his return some years later that the C.I. had hoped to have me go to Moscow and cover the Trotskyite trials. However, the decision to invite me came too late to get me over there. Darcy also told me that it was the opinion at the capital of Communism that my writings were setting a new tone for American Marxist journalism.

What stunned me somewhat at this initial meeting of the Central Committee—now known as the National Committee —was the absence of real discussion. Everybody agreed with everybody else and praised whatever Browder said. The program was for Browder to make the main report, lasting about three or four hours, followed by a couple of thirty-minute reports from more or less important members of the Political Committee, and then participation by the committee members. What they actually did was to give largely informational reports on the state of affairs in their respective sections of the country, all of which were taken down in stenographic notes and in the opinion of several National Committee members, then forwarded to Moscow. I was repeatedly advised that this was the fate of all the carefully transcribed and typed documents covering the Committee sessions. Among many other public proofs that this was true was the fact that documents denied the National Committee members in the Foster-Browder dispute—as we shall presently see—turned up in the hands of the French Communist, Jacques Duclos thousands of miles away. Moreover, it was admitted—as we shall also see—that "all leading European Marxists" had examined the documents, for they were reported to agree with what Duclos wrote. These reports at the National Committee sessions were, in effect, hymns of praise to Stalin and also to Browder, whose report was always "the finest ever made, the most impressive Comrade Browder has ever presented." The session was then concluded with a summary given by Browder. This was the Communist "scientific" method followed at all such sessions all over the world. It did not sit well with me, who had come out of the democratic hurly-burly of community and trade-union debate.

All that can be better understood in time, I assured myself. The reports are undoubtedly worked out with the members and represent the product of give-and-take and democratic discussion. Nothing could have been farther from the mark. Ukases were handed down to the members after each Central session, ordering them what to think and say. Such orders were given, necessarily, under the cover of the Communist ideological lingo and as the "Marxist analysis" of the bigger and better minds in the Party. Then, back in his own community, the district organizer, or Party secretary, opened up his sessions with a report, à la Browder, and summed up in like manner. There was no vote, in the accepted sense, and could be no dissent. And the same procedure was followed in every section and in all their branches—the section organizer and branch organizer in turn giving the "report." In this manner the "line" was passed down from top to bottom, with "centralism" fully triumphant over "democracy"—and with Moscow calling the tune.

What a travesty these "discussions" actually were can be appreciated from the fate awaiting any comrade who persisted in talking against the new line, whatever its aim. He was first "isolated," his reputation among his Red associates completely ruined, and then he was expelled from the

Party as "an enemy of the working class." In every mass organization in which he might function, he was whispered about and his life made miserable. As a matter of fact, at the end of each discussion, the leading comrades sat down in a small group and "assessed" what had been said—seeking to ferret out any hesitations or deviations from the line. These assessments were not for the purpose of amending the line but principally to discover any "alien" minds among them.

Jumping ahead of my story a bit, it would be well to say here, by way of illustration, that· Sam Darcy, the ultra-leftist member of the National Committee, bucked the Browder line in 1944 and was expelled from the Party for his "discussions." This harsh verdict was rendered on him despite his many services to the Red organization along secretive paths. Then, when the pendulum from Moscow swung around and knocked Browder out, all those whose "discussions" had favored him were disciplined. Even Abraham A. Heller, the mouselike little man who had been a financial angel for the Party and a vital "business" link between it and Moscow, was in danger of the same fate until he ran for refuge to Stalin's arms this year. We shall pursue these incidents further as we go along. But even back in 1935, when I first became acquainted with the Red methods through handling the whole National Committee meeting procedure, I was immediately conscious of the suffocating air of conspiracy which surrounded those sessions.

Two years later, when I went to Chicago, the autocratic and automatic character of this procedure became more pronounced. Out in the "I will" town, there was none of the circulation of *sub rosa* advance information on what was likely to be the latest Moscow will or whim that there was in New York. National Committee members living there merely received notice of a coming meeting of their group, sent in a few suggestions which were seldom heeded, and hurried off to the meeting in Gotham when final notice was given. There they were suddenly greeted with some new decision which was supposed to be the product of Browder's superior knowledge of Marxism, but which dealt too intimately with world affairs in which Soviet Russia was deeply concerned to be the General Secretary's own inspiration.

But this new revelation was never challenged by any member of the National Committee. On the contrary, whatever it was, it was hailed without thought or delay as the "answer" to all the problems confronting America and mankind at the moment. From the New York meeting, the National Committee members would hasten back to Chicago to ram the new line down the willing or unwilling throats of the section organizers and the active members of the sections. The process would then be repeated in every local branch in Chicago and vicinity.

The whole business was nothing but a mechanical molding of minds and memories for the dissemination of the same ideas to labor unions, civic organizations, and the press. With a casuistry never dreamed of by the ordinary American mind, afterthought arguments would be worked up to support the new position. These arguments would be slanted in such a way that certain liberals and other innocents would be induced to take them up and chant them in turn. I have often had the pleasure, if such it can be called, of seeing arguments which I confess to thinking up in this fashion, appear in newspapers of several different political persuasions. They have also appeared in speeches made by certain members of Congress. All of them had as their purpose the promotion of whatever was the prevalent policy of Soviet Russia, though usually this was unsuspected by the honorable gentlemen who made use of them.

I was well aware, before I entered the Party, that every one

of Browder's visits to Moscow had been followed immediately
by the announcement of a new line. A particularly startling
one had developed shortly before the People's Front period.
Browder suddenly appeared in Washington to favor a labor
party at the very time when Communists were then in a mass
organization meeting fighting against a labor party. This
turn-about-face was staged at the Conference on Social and
Unemployment Insurance early in 1935. I had run into
several delegates who were on their way to the conference
to oppose the Stalinists, and I told them how futile I thought
their gestures would be. Whereupon Browder, rushing from
the boat in New York on his return from Russia, upset the
whole procedure by making an address favorable to the
labor party and denouncing others for not being warm
enough in its support! After witnessing such episodes, it is
surprising that I should have been taken aback at the
imprisonment of thought which I found within the Communist movement. Only a completely controlled agency of a
foreign power could deport itself in the fashion Browder's
action had exemplified. And yet, so often had I heard from
Communists the explanation of "democratic centralism"
as the flow of discussion from bottom to top and then from
top to bottom, that I swallowed it as the truth. And I had
now, in addition, the intense desire to close my eyes to
things I did not want to see. The conviction grew, almost to
the point of monomania, that the annihilation of the Axis
would solve all these difficulties and bring about a Golden
Age of Communist democracy. Was not the word "democracy" being glorified in the Stalinist constitution of the
U.S.S.R.? Were not gestures toward "bourgeois democracy"
being made there, in talk about such things as free speech?
And would not ten million people, hearing those things,
insist that they be brought to life?

This was the case as I then presented it to myself. I

thought it a good one; actually, it was very bad. In a few years Nazi Germany was to prove conclusively, by its desperate death battle against the Allies, that even a highly literate people can by dictational methods be made to believe anything. Soviet Russia was on a par with the Hitlerite country in that respect. And the Communist party itself was to assert by its own acts that a fifth-column agency of dictatorship could thrive only by dictatorial methods.

I was soon to learn that the Soviet Government was not content with control of the Party in the United States via the Browder transmission line alone. It also had direct representatives in the Communist apparatus here. The first incident that brought this fact to my attention I dubbed rather gaily "The Case of the Cantankerous Commissar." A mysterious personage by the ambiguous name of Edwards came into the picture as soon as I was made labor editor of the *Daily Worker*. This was a few months after my entry into the Party. Ever since the day I announced my membership I had served on the Communist newspaper but at first only in a general reportorial capacity.

The heavy foreign accent that Edwards brought to the first editorial board meeting I attended belied the name he bore. It was far from his real name and was obviously assumed to deceive his Comrades as much as anyone else. Angrily shaking a copy of the latest issue of the *Daily Worker* in his hand, he broke into the session to berate Clarence Hathaway, then editor in chief.

"The editor who puts his face into the paper as much as you do should devote his brains to putting some face on the paper," Edwards spluttered out, his voice rising to a shriek. To my astonishment, Hathaway made no response, but merely smiled in a rather shamefaced manner. This only provoked Edwards to further tirades. He rapped the paper repeatedly with his hand and called it a "political disgrace," something that "can't be permitted to go on" and other denunciatory names.

The exhibition was profoundly educational. I sat through it all with my eyes half shut in contemplation. Hathaway was a member of the supposedly all-powerful Political Committee of the Party; and yet, here he was silently submitting to a most belittling blast. The baneful nature of a setup by which a stranger could appear out of nowhere and castigate an American as though he were a puppy deserving a kick, was painfully apparent. It made me uneasy and uncertain. Nowhere in the history of the labor movement or even in the records of the Communist International was there an "Edwards" of sufficient importance to justify his dictation to a political party within America. I therefore had to draw the reluctant conclusion that he was an emissary of the Soviet Government, whether he was ostensibly and technically a representative of the Communist International or not. The nameless man unquestionably remained anonymous because he was under orders from a foreign government and did not want to disclose that fact to American authorities.

My concern over finding a Soviet representative in the Central Communist apparatus was a bit hair-splitting in that muddled morality which affects all Communists in one form or another. Only a few months before, I had publicly accepted the leadership of Stalin, the head-in-fact of the Soviet Government. And yet, in my mind I had worked out such a fine casuistic distinction between Stalin "as leader of the revolutionary movement" and Stalin as head of the Russian State that I had managed to befuddle even myself. When this contradictory position—which all Communists fervidly spouted—was exposed by the immediate personal control of American activities by a Russian state agent, I was ill at ease. My American conscience revolted at the idea.

Of course, to those Communists who are Soviet-Russian patriots in the same way that a Nazi Bundist is loyal only to Nazi Germany, this situation would present no difficulties. But, being sensitive to American freedom and having functioned in it so long, I wanted to know with whom I was dealing. And so I made discreet inquiries about Edwards and learned from a comrade long in the movement that he was "a German-Jewish comrade, who represents voices bigger than those around here," and he waved his hand vaguely toward the ninth floor, national headquarters of the Party. Later, in another editorial board meeting I heard Harry Gannes—foreign editor of the *Daily Worker*—refer to him as "a German-Austrian comrade from the CI." And still later the same designation was again furnished me when, after he had been absent for some time, I was told he had left the country "for a new European assignment for the CI in Spain." A few months after this departure, Hathaway disclosed to me: "Edwards was the representative of the Communist International, whose place is now being taken by a substitute," whom Hathaway named. A man similar to Edwards in every way, save that he was older, later appeared in that very capacity as "Hans Berger" or Gerhard Eisler.

To me Edwards was always courteous and even gracious. Probably he could afford to be more lenient because I was a newcomer, but whatever the cause, he had queried me about my opinion of Hathaway as though we had seen eye to eye. Though it was clear enough that he wanted me to condemn the editor in chief, I could not conscientiously do so with the facts at my disposal. Even this did not ruffle him.

To the "older comrades" he was always much more severe. In an exuberant moment—for some of these first incidents in becoming a Communist tickled my funny bone—I had said at home: "If the mysterious Edwards were ever murdered, that would prove one of the most staggering detective stories of our day. There are so many people who would be suspect." The grimness of this jest was not yet grasped. Although I knew my way about the American scene, I believed then that the Communist leaders, as Marxists, did not hold for political assassination. Even G. K. Chesterton, the Catholic, had stated that same belief in one of his "Father Brown" detective yarns. But I should have reminded myself of two remarks Harold Laski had made at the Calverton banquet in 1935. Before I angered him he had told us of his recent visit with the Soviet journalist, Karl Radek, in the latter's Moscow apartment. When well in his cups, Radek had exclaimed to Laski, "We have Marxism here no longer; we have only a ritual."

Would time prove "Marxism," at Moscow to be like the "Socialism" at Berlin under Herr Hitler? Were assassination and kidnaping and the ruthless imposition of totalitarianism over weaker peoples to be the pattern of Soviet rule, too? How indignant would the new labor editor of the *Daily Worker* have been in the early part of 1936 had anyone hinted at such heresies to him!

The so-called "Dutch" or German, comrade—though his accent was indeterminate to my untrained ear—was the first of a long line of personages with foreign accents and foreign origins who paraded through the governing apparatus of the Communist party of the U.S.A. No one, and least of all any well-educated American, has any complaint about full participation of the foreign born in American life; our own ancestors came from afar to make up this land of the free. But the right of those who are agents of a foreign power to cross our borders under aliases and order American citizens about, is another matter. Yet, to my surprise, this was what I found in the building at Thirty-five East Twelfth Street when I entered it and began to work there.

These men of many names and no names bore aliases like

Edwards—carelessly chosen plurals of "Christian names" such as Roberts, Richards, Stevens, Michaels, Johns and, occasionally, something more distinctive taken from England or the Middle West. The second one of these gentlemen to impress himself upon me was "Roberts," then acting in a vital secretarial capacity in the Party. That is, he was one of the chief factors in the national setup. Still in the stage of pleasantries upon such matters, I had gaily referred to him as "The Cheshire Cat Commissar" because of his perpetual mechanical smile. It was not unpleasant but unreal. Like the celebrated feline, his names kept vanishing. Shortly after my labor editorship began, he suddenly converted himself into "Comrade Peters" and then into "Comrade Steve" and then, after a long time, back to "Comrade Roberts." It kept one busy trying to keep up with these transformations.

It was this smiling "friend"—for that is how these knights of the mysterious referred to each other—who let me into the secret of the "real party." That is the term he used one day in what seemed a sudden burst of confidence. "There is a conspiratorial apparatus in the Party," he had said in a quiet and even oily manner. Then he compared the Communist organization to a submarine, in which the part seen by the people and the press was the periscope. The major part of the Party—"not in numbers but in responsibility"—was hidden beneath the waves of anonymity and aliases. So he told me, sizing me up as he spoke. Then, abruptly, but still speaking almost in a whisper, he cautioned that if I were ever in touch with this "undersea" empire I must not divulge to Hathaway anything that I learned or saw. The editor in chief was too garrulous. At the time I did not appreciate the full significance of these admonitions of Comrade Roberts-Peters-Steve-Roberts. But some months later, when I was to meet, confer and co-operate with members of the Soviet secret police, I gave them more serious thought. Without doubt, the purpose of these whispered counsels had been to measure my reactions with a view to the job ahead. Evidently I passed muster.

Many big events were in the making at that moment, and my enthusiasm kept me from any prolonged mulling over the existence of the mysterious foreigners. Besides those who came and went on the *Daily Worker* and in other divisions of the Party were more concerned about the paper's foreign department than about the labor field. The late Harry Gannes was constantly engaged in conferences with these men when, in 1946, he was indicted—along with Browder—for going back and forth on false passports, his chief worry was that he might be pressed to divulge more about these political wraiths and their twilight land of semi-espionage. This obsession served to heighten the illness from which he died at so early an age. I sat in the same workroom with him for a long time and could actually feel his furtive dread of some of the people with whom he did business. His fears sometimes made him very irritable.

Soviet control exerted itself in another direction, right there on the *Daily Worker* and made another contribution to my education in the real character of the Communist party. Thousands of words of telegraphic material—translations of articles in *Pravda, Izvestia* and other Red periodicals in Moscow—were sent in to the paper every day, scot-free. They were paid for, in other words, by the Soviet Government. During the big Moscow trials, the wordage of these communications actually mounted to millions of words. These articles and statements were of the utmost value to the leading comrades here in determining the various lights and shades on any prevalent line. They were also a big aid to the paper, for they gave it an exclusive and official service from a country not given to handing out news. The *Daily*

Worker was thus subsidized by the Soviet Government to the tune of approximately $500,000 per year.

That was to go on until Attorney General Biddle ruled that this sort of free news service actually made the *Daily Worker* an agent of a foreign government. Such a ruling necessitated its filing as a foreign agent at Washington, which would ruin its influence among the trusting and uninformed. Therefore, the *Inter-continent News Service* was created to handle these wires. But the ICN was also ruled to be a foreign agency and finally had to cease operations. Thereafter, any orders or amplifications of "the line" had to be smuggled in with great caution.

I was diverted from too close scrutiny of these aspects of the Party by the tremendous outburst of industrial-unionism sentiment. Scarcely had I got settled at the *Daily Worker* than the Alantic City convention of the American Federation of Labor, in October, 1935, proceeded to make history. It was the kind of history for which I had been helping to lay the foundations for a number of years. When John L. Lewis had risen at San Franciso the year before and insisted upon industrial unionism in the basic industries, it had seemed like a new miracle. Granted that his demand arose merely from his recognition that the United Mine Workers could not maintain conditions or organization without unionism in steel, rubber, automobiles and those other big industries allied with coal, still, it had been significant. So that when the San Franciso convention of 1934 postponed the matter to the Alantic City gathering, through a plea to "study" it, and then "did nothing," in Lewis' opinion, an explosion was bound to occur. Out of that explosion the Congress of Industrial Organizations was born—first, of course, in committee form.

As the drama of the Lewis-Hutchenson punching duel and the other salty scenes of October, 1935, developed at the

Jersey resort, I watched them with the deepest interest. The actors in the drama were all well known to me, most of those on the side of industrial unionism having been associated with *Labor Age* during the ten years of its more dynamic existence. And William Hutchenson, chief opponent of the idea, was president of the Carpenters, with whom I had begun my labor journalism work. It was a great privilege to be able to edit the news as it hummed in over the wires from the convention hall. Although I had come to the *Daily Worker* too recently to arrange my personal coverage of the convention, the editorial function was equally valuable, and I was to watch the progress of this debate that was so important to the future of labor.

One month after I took up my duties on the *Daily Worker* —on November 9, 1935—the C.I.O., still as a committee of the American Federation of Labor, opened up its headquarters. That was a day of elation and a high point in my own career. In the succeeding days, during which the place and purpose of the C.I.O. were thrashed out and formed, I worked long and late at the pro-C.I.O. editorials for the Communist paper. Frequently I would be up on the ninth floor at a meeting of the Political Committee—or some important sub-committee of the body—to the last possible minute and then rush down with my notes to turn out an editorial on the big labor subject. These official expressions of the paper were inordinately long, much longer than I thought essential. Nevertheless, they were insisted upon by Political Committee members, who wanted to get in every last thought that any-one had offered. It was a sweating assignment to transform those voluminous notes into readable short sentences and dynamic passages, but I hummed as I worked, for the things to which we had so long looked forward were actually coming to pass. Many a weary evening, as I trudged around George Washington's statue and across Union Square after one of these strenuous editorial productions, I looked back on episodes that now seemed far in the past, and realized that they were the preludes to the present—to the birth of the C.I.O.

Memory turned to the struggling year of 1926 and to the painful little attempts at educational pageants, speeches and plays by District 2 of the United Mine Workers. John Brophy was then president of that district, whose headquarters were in Clearfield, Pennsylvania. The state of organization was low, and these educational weeks were designed to enlighten the community and help keep the fires of unionism burning. Out of the rugged country of western Pennsylvania, the coal diggers would come into some town like Nanticoke. There, they pitched a tent and on a summer evening produced a play—a humble effort but recording their own tale for labor history. Then would come the address, which I, among others, frequently gave. We were carrying the message of industrial unionism and of the right of association into the hills where the union banner had once been planted but where it was then being uprooted. Now, nine years later, walking across Manhattan I exulted, "the pledge made to the coal diggers is being fulfilled by their chief." My heart was glad.

Another evening came to mind, too—a summer twilight hour in Indianapolis in 1928. I had run down to see my parents, taking a treasured two days away from the Kenosha strike scene. Hurrying along North Meridian Street to catch a streetcar for home, I ran into my old friend, Thomas J. Kennedy, general secretary of the United Mine Workers. With him was John L. Lewis. They were out for an evening walk after their dinner together. Naturally they queried me about the progress of the Kenosha struggle, which had been prominently featured in the country's newspapers for days. I could still hear Lewis's hoarse chuckles as I told them how we had resorted to the "mourning picket line" when the police had forbidden shouting. A huge black coffin, labeled "Death of Liberty by Injunction," had appeared and a thousand mourners wearing black arm bands had silently marched around the mill. That created as great a sensation as the loudest Jericho shouts could have done.

We had discussed many other episodes as we walked up and down for about half an hour, and Lewis said: "The spirit which hits on such devices will not be downed. There's a promise in all these refusals of the American workers to remain dead that will put quaking trepidation in the hearts of the Philistines when new valiant men, new Davids, shall arise." He had added the name of another ancient "captain of the people"—Jesbaam the son of Hachamoni, if memory does not fail me. It sent me scurrying to my father's big family Bible to locate the man. The incident, the words, the evening hour, were all vividly recalled as Lewis shook his shaggy mane seven years later and vowed to organize the unorganized through the C.I.O.

Then there was the meeting in a school building in Pittsburgh during the organization of the Unemployed Leagues late in 1932. Two-score former employees of the Jones and Laughlin Company, then unemployed for months, sat uneasily in the hall. Although there was no prospect of jobs at the mills, the old fear of meeting together oppressed them. It had taken all my powers of eloquence to assure them that organization of the unemployed would not result in the loss of jobs, for the jobs were not then available, but with a new day and new deal the jobs would come back. Then, too, I had pledged that this "new day" would see the beginning of industrial unionism in steel, and that gave them some hope and some courage, too.

All these incidents and many more were blended in the present big reality, the campaign for industrial unionism.

That, I was thoroughly convinced, would add to the stature of our democracy by relieving men of crippling and unnecessary fears.

At this stage, I was also preoccupied with the job of advancing the "American approach." Dimitrov had swung open the gates. I had been told by returning delegates that at the conclusion of the Seventh Congress the new General Secretary of the Communist International—at least, so he became in name—had called the American delegation together to urge them to resort to American traditions in their propaganda. They were so impressed by their duty in this respect that they decided that I had been "right all along" and they had been in error. But when it came to putting the "American approach" into effect, I found there were still plenty of difficulties. To begin with, I was surprised to discover that no one among the comrades knew much about American history. It was only very much later, when it was decided that the American traditions could be a good cover-up for activities against the "decaying bourgeois democracy of America," that the throttle was opened. A number of the teachers at the Communist-inspired schools were put to writing American historical books, and the *New Masses'* Howard Fast, the author, was cheered on in "patriotic palavering." These permissions were given on guarantees that the said historians were among the furthest left of the Leftists, and that behind the scenes they adhere strictly to the new anti-American line launched under the pen name of Duclos, but actually written in the Kremlin.

When I first made mention of American history and American background, there was something like sullen resentment from many comrades at such daring. And at one meeting in Ohio that I addressed early in my Communist career, the allusion to my own American generations—even in reply to some "red-baiter"—was frowned upon by the district organizer. He was John Williamson, now occupying a high secretarial position in the present Party line-up—a plodding fellow, always straining in his effort to walk the Party line.

I was greatly surprised when, for the first time, I detected the anti-American strain bred by Soviet patriotism that runs through the Communist official ranks. To be a native American was considered convenient for certain purposes, but was, in reality, something to apologize for. To have been born in Minsk, Dvinsk or Pinsk was much more valued than birth in Minneapolis, Detroit or Pittsburgh. You were an "insider" if you came from some part of eastern Europe —preferably holy Russian soil. This was not my own observation; it was stated to me, almost in these words, by several highly placed comrades who felt imprisoned by the attitude. I realized later that such a view must prevail in any agency engaged in serving a foreign power against the interests of the United States. It would be impossible, otherwise, to maintain the proper morale.

Pat Tuohy, originally of Pittsburgh, was to illustrate how extreme were the lengths to which the comrades had gone in this regard. The Dvinsk-Minsk-Pinsk combination referred to Pat sarcastically as "our sole American proletarian exhibit in mining." He was for years, of course, a member of the National Committee, a district organizer in several key places and, for a time, one of the National Secretariat. In a moment of confidence he told to me that he had long been regarded as a police agent simply because he was both American-born and of Irish descent. "They couldn't get it in their heads," he told me ruefully, "that anyone named Pat and then Tuohy could be anything but a hidden representative of the police."

The American attitude draws no line between the native-born and foreign-born in our land, particularly after they are all on the common ground of equality in citizenship. It is incongruous, then, that an American in America should be looked upon as a person of a shameful origin, not one of "the elect"; that in order to be serviceable to a cause, the Communist cause, he must make his associations, his reading, his thinking and his speech as Russian as he can. Yet, that was the stifling lot of the "open Communist" with which I was to become familiar as I grew in experience in Party life and realities.

In 1935, though, through Dimitrov's injunctions, I had the sanction of the super-Russian authorities in my hand. In December the chance to introduce the American slant into the paper finally came. The anniversary of John Brown's assault on Harper's Ferry came around then, and well in advance I prepared an editorial for the occasion. I spent much leisure time on it so that it would stand out in style as well as in content. There was some resistance to its inclusion in the paper, and it was held up for several days while I sweated with anxiety. On December 2, however, which was the proper day, it did get in. The Dimitrov decree was too strong to be ignored. I sighed with pleasure and triumph, and saw big possibilities ahead. Immediately, I began to prepare various articles for the feature page, the one place that could be an outlet for Americana. The first contribution of any size was an estimate of Thomas Jefferson, written in popular style, but ringing in the Marxist slant. It was rather like smuggling ideas into the paper, but it began to work slowly. Others got interested, and the opposition, though it continued and never did die out, was muted for the moment.

From then on, I devoted many extra hours, in addition to my regular labor editing and writing, to promoting the articles on the "American approach." It made life rich with purpose. With high spirit, I covered the United Mine Workers convention in Washington in January, 1936, saw and heard the duel between John L. Lewis and William Green and reported it at fever heat. Anyone reading those dispatches will note the spirit which runs through them, even though they are strictly in news form. With equal zest I attended the meetings of the Party's National Trade Union Commission, of which I was made a member, and participated in working out the Communist attitudes toward the new C.I.O. development.

More and more the Communists hurrahed for the C.I.O. When the leaders of the American Federation of Labor retaliated with the charge that the new organization was "Communist," we were quick to reply. Then I wrote those phrases which were so widely used: "The Committee for Industrial Organization is not a Communist Organization. All of Green's effort to label it as such—following the lead of Weir of Weirton and other enemies of labor—will fall to the ground. That is said by way of fact, and not of apology.

"The Communist Party stands for Socialism.

"The Committee for Industrial Organization does not stand for Socialism. It is a trade union movement, which of its very nature at this hour includes American workers of all races, creeds, colors, national origins and political beliefs. The great bulk of its membership has not yet come to accept Socialism as its goal. Its leader, John L. Lewis, does not stand for Socialism. The Communist party understands that. And so does William Green." (This was specifically quoted again by Mary Heaton Vorse, in her pro-C.I.O. book, *Labor's New Millions*, Modern Age book.)

To this matter we shall return after a while. Before these words had ever been written, however, the pressure of un-American, across-the-sea interference in the Communist party itself was again felt. Lewis had frankly made use of the Communists who had been active in the "Red" trade unions in the hope of getting help wherever he might. But Foster suddenly affected to put all the Red eggs in one basket. The machinists' locals had just lately got into the International Association of Machinists, and he did not want to compel them to leave that organization. But Lewis was adamant in his demand that they get out and join. And the same applied to the Furriers' Union, then coming under "Red" control. These measures to aid Lewis were taken later, but for the moment Foster's caution was endorsed in Moscow.

This situation led to a couple of amazing and, at the same time, astounding episodes. In commenting on the opinions of the coal-digger delegates to the United Mine Workers convention, I had written what I gleaned from consulting scores of them—which was the fact—that they were overwhelmingly for an organic break with the A. F. of L. Later events proved how accurate that estimate was. But when I returned from the national capital at the end of the convention, I found Hathaway and Stachel in something of a stew. They were as jumpy as could be about my prophecy. Since what these coal diggers had told me was true, and since it was in accord with the views then held by Hathaway and Stachel, I was puzzled by their jittery reaction. Soon it all came out. They were afraid of Foster, who had been raising "the devil"—as they said—about going too fast and putting too much faith in Lewis.

Why they should so fear Foster, who was known to be only the nominal chairman of the Party, shorn of all real power, was difficult to grasp. And then I found out. It was dread of Moscow, not of Foster, that was at the root of the jumpiness. Soon an article appeared in the magazine, the *Communist International*, under the anonymous letter "R," denouncing the *Daily Worker* for its complacency and easy faith in Lewis. My own "error" was not singled out, but those made by the editors while I was in Washington were hit hard and with heavy sarcasm. The stage whisper went around: "Foster complained to Losovsky former head of the Red trade unions and later publicity director for the Soviet Union in World War II—and he panned the *Daily*."

That letter "R," written by nobody visible to the membership and after no discussion within the Party, was as much a symbol of shame as the scarlet "A" on Hester Prynne's bosom in Hawthorne's tale. The "R" stood for "Rep," that is, "Representative of the Communist International." The article was therefore a ukase or command. And it made the editors of the *Daily* look like political dolts. Everybody looked askance at Hathaway, shook his head seriously and said: "Isn't it bad that he is caught in such errors?" It made one feel that one was living in a Graustarkian world, in which fictitious characters suddenly became real and decided one's fate without one's knowledge or consent.

But there was still the People's Front to forward and many other anti-fascist duties to perform. Mussolini was dropping bombs on Ethiopia and it seemed essential to hasten Soviet-American friendship. Who could foresee that the Soviet Union would be acting in a similar manner to Mussolini within less than a decade, and grinding small countries under the heel of its Red Army?

We were busy at meeting here, there and everywhere spreading the reports of the Seventh Congress on the People's Front. Too easily we overlooked those parts of the report we did not want to see—one of these was the speech of the old war horse of the Kremlin machine, Otto Kuusinen, the Finn. To great applause he had reminded the Communist young people, in the words of Lenin, that they were to take up rifles only to turn them, in time, against their own nations. Of course, the young Communist was to use the rifle against "the bourgeoisie of his own country," as Kuusinen put it in Lenin's language, but what that meant now was that Union was an established power, sabotage and subversion for the benefit of a foreign government. Kuusinen's refrain in conclusion: "Long live the leader of the world proletariat—Stalin."

In the midst of joy at forwarding the right of association, the cloud of foreign control hung over one's every act. In joining "the Party of Stalin," a man put himself completely under the domination of unseen forms and forces that stood for world conquest in the name of Stalin. Though only partially understood then, this huge fact grew larger as my years in the Party grew longer.

SIX

Ave Maria!

B Y CHRISTMAS, 1936, the days of the "outstretched
hand" had come. The Communists, under the influence of the People's Front tactic, were talking with
a new tongue to the Catholics throughout the world. The
previous tirades against the followers of the Holy See as
"reactionaries and semi-fascists" were silenced. The men of
Moscow had hushed even those few harsh notes even at the
democracy-talking Seventh Congress of the Communist
International, when the Red youth had been counseled to
work to keep Catholic young people away from the orbit of
the priesthood.

The "outstretched hand" phrase, which was now so far-
flung and famous, had its genesis in the radio broadcast of
Maurice Thorez, General Secretary of the French Communist party, on April 17, 1936. He had been selected by
Moscow to make an advance to those whom the Kremlin had
hitherto assailed. He offered professions of friendly advice
to the Catholics, and extended the Communists' hand "in
fraternal greeting and cooperation."

During the following year, 1937, Thorez was to add:
"Unity between Catholic and Communists is necessary; it is
possible; it is about to be achieved. All that is needed is
mutual good faith and a mutual spirit of tolerance. For our
part, whatever happens, whatever people say and whatever
they do, we are firmly determined to persevere in our policy
of the outstretched hand." Every leading Communist
throughout the world understood thoroughly that these

words were not the original inspiration of the French Communists; they had been first forged at the International headquarters on the banks of the Moskva. Knowing this, the Communist parties everywhere—and not the least here in the United States—began fervidly to advocate close relations with the Catholics. Thus was a postscript being written to the People's Front—the endeavor to make the word "Unite!" the only word in the current Red vocabulary.

The Catholics, who had witnessed the results of other Communist embraces, were naturally suspicious of this sudden friendship. The overnight condemnation by Thorez of "the crude anti-Church policy," of which the Communists admitted they had been guilty, smacked too much of the Trojan horse strategy of which Dimitrov had spoken. It was one of those gift offers for prudent men to beware.

In France, Cardinal Verdler presented what was supposedly the view of Pope Pius XI on the proposal, in a pastoral letter to French Catholics. Said the Cardinal to the Communists: "In the name of Christ, who loves you, we greet you. But what do you want of me, what do you promise yourselves from us? Your teachings are not ours. Our teachings are those of Christ and the Church, and you know that our martyrs have died in their defense and that we would be prepared to do the same should it prove necessary."

On the suggested "co-operation," the papal message through the Cardinal's pastoral stated: "Our actions are inspired by spirituality, yours are influenced by materialism. And the spiritual element which is for us the soul and the true benefit of all action, is what you reject. How is co-operation then possible?"

Whatever the Vatican and Catholics may have thought of the gesture of "the outstretched hand," for me it was new proof of the healthy coming of age of the Communist movement. It gave promise of bringing to fruition all the hopes and aspirations which had been mine over the recent years. Into the campaign for the out-stretched hand I threw myself with something like a fine frenzy. The co-operation of Communists and Catholics in the United States would put APA-ism to rout, I contended eagerly—that APA-ism which had clouded the days of my Irish forefathers and had left its heritage of hatred in our land. It would assure the forward march of Socialism along with the preservation of Catholicism, a consummation for which I devoutly wished.

It must be remembered how, from my youth, I had felt that an alliance of the labor movement and the Catholic Church would greatly benefit to our nation. Now, when I considered the Communist party as an advanced expression of labor, the good that would be derived from Catholic-Communist collaboration—not only in this country but in the international arena as well—seemed tremendous.

When Christmas, 1936, came around, I expressed these dreams in a Communist message of peace and good will to the Catholic people. In the *Daily Worker* on Christmas morning, a well-displayed "greeting". of almost three columns in length appeared from my pen. It was the chief feature of that issue. "Communists Hold Out Hand of Fellowship to All Enemies of War and Oppression" said its headline. Early in its course the article asked: "Where is the peace which is our Christmas hope? And where the road that will lead to this achievement? Will the Christmas motto remain only the words 'Peace, Peace' in a world in which there is no peace?"

My fervor was inspired by the announcement, the month before, of the draft of the new Stalinist constitution in the Soviet Union. (I thoroughly believed that the Soviet Republic stood for peace.) It was also stirred by the third anniversary of the Leipzig trial, when I recalled how George Dimitrov had defied the obese Goering and the entire Nazi hierarchy. It was, in part, the enthusiasm engendered by "the battle against fascism" in Spain, the defense of Madrid and the stand of Maxim Litvinov at Geneva "against aggression." My entire being was now absorbed in the overwhelming importance of these things, and my life was a continual twenty-four-hour effort to do all possible to advance what the Communists called "the anti-fascist cause."

And so my words tumbled out that Christmas morning of 1936, hailing the Soviet Union as a citadel of peace—even though it had embarked on a war economy second only to that of Nazi Germany. "It is the Soviet Union," read my article, "which has pointed to the sole path that leads to peace—the joining of hands in pacts to halt the war aggressor by the peace-loving democratic countries of the world."

Since my appeal was directed to the Catholics in particular, I immediately took up the matter of those Catholic spokesmen who leveled criticisms at the Communists and their integrity. "How strange is it to see, in a world so set up, that the Catholic spokesmen in so many instances belabor Communism!" I exclaimed. "Monsignor Fulton J. Sheen of the Catholic University at Washington has been perhaps the most persistent of these spokesmen. As late as December 14 —almost on the very eve of Christmas—he again speaks out against the Communists who fight for peace."

Thus it was that I took up my doughty lance against Monsignor Sheen, and almost all the rest of the Christmas message was devoted to "replying" to him. I acknowledged that he had said in his December 14 address or sermon that "there is something very good in Communism. That good is its protest against low wages, accumulation of wealth, the conditions of the poor, imperialism and the condition of the workingman. That is its appeal."

He had gone on, however, to repudiate the Communist

merits. Among his statements to which I took heated exception was this: "The Communists' protest against fascism is
not a just one. When a Communist uses the word 'fascist' he
means 'anti-Communist.'" Then he added that "all who
oppose Communism are fascists" in Communist eyes.

It was this assertion which caused me to burst forth with,
"Come, come, Monsignor Sheen," (which I thereafter heard
repeated by Communists in meetings large and small all over
the country) and I challenged him to give proof of his statements. "Is it not the Communists," I asked, "who are fighting in Germany for the freedom of worship for the Catholic
priests, hunted and hounded by the madman Hitler? Is it
not the Communists who have opposed to the limit the
Black Legion and the Ku Klux Klan in America, the same
dark organizations aimed at attacking the right of worship
of the Catholic priests? Is it not the Communists who have
stood with the Basque priests, not only for democracy in
Spain, but also for the right of those priests to freedom of
worship?"

Then I again proceeded to offer "the hand of good will and
fellowship to the Catholic people of America—to make united
resistance to the Black Legion, the Ku Klux Klan, the
American Liberty League and to those other anti-democratic
forces who aim to destroy the liberties of the mass of the
people."

Although there was an imprudent and impudent element
of "distortion" in my "reply" to the Monsignor, it had
none of the anti-Catholic spirit that now rages in the Communist press. It now follows the old "ex-priest" scandal line
of the deceased *Menace*. Only recently Joseph Starobin, the
foreign editor, referred an inquiring reader to one of the most
notorious of the ex-priests for information concerning Monsignor Sheen. Although any such antisocial attitude—
reminiscent of the Klan—was totally absent from my

Christmas article, I had, nevertheless, put the burden for failure to co-operate on the Catholics and not on the Communists' long record of disruption and deceit. In my earnestness to forward the anti-fascist cause, that consideration of Communist bad faith was far from my mind.

With my present deep distaste at this attempt to put Monsignor Sheen in a false position, there is this thankfulness: that it was this very article and its occasion that were to lead to the jolt that changed my life, after many years, and made me see the Red cause in its proper colors and brought me back to Christ. A young man named Saul displayed false fervor of this sort a long time ago, and even consented to the stoning of Stephen. I had not thought of the man of Tarsus when I worked out my response to the Monsignor, but only a few months later I had him very much in mind.

It is no more possible for me to explain how I could help Catholic-Communist co-operation by assailing Monsignor Sheen than it was to say why I thought I was serving social justice years before by leaving the Catholic Church. At the time of my departure from the Church, I knew in my heart that it was solely to defy the Catholic moral law. For both of these incidents I can best give as explanation, but not excuse the words of the great St. Augustine. He who was to teach me so much about myself through his *Confessions* has this to say, addressing himself to God: "If any man has heard Thy voice and followed it and done none of these things he finds me here recording and confessing, still he must not scorn me: for I am healed by the same doctor who preserved him from falling into sickness, or at least into such grievous illness."

However, in those days of the People's Front, because of my horror at the aggression of the Axis powers, and the "nonintervention of the democratic nations" in Spain, I had the feeling of being in the right that only the future was to prove wrong. Though little did I know it, the doors were even then swinging open, for that very revelation.

Monsignor Sheen was well able to take care of himself. In a surprisingly short time he sent me a long manuscript answering each one of the questions I had asked of him. Its title was, "Communism Answers a Communist," and it was replete with damaging admissions of Soviet crimes and crudities taken from the official Soviet press. Monsignor suggested that I print it in the *Daily Worker*, since I had taken up considerable space with the Christmas message. I took the matter up with my colleagues but they were loath to do anything of the sort. Then I hit upon what I thought was a clever idea: we would do what the Monsignor wanted, if our reply could be published at equal length in several well-known Catholic papers which I planned to name. But that proposal was frowned upon by the editorial board of the *Daily Worker*.

The lame excuse given was that it would be inadvisable to conduct a "full dress debate" with a Catholic church dignitary just then. This did not satisfy me at all. It sounded too much as though the Communists were capable of entering upon debates only when they felt free to hurl the usual "liar," "slanderer," Trotskyite" at anyone on the slightest provocation. And that was exactly the case. The consensus was that it would not be a good reply unless it was "a vigorous reply," which meant a Niagara of abuse and near-gutter accusation. That is the convenient form which the Communists employ in so many of their polemics and which I strongly resented.

But while the hesitation continued, I took the Monsignor's pamphlet home with me and studied and underlined it with care. It was a definite and devastating rebuttal to my queries. "If Communism is the friend of the downtrodden," he inquired, why do so many oppressive laws and regulations exist in the Soviet Union? These he cited on page after page, as quotations from official Soviet decrees or from the leading Soviet publications. Concerning the Communists' new-found affection for religion, Monsignor Sheen retorted with, "Come, come, I will show you." He then turned to such official Soviet declarations as that of Otto Kuusinen's pamphlet, "The Youth Movement and the Fight Against Fascism," in which the Finnish Red specifically assails the Catholic priesthood as youth's enemy in the battle against fascism. He also quoted Ercoli's article in the *Communist* of December, 1936, in which, while appealing for a People's Front, that Red spokesman links "the clergy and the Jesuits" with the Fascists. There was much more to the same purpose.

As to the Catholics in Germany, the Monsignor showed that the Communists had been their enemy no less than had Hitler. The Catholic bishops at Fulda were his authority for this and also the fact that when Hitler came to power five million German Communists were enrolled as members of the militant atheists' society of Moscow. As to the Black Legion, he said that it had been combated by forces and authorities who had no common bond with the Communists at all. And he quoted the Basque bishops' strong terms comdemning the "modern monster, Communism."

The Monsignor's pamphlet, which could well be read extensively today throughout America, concluded, in part, with these words: "The more I read about Communism, the more I am convinced that its greatest propagandists know practically nothing factual about it. They talk of Russia either in general terms or in the stereotyped language of its propaganda. That is why I believe many Communists are in good faith, and here I include you, Mr. Budenz." In his final fusillade he said that Catholics would neither be fighters for fascism nor dupes of Communism. "We know your tactics from your documents; we know your purpose from your writings; we know your failures through Mexico, Spain and Russia. No! We will not join with you. We prefer to be loyal to our God and to our Country."

Powerful as was Monsignor Sheen's plea, it did not dissuade me from preparing a counterreply. Many of his accusations I knew to be true; others I would have to check up. It was my intent to prove that those which were true were thrown out of focus and made to loom too large. I would then play up those things which were subsequently made much of in the Soviet Building at the World's Fair. I would dwell upon the wonders of Magnitogorsk and the great wedding there of iron and coal, and of the building of a huge metropolis on short order in the desert. I would list the cultural palaces and the educational enterprises within the U.S.S.R. Behind my proposed reply was the conviction that was causing me to write my earnest, eager words in the pages of the Communist publications. The essence of it was that a new day was dawning in Communist thought, that the Seventh Congress and the subsequent People's Fronts were breeding a Communism which would not be hostile to religion. There had been a change in the sons of the French Revolution in this respect; there would be a similar change on the part of the sons of the Bolshevik Revolution of October. In later years I was made aware of the falseness of these hopes and their expression, but at the time they made the Communist message ring out in many places in America.

In the midst of these preparations, I was stricken by an influenza bug which put me in bed for two weeks, so that I could not reply to Monsignor Sheen. When I returned to the office I had a letter from him, or some other notice, that his pamphlet had been published by the Paulist Press. I wrote him explaining my illness, and on March 21, 1937, received a short note from him asking if it would be possible for us to get together in New York some week end. I answered that it would, saying, "I am leaving on a speaking tour of the mining, steel and automobile areas" but would be back in time to meet with him on April 17.

In his startling success in winning souls to the Church of Christ the Monsignor has frequently been aided by his spiritual audacity. On a number of occasions he has boldly told an erring person that it was his duty or hers to return to the Church or to embrace it. That was his intent in making this engagement with me, and in this instance he was assisted by one of those humble but holy souls who are the glory of the Church Militant.

Monsignor Sheen told me, at the time of our meeting, that when the pamphlet directed at me had obtained a wide circulation, several hundred Catholics who had known me wrote to him. He said they all spoke well of my youth and that had impressed him. Among these, I was to learn after my conversion ten years later, was an old acquaintance of my school days. He had asked the Monsignor to pray for me always and to make every effort to get in touch with me, and then expressed the hope that I would return to the Cross and to Calvary.

It was in the grill room of Manhattan's Hotel Commodore that the odd meeting between the most noted Catholic pulpit orator and the member of the editorial board of the *Daily Worker* took place. In an obscure corner we talked for an hour in earnest, quiet tones.

With a smile in his intense blue eyes, Monsignor told me that he was leaving for England in the early summer. Each year he preached in Soho, living near the house where Karl Marx had labored. Our talk drifted from London as the workplace of Marx and Engels, to a discussion of what his pamphlet had said in establishing a parallel between fascism and Communism. Here I objected. "There is this merit in the Communist view that does not inhere in fascism," I contended. "Communism has within it the promise of democracy and the end of dictatorship in its doctrine of the withering away of the state." I was still at the old theme, which had been on my lips and in my mind since the St. Louis days when I read Engels and swallowed his estimate of how the Socialist revolution would proceed. We then went on to talk of the new Stalinist Constitution which I considered further assurance of the inherent democratic tendencies in the Communist movement and the Soviet state. Stalin had not yet written that judgment in *The History of the Communist Party of the U.S.S.R.* which was to discard the "withering away" theory as outworn. And in the elections following the adoption of the Constitution, the one-slate electoral machinery of fascism had not yet been installed to make a mockery of its democratic pretensions. Therefore, on the basis of the facts at my disposal my argument was good. Unfortunately, those facts were eventually to be proved utterly false and fictitious.

Monsignor Sheen knows the secret of dealing with people who have broken with the Church. It is an outgrowth of Catholic charity, but it also springs from a deep knowledge of human nature. He was not disposed to contradict me, in our face-to-face discussion. That would only have aroused my personal pride and incited me to further argument. What he did, instead, took me totally by surprise.

Pushing aside the remaining cutlery on the table as though to waive any argumentation, Monsignor bent forward and exclaimed: "Let us now talk of the Blessed Virgin!"

For those who are beyond the bounds of belief, this incident will have little significance. They will not comprehend what went on in my soul at those words. But at some time in their lives they may have experienced the electrifying moment in which a series of intellectual concepts on which they have long labored without result suddenly become clear. What happened to me then was something like that, but it was much more.

Immediately, I was conscious of the senselessness and sinfulness of my life as I then lived it. The peace that flows from Mary, and which had been mine in the early days, flashed back to me with an overwhelming vividness. There rang in my ears for a moment the prayer which comes from the salutation of Gabriel: *Ave Maria, gracia plena!* "Hail Mary, full of grace!" How often, I thought, has that supplication gone up from thousands in distress and brought them peace—and I, who know better, reject it! This world is a madhouse, my thoughts went on rapidly, without the blessings of the Magnificat: "His mercy is from generation to generation . . . " went the rhythm in my mind and heart. "He hath put down the mighty from their seat, He hath exalted the humble. He hath filled the hungry with good things, and the rich he hath sent away empty."

The drabness of life without Divinity, the slaughter which science will wreak on mankind without Divine Law, pressed in on my consciousness. "Very well," I said simply to Monsignor. He saw that I was deeply moved. And so he spoke of the Mother of God and of the peculiar blessings which she has conferred on so many who have had recourse to her.

The wholeness and holiness of the life I had deserted were laid before me. To regain the peace that is the product of devotion to Mary was still possible. I caught my breath at the prospect; I was quietly laboring under an intense strain.

I record my thoughts during this conversation, because these are what I best remember. The conversation itself had to do with Lourdes, with the promises of Our Lady, with the prayers of the Church for the conversion of Russia and Our Lady's power to see them fulfilled, and with the need of faith in her graciousness—but it is not vital now to recall the details. What stood out in this discussion was the dignity of the human personality represented by the whole spiritual concept centered in Mary. One statement of the Monsignor remains vividly in my memory, "I shall always pray for you because you have never fully lost the faith," he said. That startled me as much as the suggestion with which he had opened this part of our conversation.

Of all the episodes that have crowded my varied career, this memento to Mary was the most electric, the most awe-inspiring. In the course of the years I have met many magnetic men and women, have conferred with governors and senators, have stood in court twenty-one times as a result of labor disputes—breathlessly awaited the verdict and each time experienced the triumph of acquittal—but never has my soul been swept by love and reverence as it was that April evening.

There will be those who will look upon this event as just so much imbecillity—their lack of faith will lead to that comment—and them I will have to let pass. There will be those who will appreciate the integrity of this report from the very fact that it is made; in an age which sneers and scoffs at holy things it takes a certain courage, too, my friends, to testify to truths which prevail despite the sodden state of man's spiritual existence. There is a certain reluctance to lay bare what occurs in one's inner heart and soul. To those who understand and respect such a reality, I would say to look deeper into the truths of the Catholic Church, learn to know these truths fully and to hold them dear.

It would have been well had I heeded that experience nine years ago. However, when Monsignor Sheen and I parted in the main lobby of Grand Central Station that night, it was the last time that we were to see each other for nine long years. From Atlantic City, on the following May 10, I wrote him a hurried note to the effect that I was covering the

International Ladies' Garment Workers' Union convention, which precluded writing about "the future meeting to which we had agreed." To this I added: "The relations between American Catholics and Communists are of such great moment that I had hoped we might continue our discussion before this. It may have to wait now, until your return from England."

The communication concluded with this sentence: "Meanwhile, I hope that you will have the *Daily Worker* forwarded to you in Great Britain, as I shall very shortly have an article or two on your pamphlet." I wrote those lines with full confidence. In spite of the leading comrade's original reluctance to print any such reply, I was making progress in that direction. I had obtained an interpreter of long standing to translate the *Pravda* and *Izvestia* articles for me, so that I might have at hand exactly what they said. I was carefully collecting all the material regarding the Soviet Union which is regularly ground out by the various pro-Soviet agencies in order to refute Monsignor Sheen indirectly, even if it could not be done directly.

Monsignor replied on May 17, and asked to be allowed an equal space in the *Daily* to answer my article. "Whatever you write," he said, "I shall read with great interest." Indeed, he went further: "It will be a great joy for me to know that you are going to answer my pamphlet in the *Daily Worker*. I shall have my secretary forward it to me."

Finally, he stated: "I shall remember you, particularly, at the Shrine of Our Lady of Lourdes, that you may once again recover not only the faith which once was yours, but also the peace which surpasses all understanding, and which only Christ can give."

What, then, did I proceed to do? Far from preparing my return to the Church, I began to work even more eagerly for the Communist cause and planned article upon article in behalf of "closer Communist-Catholic relations." Even to me this was a mystery after I had begun the actual journey back to Rome. It was Augustine, that mighty light of Christianity, who again showed me the meaning of myself in this unholy, unpleasing aspect. Nine years had also passed after St. Monica, through Catholic charity, again invited her son to her table—which affected him exceedingly—before he entered the gates of Rome. And after that blessed incident, which taught Augustine so much of Christian love through Catholic tenets, he performed even more services for the heresy of Manichaeism than before. In the same way, after my meeting with Monsignor Sheen I did much more for Marxism-Leninism than I had before. I wrote more of its leading pronouncement and propaganda pieces in America, spoke to more meetings on its behalf and advanced its purposes in more varied ways.

The "why" of this must be laid to the perversity of the human soul when once it has been led into a camp of error through the delusion of being led by reason. With his intellect clouded by fumes of unbelief, the victim of this stupefying rationalization intones pompously the magic word "clarity." In my case, the spiritual fire which was rekindled momentarily, at least, by my conversation with Monsignor Sheen, was gutted by the secularist spirit which again enveloped me. "Intellectually," I would say, "there had still to be a recognition of the existence and expansion of the Soviet Union's strength." Two considerations did much to convince me—or at least, that's what I called it—that there should be renewed gestures toward Communist-Catholic *rapprochement.*

One of these current phenomena which kept me on my course was the Communist overestimation of what was going forward in Soviet Russia. We Communists literally doused ourselves with Soviet "good points." Everything in our United States had defects; everything in the U.S.S.R. was perfect. That's the way the theme went, and even I who had always been cautious in my estimate of the Soviet Union and had merely related it to Dickens' asperities toward early America, was swept off my feet by the reiterations. Though this may seem strange, it is no more surprising than that scientists, physicians, lawyers, "practical men" and alleged statesmen are today taking an even more one-sided attitude toward Soviet Russia and what it is up to—and much more water has flowed into the sea of history.

What were we Communists saying to ourselves and others, during those years of 1935, 1936 and 1937? On his return from the Seventh Congress of the C.I., Earl Browder gave his report on the Soviet Union to a crowded Madison Square Garden on the evening of October 3, 1935. Said the General Secretary of the Communist party of the U.S.A.: "Since 1928 the number of workers employed in the United States has declined at least ten million and the sum total of wages has dropped by more than half. In the Soviet Union the number of workers has doubled, and the sum total of wages has multiplied by five. In the United States, where the need is greatest, social insurance is still a vague aspiration, while in the Soviet Union, where unemployment is unknown, the social insurance funds have been multiplied sevenfold and run into billions of rubles. . . . In the United States, millions of the population are moving from their homes to cellars and shacks. In the Soviet Union they are moving from cellars and shacks into great, modern apartment houses."

Knowing some of our ills at home, we began to build a Paradise on the Volga and Vistula and across the Siberian steppes. Tons of literature—books, pamphlets, reports, issues of the *Communist International*, issues of *The Communist*— the American theoretical organ—constantly filled our heads with visions of Soviet magnificence. This was not infrequently contrasted in the most extravagant manner with "American decline and deficiencies."

The only trouble with this whole line of argumentation was that it was founded on utter falsehoods. World War II was to supply the most devastating proof of that. It was the much-derided United States that produced the sinews of war to save Soviet Russia from Hitlerite efficiency. It was this "declining" nation of ours that finally turned out almost as much of the material of war as all our allies and enemies combined. It is this U.S.A. right now that is educating ex-soldiers, our G.I.'s, on a scale that no other country could dream of. This is taken more or less as a matter of course; nor is there any propaganda afloat to undermine other nations because they cannot approach such an achievement. We know from countless sources—one of which is David J. Dallin's *The Real Soviet Russia*—that the standard of housing on the whole and of living in general in the U.S.S.R. is so low that it is probably beneath that of the poorest groups in the United States. We have had our eyes opened—and by no less than the astounding "war speech" of Stalin early in 1946—that such economy as is flourishing in the Soviet Union is still a war economy. It is much like that in Germany under Hitler, and is continuing as such even after the Nazi menace has been removed from the Soviet borders. It is an economy for manufacturing tanks, planes and munitions of war for conquest of other nations, as the recent acts of the Soviet Government and its puppets in "Soviet China" and other places have made obvious.

So far as the absence of unemployment in the Soviet Union went, which Browder and the rest of us stressed at that time, we know so little of what is actually happening in the U.S.S.R. that we are only making guesses. There can be such a thing as slave labor without idleness, too, as Hitler demonstrated. One of his boasts was likewise the ending of unem-

ployment. The denial of free speech and free press in the
Soviet Union makes every estimate difficult and doubtful.
But far from recognizing that, the Communists of 1936–1937
were shouting in a shrill key that these rights were vague or
fictitious in the United States. The Soviet Constitution was
actually much "more democratic" than our own! And in the
September, 1936, issue of the *Communist International* that
assertion was actually made, not once but several times, in a
long article comparing the two constitutions.

Americans will scarcely agree that an extensive and all-
seeing secret police, concentration camps filled with millions
of prisoners, denial, at the point of a gun, of the right to
worship, and elections in which the electors can vote for
only one slate, are reaching the heights of "democracy."
And yet, Communists were telling themselves then—and
are telling themselves now—that "the Soviet Constitution
now establishes the rights of man upon a plane that history
has hitherto never known." ("The Constitutions of U.S.A.
and U.S.S.R., by Harry Owen, *Communist International*, Vol.
XIII, No. 9.)

It would have been too much for us to have attempted to
convince ourselves, or anyone else, that the Soviet Union
was superior to the United States in technical advancement.
That was not the manner in which the Communists ap-
proached the matter. Our way was that taken by Browder
in his October 3 speech: "There can be no doubt that in the
United States we have a much higher development of technical efficiency, that in the Soviet Union they are still
technically backward compared to us, and yet over there
they are rising out of a poverty to a general well-being for
all, while here we are sinking into a swamp of misery that
seems to be created by the very wealth of the country."
There were enough weak spots in our own economic scene,
and some of them obvious enough, to make the American

Reds readily accept this interpretation of history by the servants of Moscow.

Furthermore, there was the emotional whipping up of Soviet patriotism which was adopted in varying degrees by different persons, but which affected all Communists. Up to the rafters at almost every Communist meeting went the song of the Red Air Fleet:

> *Fly higher and higher and higher*
> *Our emblem is the Soviet star,*
> *And every propeller is roaring—RED FRONT!*
> *Defending the U.S.S.R.*

For our American air pilots and pioneers there was no Red singing in those days; there was only derision for any plan or proposal of American national defense.

The mere existence of a "Socialist country on one-sixth of the globe"—which would have been regarded as a dream by many Socialists thirty years before—stirred us to dreams of our own in making it more perfect and promising than it was. The urgency of bringing all institutions and movements into line with its aims pressed on me day by day. I regarded that as the major undertaking of the age. Every night in our small Manhattan apartment I worked on arguments for it, to be published later in the *Daily Worker*. To me it was not just an assignment, it was a duty.

No one should harbor the idea that I was so naïve as not to attempt a measured judgment of all these things. There was constant recognition on my part that there were plenty of defects in Soviet life. One of the members of the Political Committee of the American party, who from the beginning had shown me considerable respect, had privately presented a none too pleasant view of Soviet living and labor on his return in 1936 from a secret visit to Moscow. He did this in sympathy with the U.S.S.R. of course, as he might speak of some weakness of his father or grandfather. But he gave startlingly frank, though scattered descriptions of utter poverty in some places and of prostitution and other crudities which the Communist press either consciously ignored or denied. Perhaps noting a thoughtful or disapproving silence on my part, he had smilingly and apologetically added: "It's like your reference to Dickens and early America. The spots which are there will be cleansed as the years roll on."

Though this report, made almost secretively, cast a momentary cloud over my vision, I soon reassured myself by reasoning that every system has its weaknesses and that they are bound to show up in something newly fledged and immature. The materialistic concept of history, too, continued its powerful pull. The bravado of its promise that Socialism was next on the calendar of history and the deduction that "here it is in the Soviet Union" furnished a strong motive for overlooking any blots that might appear on the escutcheon of the Socialist Fatherland. That promise steeled my conviction that many shortcomings could be ignored when the greater goal of "a new society" was being won. I hid from myself what I knew to be the case, that this very materialism had to rely on terror as its only law. It wiped out intellectual integrity, but to that I closed my eyes.

Then, too, it was heartening to observe the new Communist tactics in handling religion in 1937. The outstretched hand had given me a chance to have some real effect on Browder's thinking—or at least on his statements—about this time. I was able to insist with him and other leading comrades that a better understanding with all religious groups, and with the Catholics in particular, was essential. I continually pointed to the 300,000,000 Catholics in Europe and the 30,000,000 or more here in the United States. "They are the largest minority group in America and on the increase in numbers. The building of the unions, the strengthening of the People's Front, the buttressing of the defense of the Soviet Union depend upon their good will." It was also my own belief that the measures which would be necessary to bring about this affiliation would tend to widen the viewpoint of the Communists and give them a more democratic outlook than prevailed either in the Soviet Government or in the Red ranks here.

It was not long before Browder began to criticize "anti-Catholicism" along with anti-Semitism and Negro-baiting. How far this was from the official Communist slant of only a year or two before can be appreciated by consulting the piles of antireligious and audaciously atheistic pamphlets and articles which appeared in popular form from the Red express up to 1935. I will cite only the mildest one of these, to serve as an example. It is "The Church and the Workers," International Pamphlets Number fifteen. It was issued by the Labor Research Association, supposedly an agency to promote the unions and therefore not so extreme as the *Daily Worker* and similar publications.

"The main contribution of the churches to an unemployment crisis," said this pamphlet, "are prayers and charity. Prayers, of course, provide neither bread nor jobs. But they serve the purpose among church-going workers of turning attention and bitterness away from the real cause of their suffering—the capitalist system—and make it appear that change is only in the 'power of God.' This faith in the supernatural tends to prevent the workers from organizing and taking matters into their own hands, do away with those periodic crises which are characteristic of capitalism."

Any stand for social justice taken by the churches, and especially by the Catholic Church, was labeled "hypocritical." And the pamphlet continued: "'Justice to the workers has been a slogan to keep the workers under the church's domination and to prevent them from participating actively in a movement that has for its aim the overthrow of capitalism." And so the churches were contradictorily damned both as being against and for the workers. Those religious organizations in general were declared to be "bulwarks of reaction and ignorance" and the pamphlet proudly and exultantly reported that "the anti-religious campaign in the Soviet Union succeeds." The thirty-one-page document concluded with the assertion that "religion cannot be reformed" and called for an intensification of the "fight against the churches and religion."

This publication appeared as late as 1932, the year that Franklin D. Roosevelt was first elected President, and was, therefore, the "popular education" spread far and wide by the Communists a very short time prior to the period of the outstretched hand.

There were many among the leading Communists, then and later, who were against wooing the Catholics and other religious groups. They had understood Marxism-Leninism to be the extermination by fire and sword of all religion. Their hatred of Catholicism was intense and remained so. Then, there were others who, though with less hatred were, nonetheless, of the opinion that a religionist could never be a tried and true Marxist, even in the lower ranks of the Party. They considered these peace offerings debilitating to the Red organization. One of the leading comrades in charge of trade union work for the New York district, Rose Wortis, came to me as late as 1941 to discuss this question. She had been perturbed about it for years. She told me that the "comrades in the Transport Workers Union" had insisted on remaining Catholic when they became Communists. That had been in 1930 or 1931 and she was still worried about the matter and wanted to know whether or not I thought the Political Committee had made a mistake in allowing them

to retain this "peculiar dual allegiance." The Transport
Workers Union comrades had urged that "tactically" they
would have to be Catholics or they could not hold leadership
among the Irish workers. But the woman comrade was afraid
that constant attendance at Mass and the like would
make them "uncertain in their loyalty to the Communist
movement."

By that time—1941—I refused to give an opinion, pleading
that I was not present at the enrollment of these men in the
Party and did not know all the circumstances. In reality, I
was pretty well convinced that the Communist party intended to destroy religion by force, and would turn back to
that path whenever Moscow gave the word. But I was still
hoping earnestly that this would not be the case. As to the
Party members in the Transport Workers Union, I knew that
persons acting in various auxiliary capacities had been
instructed to watch their conduct and to report any tendencies to stray from the Communist movement. They were
under strict surveillance.

Browder was to some extent influenced by those who held
the cautious position in regard to being "too liberal" on the
rights of religious groups. While cheered on the "growing
friendly contacts between Communists and religious com-
municants," he was not free to go so far as he might have
liked. This I know from a number of talks with him on the
subject, both on the ninth floor and at luncheon at Wana-
maker's. Through my constant insistence, he did bring
forward the evils associated with the old APA, Know-
Nothing and other anti-Catholic movements and pointed
out that their revival would be harmful to the entire nation.
He also got hold of *The Protestant Crusade* by Ray Billington
and made wide use of it by warning of the deadly venom
wrapped up in anti-Catholic propaganda. But he was compelled by the religion-hating comrades—with some secret

pressure from Moscow—to interlard this cajolery of the Catholics and other religionists with indirect antireligious argumentation. A classic example of this method is his "Religion and Communism," issued in pamphlet form in 1939 and taken from his speech at the Community Church of Boston on March 5 of the same year.

This speech was a compound of two that I had recently made as a substitute for Browder, in Pittsburgh and Johnstown, Pennsylvania—with one addition. It was the addition that I did not like, though the speech as a whole I marked down as a gain. One of the thoughts that I had contributed was an emphasis on the triumph over joblessness in the Soviet Union. In my debate with the Catholic, Arnold Lunn, at Pittsburgh, I noted that this made a marked impression on the Catholic portion of the audience. I had often contended to Browder that in dealing with the Catholics we should stress the homes that would be saved by the Socialist practices prevalent in the U.S.S.R. The second thought that I presented was one that the audience at Johnstown, though far from responsive to my views at first, had accepted with something like satisfaction. It was an interpretation of the Communists' "scientific" view of religion. I represented it as being firm in its defense of the right to worship, but always reserving the right to judge religious movements and organizations in the light of history.

The part of Browder's Community Church speech which was not mine was an outline of the "materialist" attitude of the Communists as Marxists. I felt that the antireligious aspect would cancel out the good features of the address, and as soon as I could get hold of Browder after his Boston trip, I told him so. He seemed inclined to agree with me, but, as was the provoking case in so many other instances, was very vague about why he had inserted the antireligious clauses. I got the impression, as often I had before, that he was as uneasy as though someone were looking over his shoulder and dictating what he should say.

The Pittsburgh-Johnstown speeches on "the Catholic Question" were staged while I was located in Chicago and it was in that city that I had considerable success in "Catholic-Communist co-operation." This success gave me high hopes for a number of years that it would be repeated on a larger scale. But without knowing the circumstances, the leader will be unable to comprehend fully how I could experience so many rebuffs in this endeavor later on and yet continue to press it forward with such great expectations. Let us, therefore, review these events.

The *Midwest Daily Record* first appeared on Feb. 12, 1938, as a People's Front paper, and was frankly manned by a Communist staff and under a Communist editor. I stated this setup quite definitely in print in subsequent discussions on the paper. We had to hit upon some way to make that publication both Communist and non-Communist, and the phrase "the Communist party's gift to the People's Front" came to me as an inspiration. It was helpful in keeping the paper in good odor in many quarters.

From the very beginning, the publication expressed a sincere regard for the Catholics and their problems, in the language I felt Reds should use. George Cardinal Mundelein's address to the Archdiocesan Union of the Holy Name Society on January 2 gave me a foundation on which to build. The Cardinal urged greater co-operation on the part of Church agencies with labor, and also, inferentially, frowned upon what is commonly known as "Red-baiting." Since the Communists always identify themselves with labor, the *Midwest Daily Record* took advantage of this declaration to hail the Cardinal's utterances all through the year.

The official organ of the Catholic Archdiocese, the *New World*, began in its turn to reprint editorials and columns from the *Daily Record* and to comment favorably on its statements. Without recounting all such incidents, here is an example. On May 18, 1938, an editorial appeared in the *Daily Record*, entitled "Chicago's Cardinal Speaks," praising Mundelein for his stand on dealing with delinquent young people. Characteristically, the editorial opened with this eulogy, "Cardinal Mundelein has recently taken one progressive position after another." It was prominently reprinted in the Chicago Catholic organ of May 27.

Again, skipping to the next year, on July 1, 1939, the *Daily Record* ran a large picture of His Eminence as a salute to his birthday, which was the following day. The caption read: "Catholics as well as other people will greet Cardinal Mundelein, the democratic leader of the Chicago archdiocese, on the occasion of his sixty-seventh birthday tomorrow." Editorially the publication wished the Cardinal a happy birthday. It reviewed his life and accomplishments, from a humble beginning, and proclaimed him "a defender of democratic principles."

With a gesture of good will, in the next issue (July 14) the Catholic *New World* devoted a considerable portion of its column, "Keeping Pace with the News," to comment on this courtesy to the Cardinal. "A Salute to Our Cardinal" was its heading, and after describing the *Daily Record's* gesture, it went on to say good words for our paper. It referred to the advance "dire predictions" that had been made with regard to the character of the paper and then showed how it had not lived up to them. "The heartfelt birthday wishes to the leader of the Archdiocese of Chicago is typical of just how irreligious and anti-Catholic the *Midwest Daily Record* has been from its inception." It then added that if every paper was similar minded on irreligion and anti-Catholicism, "this would be a much better world for everybody."

These were unusual words from a Catholic official organ for a publication under Communist auspices. I made the most of them in pressing the Communists for a more understanding view of the Catholics. The writer of the column in the *New World* did not know at that time how far from the official Communist outlook on religion and the Catholic Church my utterances were, or what a rocky road I had to travel to get these sentiments expressed in the paper. The outstretched hand was my cudgel, and I brandished it whenever there were maneuvers to shut me up. It would look very bad indeed for the Reds were my views publicly criticized by any leading Communist while they were professing to grasp the Catholics by the hand as brothers. It simply couldn't be done. The moves to curb my "zeal" were, therefore, subtle and temporarily unsuccessful.

There were some comrades, nurturing the false view that all religious Christians are anti-Semitic, who assailed me for cultivating the good will of "the pogromists." To them I could reply that the Ku Klux Klan made anti-Semitism, anti-Catholicism and Negro-baiting its joint goal—and that Catholic, Jew and Negro should uphold each other's rights. There were others who contended that I was sowing "illusions" among the comrades, and that Catholics were "inevitable enemies of progress." To them I could quote the words of Thorez, but of course I forgot that they were said only for Moscow's benefit and could be completely changed whenever Moscow so decided.

That was exactly what happened. The outstretched-hand policy was to be specifically repudiated by V. J. Jerome in *Political Affairs* in 1946, shortly after my departure from the Party. What his article held out as the course for the future was actual war upon the Catholics under the guise of "warring on the hierarchy."

You need but contrast the expressions of respect to

Cardinal Mundelein with the gratuitous insult offered Francis Cardinal Spellman by the Communists in New York's city council this past year, to understand how far I had stretched the outstretched hand. That was possible only because Moscow then wanted Catholic support, in its fear of the German military machine. When the Soviet leaders came to grasp Hitler's hand, instead, Moscow forgot all about the rights of Catholics. Today it has completely thrown aside its sheep's clothing on this subject, and has unloosed a savage persecution of Catholics in Hungary, Lithuania, Ruthenia and Yugoslavia.

Back in Chicago in 1939, however, the animus of anti-Catholic bigots gave me the opportunity to put the paper on record on the Catholic question for a long time. A flood of letters came into our office, threatening a boycott of the *Record* if it went on printing anti-fascist comments from Catholic papers. We had resorted to this practice in order to acquaint all "liberals" with the stand of prominent Catholic organs in America against fascism. The boycott threat was accompanied by attacks on the morality of the Catholic priesthood, particularly in Germany. In my own column, titled "the Heart of America," I strongly condemned such "poison," and paid tribute to a number of Catholic papers for their valuable contribution to "the preservation and extension of American democracy."

Eager to make our position permanently understood, I replied to these scurrilities further by saying that reflections upon any group because of their religious beliefs or racial origins would not be tolerated in the *Record*. In order to get all the common people together for the defense of their common democracy, "the base slanders against the Catholic people must be swept aside." And the *Midwest Daily Record*, I added, "will adhere to that stand no matter what ultimata it will receive."

It was with much satisfaction that I wrote this last sentence. It disposed of the bigots for good, and it gave me a little lever with my comrades, since the *Record* was now committed for some days ahead. Naturally, I was quite well aware that among Communists the whole business could be readily repudiated; that some fine day I could be asked to run an article in the Record by some comrade, known or unknown, stating that what I had written was off color. But I also knew that during the People's Front period they dare not carry through anything so crude. The only hint of criticism I got was the comment by Morris Childs, District Organizer in Illinois, in a state committee meeting, that "we are giving Louis enough rope to let him hang the Catholics." It was supposed to be a jest, but among Communists political jests have ironic aftermaths. Childs apparently felt he had to make some such comment to keep the record straight for "the next turn around the curve of history's railroad." The most active comrades would thereby know that we were not taking the rights of Catholics too seriously.

Meanwhile, the official organ of the Chicago archdiocese was saying of my statement: "This is the 'kind of boring from within' that our alarmists warned us about. If 'boring from within' consists in defending the civil rights of Catholics we need more of it, to say nothing about 'one good turn deserves another.'"

This was of a mettle I admired, and it aroused happy anticipations of what would follow. Unfortunately, both the *New World* and I were then predicating our acts and words on false premises. This was "boring from within" that would later be used for the crassest antireligious purposes, as the present Red flood of anti-Catholic persecution in Eastern Europe proves. Even then, it was but a short while until Soviet Russia would join hands with Hitler, with Munich as an excuse. Cardinal Mundelein died of a heart attack a few days afterward. The scene changed swiftly and was never the same again, though many like myself tried to pretend that it was later restored by the anti-Axis war. The Soviet Union's "distrust" of the United States, which is in reality the enmity that totalitarianism must have for the democratic process, was to be revealed as just as deep and dangerous as that which Hitlerite Germany had harbored against the U.S.A.

In Chicago I had deceived myself into believing that the totalitarianism of the Soviet state would fade out after Hitler's demise, and that a new attitude toward Catholicism would prevail. This self-deceit, because of its very earnestness, had to some extent served to deceive others, including the *New World*.

Throughout this Chicago chapter, I was conscious of the close watch kept on my conduct in regard to the Catholics. I could not signal that fact to the leading Catholics with whom I came in contact, nor could they know anything of my rocky road inside the Party. This watch was dramatized by the jitteriness of Morris Childs on many occasions, the uneasiness of the Chicago comrades on this "Catholic business" and the general attitude in our Party council discussions that I was doing something wrong, something that would later have to be corrected.

These veteran Communists were right, as things turned out, and I was naïvely wrong. "This goody-goody talk to the Catholics," as one comrade designated the 1939 Red view, was merely an interlude of deception such as the Soviet leaders and the Communist parties resorted to from time to time. I was about to get a jolt that would let me know that the Soviet rulers intend to root out religion even by bayonet and bullet, if other agencies fail.

But before that big jolt came, my friend Heywood Broun's conversion to the Catholic Church re-enforced my conviction that co-operation with Catholics was essential for the

Reds. I had first known Broun during the abortive attempt in the twenties to organize newspapermen into a union. This was prior to the successful launching of the American Newspaper Guild. A small handful of us had sought affiliation with the International Typographical Union, which originally claimed jurisdiction over reporters in the American Federation of Labor. We were unsuccessful. Later on, Broun and I had had many talks in many places—chiefly hotel rooms and taxicabs—as we met each other in Toledo, Washington and other cities. When the *Record* had got under way, we secured his column for it as one indication of our devotion to the People's Front. Broun was then pursuing the Party line pretty well, and had told me during the course of a long talk in Washington in 1936 that he planned to "serve as a liaison officer between Lewis and the Left in the labor movement."

Now, however, it was 1939, and the strike at the Chicago Hearst paper was on. Broun came into Chicago to walk the picket line and to visit the Guild. As our columnist, he also made a trip to the office of the *Record*. In the taxi, on the way to the *Record* from the strike headquarters, he tried to tell me about his becoming a Catholic, but he did it so shyly that I did not appreciate, until too late, what he was trying to say. Recalling that I had been a Catholic and that I still stood for working relations with them, Broun said, "These Catholics have been troubling me a lot of late." Or he may have said, "the Catholic Church has been troubling me." I thought he was referring to some runin with Catholic critics and had no idea that he intended by the word "trouble" to stress his mental and spiritual concern. Consequently, I hastened to assure him that there were ways to work well with the Catholics, that we had been doing it in Chicago. He replied with a laugh that he was aware of our work.

I never heard the rest of what he wanted to say, as my remark diverted the conversation until we reached the *Record*. Shortly afterward, his conversion, or the rumor of it, was announced. Monsignor Sheen's name was associated with Broun's act, and once more brought to mind our meeting of 1936. It made me long again for a return to the Catholic fold, but so paralyzed I was by my preoccupation with "saving the world from fascism," that I let it remain a longing.

A few weeks after Broun's conversion, Jack Stachel came into Chicago. He immediately mentioned the matter to me, saying, "This is undoubtedly a blow to us and might under certain circumstances be a calamity. But in this People's Front period we can afford to grin and bear it." Which was an interesting side light on the Red view of Catholic affiliation from a leading Communist who followed each turn of the line with skill.

The days of the *Record* were numbered, though, as 1939 drew near its end. You cannot long maintain a People's Front paper when there is no People's Front, and the Hitler-Stalin pact of August had killed off all that. The paper managed to linger on as a weekly until February, 1940, when it was decently interred. Its life would have been shorter had it not been for its warm endorsement by Representative Adolph Sabath, who gave it as his opinion that "the *Record* does a better job for the New Deal than the New Deal itself." He was actively getting subs among the members of his Democratic organization, even after the pact with the Nazis—which we dutifully had to defend.

Another admirer of the paper was the late Harry L. Hopkins, who subscribed to it and received it at his home in Washington every day. He said he considered the *Record's* defense of the W.P.A. the best made throughout the nation, and that that was what originally attracted him to it. He could not know that the "good points" in the *Record's* labors were solely to win friends and gain influence for the Soviet Union in our country. The *Record's* editor, though he should have been better advised, was not too conscious of that himself.

All of these Windy City achievements—the respect of men in high political posts and the good will of many Catholics—inspired me with the idea that all this could be resurrected again on a larger stage. When the *Record* ended, I went back to New York to be associated with the *Daily Worker* in the capacity of leading executive. Although the darkness of the Hitler-Stalin understanding made things difficult, I went back with the resolve to improve on the relationships begun in Chicago.

And then came the big jolt! It depressed me, deflated many of my hopes, and gave me a glimpse of the innate hatred for religion of the Soviet state and its emissaries.

This is what happened. Fired by "the Chicago Chapter" with enthusiasm for more extensive Communist collaboration with the Catholics, I had prepared an article for *The Communist*, which was published shortly after my return to New York. For this piece, "The Vatican's Political Policy," I am now thoroughly regretful. For it endeavored, in effect, to place the responsibility for the failure of any such collaboration on the papacy and to its "reactionary" position historically. Thus does a Communist, in order to stay within the prevalent line, twist and torture even the very ideas he is seeking to get across. The theme of the article was the civil rights of Catholics and the urgency of that matter to America's life. On that score it was effective in its pleading. The comrades thought the piece a unique contribution to Red writing; Foster in particular commended its "scholarship."

But behind the scenes the following incident had attended its publication. All articles in *The Communist* were looked over, not only by V. J. Jerome and some member of the

Political Committee, but also by one of the "Mystery men." We shall call him, in this instance, Comrade *B*. He was a dark, quiet-spoken, quiet-walking little man, with a foreign accent, and had never been heard of in the proceedings of the Party or in its public life. In the course of writing this article, I was asked to confer with Comrade *B* and therefore knew immediately that some "correction" had to be made in the manuscript, and in a special way.

I was asked to see him, not on the ninth floor where Jerome's office was, but over at the Workers Library Publishers—now the New Century Publishers—on Fourth Avenue. They publish the magazine and are one of the many corporations under direct Party control. Very apologetically he pointed out to me that I had used the expression, "Religion is a private matter." This could not be used in any Communist theoretical organ, he said.

"But that is a very common Marxist phrase," I replied, "it is even criticized by the Catholics as being incorrect. It is not an enemy expression. We employ it every once in a while in the *Daily Worker*."

"In the *Daily Worker* it is all right," he went on with a patient, wry smile. "We can use it in our agitation, our popular papers. But to put it in our propaganda, our educational work for our own comrades, would be to create illusions." Then, seeing that I was perturbed and puzzled, he went on: "It is just like the expression 'Separation of church and state.' That we use also, but in a different sense entirely from the bourgeois democrats. We mean by it the subjugation of the church by the state, the complete control of religion by the Socialist state so that finally we can abolish it. So here, too. The Socialist state must pursue religion into the home, if necessary, and wipe it out there—by persuasion if possible, by force if that is required. We shall probably have to destroy it by force—and we have no illusions on that—by the secret police, the Red Army, and the various Communist parties. We can't suffer any false ideas among ourselves on this matter; religion has to be completely torn out by the roots."

And so the expression did not go into the article. Today the murder and imprisonment of priests and the members of religious orders in Soviet-occupied countries is a stench in the nostrils of those who fought for "the four freedoms." And Comrade *B*'s contention of six years ago has been proved by the current brutality of the Red Army and the Soviet secret police.

But in 1940—deeply disturbed as I was by this refusal to let even the phrase "religion is a private matter" remain in *The Communist*—I still hugged the Chicago experiences to my heart and decided that further "education" among the comrades was required. But it was my own further "education" in the Red determination to abolish religion that really transpired.

SEVEN

From Nazi Pact to Nagasaki

ALL THE American Communist leaders with whom I
became intimately acquainted had one common
characteristic—a form of fright. In off-the-record
conferences, and private discussions, this was very noticable.
Around each one of them there hung an atmsophere of
mystery and suspicion, accompanied by this stigmata of
fear.

Although he was General Secretary of the Party for more
than a dozen years, Earl Browder was no exception to this
rule. He was a startling confirmation of it. My position, both
as a member of the National Committee for more than six
years and editorial head of the Party organ for a considerable
time, threw me into close contact with him. When visiting
the House Committee on un-American Activities on April 3
of this year, I observed a huge chart on the wall, giving the
Communist setup of the recent past. My name was prominently listed as chief of the Party's "Popular" press—a
striking reminder of how confidential were my relations with
the General Secretary.

During the last five years my office was just under his—
mine on the eighth floor, his on the ninth—and many times
a month I went up to confer with him. There was, at many
of these meetings, a disturbed look in his light blue eyes,
as though some shadowy censorship were haunting him.
Sometimes he would give a definite opinion on a course to
pursue and then suddenly ask that we "sleep over the
matter." Then the next time I brought it up, he would be

just as decisively on the opposite side of the fence. I understood very well that he had presented the matter "in consultation"—a phrase often employed in Communist circles—but in this instance meaning with Moscow men. Thus there was always an unseen "third party" at our confidential conferences. The girl secretary, supposedly of a business house, did not want me to recognize her as she waited in Browder's outer office, but whom I identified from my own sources of information as the bearer of some of these messages, and the well-dressed, debonair businessman sitting there quietly with his brief case bore others. A number of these runners were known to me. And then, there had been the direct and intimate relations that I had unexpectedly had with the Soviet secret police on American soil—of which you shall hear later. But before my eyes, they had threatened Stachel and sent an ultimatum to Browder that told a thousand tales of where the power in the Party lay.

Jack Stachel had his share of fears, too. The ex-Communist, Ben Gitlow, may describe him as an arch-villain and a former patent medicine salesmen, who stayed in high Party position only by becoming a Red Vicar of Bray. But that's a little too simple. Stachel had a fine, intelligent son, and that was proof enough for me that his home was a pleasant place in its way. But anyone who heard Stachel nervously pattering down the hallway as though someone were pursuing him, was aware of the fact that he was driven by secret furies. I had seen several of them and knew how he was buffeted about by these underground Soviet agents and I felt sorry for the man. It was the same with the others of the Political Committee—but especially with Gene Dennis, the man of so many mysterious missions during which he completely disappeared for long periods of time. Dennis hid his own fears with an air of bravado and brusque humor. But I was experienced in sizing men up, and it wasn't long before I fathomed the real motive power behind Dennis in the unnamed, unseen gentlemen who run the Communist Party of the U.S.A. from several political leagues under the ground.

Naturally, there were some men so fanatically pro-Soviet that they were willing and ready to be driven or to drive anywhere. Several of these had such a blind hatred of America, which had given them refuge, that they were well-nigh deranged on the subject. Interestingly enough, some of these men were placed in the foreign editorships of the Party's publications, where they had the closest and most constant connection with underground anti-American agencies and agents. And they gloried in being able to do damage to "American imperialism" in that capacity.

None of the Communist chiefs here could be charged with being mental giants. They were, indeed, quite ordinary minds—Jack Stachel the most facile of them all. And yet, they handed down opinions on every conceivable subject as though they were gifted with some secret second sight of political genius. This combination of bureaucratic omniscience and over-the-shoulder fear puzzled me considerably at first. Then I learned, firsthand, how these men—and others like the now expelled and expunged Cannon and Lovestone—had gone with hat in hand from Bukharin to Stalin begging for post and place.

These accounts kept bobbing up. In 1944, at a private dinner given in honor of Ella Reeve Bloor for the National Committee and active Party workers, Bob Minor told the assemblage how proud he was that he had been representative of the American Party in Moscow when Stalin made Browder the leader here. It was plain that both the omniscience and the moral dread arose from the same source—the ruthless bosses to whom the Red leaders in America were accountable. I have often sat in Political Committee meetings and *Daily Worker* editorial board sessions observing the jittery effects of the presence of the hidden hand of the Kremlin.

Some of this narrative has taken us several years ahead of the time and place to which I wish to direct your present attention—Chicago and late 1939. But it was essential that you be given a glimpse of the fog of underground thinking and anti-American plotting which surrounded the Communists all along. It was to an organization thus trained in advance for conspiratorial activities that the bombshell of the Hitler-Stalin pact of 1939 came, one fine September day. Every well-disciplined Communist knew what this entailed. He did not have to wait for the central committee to send out the slogan, "imperialist war" to appreciate that that was what the anti-Hitler campaign would now be called. Any war in which the Soviet Union did not participate, directly or indirectly, was an "imperialist war." You knew that automatically without reading *Pravda*. By dubbing this conflict an "imperialist war" the Soviet authorities knew, and the Communists here knew, that they were helping Hitler. And there was plenty of inside comment to make that clear. The justification was, of course, the mandate of Munich under which Chamberlain had weakened before the Nazi overlord. The Soviet Government had decided to out-Munich Munich and the explanation had to be wrapped up in the ancient Leninist phrase, "imperialist war."

In October, 1938, *Pravda* had commented bitterly: "The whole world clearly sees that behind the well-turned phrases, acclaiming Chamberlain as the saviour of universal peace, an outrage has been committed far surpassing in its impudence anything which took place after the first imperialist war." The *Daily Worker* followed suit to the crossing of a *T*. One year later—after the Soviet-Nazi nonaggression pact— Foreign Commissar V. M. Molotov granted Hitlerite Germany complete absolution so far as aggression went, stating emphatically that the Nazis were not the aggressors. The *Daily Worker* had to echo that view, too—and did so promptly.

The official estimate of Hitlerite Germany was given in the speech by Molotov to the Supreme Council of the Soviet Union on October 23, 1939: "Today, as far as the European great powers are concerned, Germany is in the position of a state which is striving for the earliest termination of the war and for peace, while Britain and France, which but yesterday were declaiming against aggression, are in favor of continuing the war and are opposed to the conclusion of peace. Roles, as you see, are changing."

It was then that Molotov decided the whole idea of a "war to destroy Hitlerism," comparing an anti-fascist war to the religious wars of the Middle Ages. He said specifically: "Is it back to the Middle Ages, to the days of the religious wars, superstition and cultural deterioration that the ruling classes of Britian and France want to drag us?" And wasn't it in that speech, too, that he guaranteed the integrity of the Baltic states? "All these pacts of mutual assistance," said he, referring to the treaties with Esthonia, Latvia and Lithuania, "strictly stipulate the inviolability of the signatory states and the principle of non-interference in each other's affairs." (*World News and Views*, Vol. 19. No. 52, Nov. 4, 1939.) These sugary words were but preliminaries to the conquest of those little states by the Red Army, with the aid of a fifth column in the most approved Hitlerite manner. The U.S.S.R., Soviet authorities stated boldly, was in congenial company—both in political views and in invasion techniques—when it embraced Hitlerite Germany on August 23, 1939. Molotov had already hailed that date as historic in his August 31 address to the Supreme Soviet when he submitted the pact for approval. It would constitute "a new turn in the development of Europe," he averred. Fascism, he said, was, after all, a matter of "taste."

The impact of this turn-about-face on the comrades in Chicago and elsewhere was immediate and sweeping. The master had spoken and every Communist was supposed to obey without question or quibble. The entire "anti-fascist campaign" was to be dropped, forgotten, and all its literature burned and buried. The new political alliance demanded every act of sabotage in behalf of Hitler and against aid to Britain that we could manage. As usual in these crises, there were a number of members who could not go along; they got off the train, as the saying went, from Lenin's famous metaphor about the train of history.

The Party found itself in this peculiar position at every turn because of its composition. There was the core of comrades who were Soviet patriots, either by birth, family origins, or marriage. They were the dependables. Around them gathered the trade union officials and always a considerable number of fanatics of the current "line." At this period many of these last were Nazis and black-shirted fascists and friends of the fascists. At others, they were those who wanted to prosecute the war with vigor beyond the possibilities of reality and who turned to the Party in its later pro-war period as a center of upheaval and uproar.

Some prima-facie case could be made, and was made vociferously, for the signing of the pact with Hitler. The ground was that the Soviet Government couldn't count on a British Government headed by Chamberlain and had to have time to prepare for war. Examination will prove this a weak argument, indeed. After Soviet Russia's battle with Hitler had begun, Stalin again gave that reason as the one which justified the pact. But the need for preparation was also the reason given by the British for Munich, and when Churchill gave his final report on the condition of England at the outbreak of the war against Germany, it was plain that Britain had been in a bad way militarily. The number of planes at London's disposal was pitifully small. If anyone had an excuse for delay, it was England.

Years before World War II, the Soviet press and its echoes, the Communist newspapers everywhere, had set up a din about the super-militaristic preparations of Britain and the United States. When the test came, the falsity of all these cries was quite apparent. By then, everybody had forgotten the Soviet clamor, but the reputation as "war mongers" and "imperialists" given to America and Britain had stuck in the minds of many "liberals."

No case at all could be made for the aid to Hitler that the Communist party in the United States decided to give. But Moscow wanted that, and Moscow had to be obeyed. On the tragic September day in 1939 when the British-German war was declared, the National Committee of the Communists was meeting in Chicago. It was one of the very few times it had met there; most of the meetings took place very secretly in New York. When the news came of the outbreak of war, the Committee hastily concluded its business and everybody rushed home to take up new assignments. The kind decision to help defeat England in the Battle of Britain had not yet been made, but it was soon to follow. The political "reports" and "resolutions" by the Communists always state—in concealed form—the practical moves that have been decided upon. From the involved verbiage of the official declarations, any intelligent Communist, as we shall have opportunity to see later, can decipher what is to be done. These orders are quite plain once they are unraveled by the faithful, and always contain very specific instructions.

If you look up the copy of the *Daily Worker* that carries the resolutions of the "Plenum" of September, 1939, you will find that there was still some uncertainty about how to proceed. There was still some hankering after the pro-Roosevelt line which had been adopted in 1936 and followed so vigorously ever since. But word soon came from Moscow that "the Party was too slow in fully drawing the main conclusions from the new national and international situation." The Party had to "reorientate itself"—and that it did with a vengenace. (In England, the Communist party's General Secretary, Harry Pollitt, was slow about this "reorientation," and was summarily dismissed from his post by Stalin.)

In October, therefore, as you can see from the files of the *Daily Worker*, an entirely new statement was issued in the name of the National Committee. The Committee members with the exception of a few in the Political Committee had not seen it in advance. This call for widespread action against any aid to Britain—which is what it amounted to—was headed "Keep American Out of the Imperialist War." It was the beginning of a nation-wide drive to cripple lend-lease and keep the munitions of war from being sent to Great Britain. But even with that statement the Political Committee had not yet put itself on record as sufficiently against President Roosevelt; a month later it had to make another declaration. Just a little while before, Earl Browder had been busily engaged in proving that Roosevelt would fail in his duty if he did not run for a third term. Now, in November, 1939, the Party launched an all-out assault on the "war-mongering tendencies" of the President, Sidney Hillman and the Social Democrats, and grew shrill in its outcries against a third term. This, an anti-Roosevelt campaign, was to end in 1940, in the Daily Worker's acceptance of an ad for Wendell Wilkie.

Shortly after these new "revelations," which put the Communists four-square against Britain in its war for survival, orders came to Chicago that the "open" Party was to go underground. Every branch was reduced to only five members and meetings were held in homes instead of halls or other semipublic places. Something like the old "phalanx" system, which the Trotskyite-to-be, Jim Cannon, had told me about so many years before, was adopted. Each branch had its secretary, who sent reports to the sections by numbers. The members' names were kept in secret files, of which triplicates were made and put in safe places outside the headquarters in each city. Meetings of the State Committee in Illinois were held only on a few minutes' notice, and were convened in out-of-the-way places.

Suddenly, one evening, the most active and responsible members of the Party leadership in Chicago received an alert to attend a vital meeting. Under the most secretive conditions we assembled, in the basement of a building we had never entered before. Gene Dennis was there from New York and gave a brief report. In almost sepulchral tones he said that the time was approaching when we would have to "turn the imperialist war into something else." That was plain enough; it meant to be prepared to do anything to wreck American loans to aid Britain, either directly or indirectly. As a consequence of that meeting, it was decided that the local leaders should also disappear into thin air.

Everyone was instructed to stay away from his home in order to avoid any arrests by F.B.I. agents or the anti-Red squad of the Chicago police. The specific order was to register in a different hotel every evening under an assumed name. This was too much for me and I refused to comply. The Party line would be carefully followed, I said, and the *Midwest Daily Record* would carry it through vigorously. But it would be an invitation to a serious frame-up to go to a hotel and be found registered under some name other than my own. "That would look guilty as the deuce," I said with some show of sarcasm, "and I prefer not to look guilty when I am innocent of any wrongdoing." I then orated on how it would look for the editor to be caught in such a predicament and how gleefully the *Chicago Tribune* would play up the conspiratorial angle.

At first this was displeasing to the leading comrades, particularly to District Organizer Morris Childs. He was rushing hither and thither, most mysteriously, with a newly sprouted mustache, and saying dramatically: "I have seen the enemy and the white of his eyes. He has passed me by and I have felt his breath on my cheeks." This reference was undoubtedly to the F.B.I. The comrades had somehow received a tip that the F.B.I. was going to round them up on such charges as were subsequently filed against Browder and which sent him to Atlanta. When I continued to explostulate with them, pointing out that there was "no principle involved here"—a ritualistic phrase always prominent in Communist discussions—they finally gave in. They didn't agree one way or the other, and that left the decision up to me. I decided to act like an American and walk, talk and live out in the open.

Most of the leading comrades had been mollified by my agreement with them that anyone with "technical difficulties" should certainly not imperil himself. This term "technical difficulties" was often heard among Communists. It signified either that the person to whom it was applied had traveled on a false passport, or that he was not a naturalized American citizen—through some default of law; or that he was unlawfully in this country and had not yet been caught. Which one of these "difficulties" attended the individual comrades was not known generally. One Communist social grace was not to ask questions about such matters unless it was necessary in order to make a decision.

These "technical" defects seemed to be pretty widespread among the Communist, because the number that went into hiding was considerable. To evade the authorities, some of the comrades—keeping always on the move—even traveled as far south as Florida to evade acquaintance with their newly acquired mustaches or other disguises. I chose to remain in the Windy City, occasionally visiting or dining with certain irresolute "liberals" the Party wanted to keep attached to it. Even so, the circumstances under which I worked were highly conspiratorial. I was constantly forced to duck into side streets or waiting automobiles to be able to get a face-to-face interview with the comrades I had to see in connection with the *Record*. My position, as I described it on one occasion, was "like that of the boy eating the peanuts. I am out on the burning deck, but I'm at least visible to the naked eye—and I can get a good view of what's happening for my own part."

During the following period I was one of the very few national leaders of the Communist party still functioning "out in the open." At one National Committee meeting besides carrying on my editorial work I had to serve as secretary of several vital Committees, so completely had most of the leaders disappeared! Of course I heard from them off and on, through secretive channels. But for the most part, in city after city if comrades wanted to write the Party or hear from the Party, they had to do so through me.

Later on, Browder and other leading comrades advised me that it was my successful "open functioning" which led them shortly afterward to put the "destinies of the *Daily Worker*" in my hands. It became clear, as the years passed, that the secret bosses of the Party found me a valuable person for "protective" and public political purposes because of my native American background and viewpoint. They listened carefully, for the same reason, to my proposals to "Americanize" the Party—but did little or nothing about them. During the Foster-Browder debate, one leading comrade admitted to me, privately and cautiously, that my "American" and "democratic" proposals were "humored," but that it was known they could not be put through. Those who understood Moscow's views knew that the Soviet hand had to be kept directly on the throttle.

The following February—that is, in 1940—we members of the National Committee had to hurry off to New York to a new "plenum." We met in redoubled secrecy, while Browder addressed us in his new character as an opponent of the "aggressive imperialism of the Roosevelt administration," and he demanded "the Bolshevization of the Party in the struggle against the imperialist war." Everybody agreed double-quick that this was a mighty fine stand, loudly applauded Browder and unanimously voted resolutions of the most drastic nature. These inveighed against "the increasingly aggressive imperialist policies of the Roosevelt Administration and Wall Street." They declared that the President had "drawn the United States deeper and further into the imperialist war and brought about the immediate danger of the direct involvement of our country as a militant belligerent."

During this gathering of the National Committee there arose, in whispers, the question of just where the Soviet Union was going. Wherever it went, the Committee members would, in the course of their puppet service, follow with alacrity. Was the Soviet plan one that would lead to closer and closer collaboration with Hitler? Could we expect the Land of Socialism to join up as a long-time partner, perhaps war ally, with the Nazis? Such speculations were not uttered aloud in the Committee sessions. That would be equivalent to a kind of Red treason, and anyone attempting it would find himself sprawled out politically under a withering fire of denunciation. Around the periphery of the meeting nonetheless—at restaurant tables and in hallways—the question was brought up in all sorts of roundabout and "ideological" ways.

The view of many of the comrades then was that co-operation with Hitler would last a long time and that it would end in the advance of Communism across Europe. Had not the leading English Communist, William Rust of the London *Daily Worker*, just resurrected Marx's famous phrase about "the specter of Communism is haunting Europe."? Hitlerism might be a partner in that direction!

They received no contradiction of this opinion in the pronunciamentos from Moscow. In the *Communist International* magazine for February, 1940—issued just when the Committee was meeting—the whole burden of the conflict was put on England and not on Hitler. The special editorial in that issue was entitled: "England Drives for a New World War." The article commented that former patrons of the Nazi party were greatly disappointed by Hitler's arrangement with the Soviet Union. It then congratulated Germany for refusing to play England's game and denounced Britain as the strongest pillar of world reaction." That land which, with all its sins, was being blasted by the Nazis in desperate battle, was scored as "the most dangerous incendiary of war" and "the chief enemy of the international working class." It is miraculous how the Communists can discover an "enemy of the working class" in any individual or country that disagrees with Soviet Russia. They always associate Communism with the workers, whereas I was to discover that actually it is one of the worst enemies of the working people.

My own opinion was that eventually the Soviet Union would not aid Hitler. A close friend of Harry Hopkins and President Roosevelt asked me especially what I thought on that matter. This was just before Hopkins went on his first mission to Moscow. My answer was without hesitation: "Who began the original fight against fascism? Has that antagonism been resolved?" In other words, I gave it as my strong belief that Soviet Russia and Hitler would not be allies in actual warfare against the "democracies." That conversation took place in New Orleans in November, 1940, at the American Federation of Labor convention, which I was covering. I had held the same opinion in February of that year, as well. However, governing reason was not precisely that given to the President's friend. It was the product of deeper thinking on the subject. Totalitarianism can never brook any rival and two totalitarian states like Soviet Russia and Nazi Germany could not live together on the continent in harmony. They would inevitably clash just as Czarist Russia and Napoleon had done.

The word "totalitarian" was not even privately whispered to myself in connection with the "Land of Socialism." What I said was "a fascist state and a Communist state," but in the manner of my saying it I was drawing a parallel. Molotov's declaration about "taste" had been a hint of some similarity between the two states. As a matter of fact, a number of leading Communists were noting certain resemblances—and they were not so difficult to discover.

Whatever the long-run goal of the Soviet-Nazi pact, there was short-run work in abundance for the comrades. The Roosevelt administration was now being accused of promoting "a war and hunger budget." New and greater agitation was to be spread through the nation for "higher wages, shorter hours, an American standard of living." Therein could be found a gauge for our future conduct. That schedule forecast strikes, commotions, demonstrations—anything to block bundles for Britain in the form of munitions and planes.

Some of the comrades even ventured the thought that the Soviet Union might persuade Hitler to abandon "anti-Semitism," and that thereafter the two totalitarian regimes might march together across the world. The *Daily Worker* was given strict instructions by the ninth floor not to deride Hitler in cartoons, but to open both barrels on Britain. This suggestion was unnecessary, as the documents coming out of Moscow made it crystal clear that England, with its back to the wall, "was the main enemy of mankind."

Foster, whose congenital leftism had once even drawn a rebuke from Stalin, was now in his glory. I can see him clearly, as the National Committee sessions were drawing to a close, standing at the side door in the meeting hall, talking with William Schneiderman, the Russian-born secretary of the Party in California. Foster, always conscious of his weak heart, was leaning against the doorpost, speaking in a complaining tone. The former Wobbly was telling the man from the West that the opportunity is at hand to raise every demand of the workers to the highest scale." More had to be done about it. He ran over the fight against "profiteering," the fight for "better wages and shorter hours" and unemployment relief. Then, with his dry but pleasant laugh, he summed up by saying, "We can give'em hell!"

The Communist leaders went out of that meeting to make use of the workers wherever possible—not for the workers' benefit, but for the purpose of paralyzing production that might hurt Hitler. While "cynical" was a word the Communist resolutions then applied freely to Roosevelt, there was nothing more cynical than the North American aviation strike and the Allis-Chalmers walkout. Both were called by the Communists for one purpose only—that of embarrassing the Roosevelt administration and keeping arms from Britain. The offense against the nation was nonetheless vile in that the men who committed these acts did so as concealed Communists, unidentified as Reds, so far as most of the workers were concerned.

Communists can never go halfway, and consequently

Roosevelt was not merely damned for giving aid to Britain against Hitler; he was also accused of plotting to annihilate the labor movement and all his own New Deal social reforms. This accusation appeared in the resolution entitled "Defense of the Communist Party." It started out by bitterly scoring F.D.R.'s "reactionary war regime," and proceeded to say: "This imperialist course necessitates also a headlong attack against the American labor movement and against all the social measures and organizational gains of the workers and other exploited sections of the American people."

I still had enough sense of reality to object to this phrasing. "If we put out a statement like that, the workers will know that it isn't a correct estimate," I asserted, "and we will be discredited. In any coming war status the workers are very likely to have higher wages than at present out of the war production. The production for Britain will provide employment and there need be no diminution in wages. Quite to the contrary, Roosevelt is a keen politician and he will do the best possible for the workers to retain them in his camp." Of course, both Foster and Dennis told me plainly that this was not the "fundamental purpose" of the resolution; that the "subsequent events would, with our guidance, inform the workers of the exploitation which was being imposed upon them." In other words, by the creation of more or less artificial demands, the whipping up of agitation on any and every conceivable subject, the Communist leadership proposed to sabotage production which might harm Hitler. The workers would be made to think the demands were the natural outgrowth of the defects and scullduggery of management.

Far from being deterred by my critical attitude toward the Communist slant on a number of these matters, I prepared to plunge still deeper into the Red work. As part of the side business transacted there at the February plenum in New

York, on my recommendation it was agreed to put an end to the *Record*. The "decision" was for me to go to Chicago, close the paper quickly and return immediately to New York. I was to labor again on the *Daily Worker* and was told that I would be called on to take over a most responsible position there.

Elizabeth Gurley Flynn, who had always been generous in her good opinion of me, told me of the proposal when we met down in "Benny's candy stand" just before I left for Chicago. The ability with which I had stood up "out in the open" in the Windy City had made an impression at headquarters. It was thought that I might take over a key position on the *Daily* and "contribute to the defense of the paper." I knew, very well, what that entailed. I was to be the man who would be in danger of going to jail if "the defense" did not work out well. As an expert on newspaper libel, I felt that the paper would be much better off than it had been under Hathaway. The *Daily* had been bedeviled with libel actions and Hathaway had finally gone to jail on a criminal libel conviction. That would not happen in any organization that I had anything to do with, I was certain. About the wide "defense" of the paper while it was warring upon American policy, I was not so sure. But even in that respect I finally concluded a competent job could be done.

In a few days I was back in New York, ready to tackle my new field. Six lonesome weeks at the Hotel Albert, one minute's walk from the *Daily Worker*, followed. My family did not arrive from Chicago until Good Friday, March 25. The two girls—for that was our sum total then—had been presented with huge Easter rabbits by some kind-hearted and big-pursed man in the La Salle Street Station, Chicago, and were carrying them when they arrived in New York.

Those six weeks of waiting for my family had been devoted

to writing that article on the Vatican which I now so much regret. What magic caused me thus to go on and on, with considerable vigor and zeal, for a cause which I continued to look upon critically? There is the mesmerism of unbelief, I must repeat, of which the great Bishop of Hippo has written so eloquently. Marxism had provided me with a "philosophy"; it gave me a yardstick by which I could explain why a certain course was being followed. Each time this course merely turned out to be the one that Soviet foreign policy favored, but amazingly enough, I again thought up arguments to justify the 1940 turn. In the contest over my soul between Marxism and Mary, Marxism was still in the ascendant. As an example of my thinking, one argument I forged was that the Soviet Union's course was letting Hitler and Britain bleed each other to death, which I considered highly desirable.

Not the least of my incentives to renewed work in the vineyard of the Party was the new stand taken on Ireland and the Irish. Since Great Britain was now the chief enemy of mankind because it was battling Hitler, overnight the Irish were rediscovered by the National Committee. A resolution, most of which I wrote, was adopted, for a special "Irish Commission." We were going all out for the wearing of the green. Prior to this February of 1940, general indifference and worse to the Irish had marked the official Communist attitude. Ever since my entry into the organization I had urged the comrades to do something real for these people from whom I was half descended. But the best that could be won was a grudging agreement to an article in the *Daily Worker* on St. Patrick's Day which never got any wide distribution among the Irish-Americans. Now the Irish community in America was being told through this new resolution that "President Roosevelt and the camp of reactionary 'National Unity' are giving American imperialist assistance for the continued division and exploitation of Ireland."

The Irish kinsmen in America were urged to help the Irish in Ireland by "participating in that growing movement of the American masses against the present imperialist foreign policy by which our country is being led, against the popular will, into a reactionary war in alliance with British and French imperialism." My hand is to be noted especially in the final paragraph, which read: "To the American people we repeat the slogan of the early champions of democracy— the Jeffersonians: 'For an independent, united Ireland.'"

Although from time to time the Communists had made a pretense of remembering the oppression of the Irish people, these gestures were merely formal and for the record. Of all the uphill struggles I have had, the constant attempt to get the Reds to start some work for and among Irish-Americans was the most grueling. The bizarre view prevailing among Communists about the character of those who had sprung from Erin was the root cause of my difficulty. Israel Amter, who was in charge of work among "national groups," had told me frankly that the Irish were among the ruling groups of America. "They have no feeling as a minority group," he said.

"All of which proves that you have never been an Irish-man or an Irish-American, Comrade Amter," was my retort. There flashed to my mind the peculiar minority position that I had recognized was mine in Indiana as a part descendant of the men of Cork and Kerry. "Beyond that," ran my argument, "the Irish are important in the Democratic party, in the trade unions and in many walks of American life. We can't act deaf, dumb and blind where they are concerned." With a persistence worthy of a better cause than Communism, I pressed National Committee offices and the Commission on National Groups to do something serious in the field. You can understand the joy with which I beheld this 1940 National Committee venture in that direction.

It was, alas, something very ephemeral indeed. The prevalent Communist concept was that the Irish were a degenerate national group that would get completely on the right side of the fence only when forced to do so by "the revolution." A standard Communist stunt was slyly to berate and degrade the Irish communities. Every time any group of boys of different national strains got into fisticuffs, if the Irish were involved they were always pictured as the hoodlums. It was a standing joke around national headquarters that "Mike Quill is pulling the Irish along in fine style; they're a pretty ignorant lot to handle." This made me more conscious than ever that something had to be done to change this anti-Irish animus. Confessedly, it got my dander up, too, though I was still inclined to put the expressions down to the bad upbringing of certain comrades rather than to an established policy. The official pronunciamentos of the Party, whenever made, were sympathetic to Irish aspirations. But well did I know by now that official pronouncements could never be read literally. They had always to be gauged in relation to the emphasis with which they were worded, the time at which they were issued and the persistence with which they were reiterated. By these standards, the Irish were of little or no account in the Reds' eyes.

In order to maintain their record as champions of all national groups, the Communists would never come out publicly and denounce the Irish as stupid or as given to hooliganism. But their "pro-Irish" statements were merely perfunctory, and nothing real was ever done to follow them up.

Most baffling of all was the indifference of men like Foster to the Irish Americans. Although of Irish descent, he continuously refused to appear at any commission or discussion on the Irish. A number of private talks with him led me to the conclusion that he was actually inclined to be ashamed of being Irish. For one thing, he told me one day, when I was particularly persistent, that the Irish were "on the whole hopelessly committed to reaction and superstition."

An insight into the estimate of the Irish generally held in the Red ranks was given by a girl Communist who reported effusively in the *Daily Worker* that she had canvassed the Irish districts and had not been insulted or assaulted by anyone. The implication, of course, was that the Irish were a rough and immoral lot; that a woman in their midst could rejoice if she got by with no harm to her person. I insisted that something be done to correct this story and that Amter, as head of the National Groups Commission make some sort of explanatory statement. He agreed that it should be done, but if my memory is correct it never was.

If anything was cynical, it was this Communist wooing of the Irish whenever that would serve the Soviet interests. As soon as the Irish were of no potential help, they were dropped and even derided. Elizabeth Gurley Flynn finally blurted out the truth in the National Committee meeting of June, 1945— the meeting that politically beheaded Earl Browder. Though that incident is ahead of the story, it is well to note it here. Miss Flynn, a member of the Political Committee, stated that all her efforts to work among the Irish had been snuffed out. One of her great joys in scuttling Browderism, she said, would be to be able to talk about the Irish again. Almost everybody among the sixty Committee members present laughed heartily at this. They knew well enough that it wasn't Browderism that had been responsible for such a condition, but Communism, which regarded the Irish as in the "camp of the enemy."

We could quote James Connolly and his Marxist works on

Ireland until we were blue in the face. We could go back to Fintan Lalor and claim that he foretold Socialism for Ireland. It didn't really matter; no one was interested in anything except that Quill should "put it over" on the Irish in the Bronx.

Early in 1946 the City Council of New York had a good illustration of this Communist animus against the Irish in the insult offered Francis Cardinal Spellman by the two open Communist councilmen. This was more than an anti-Catholic gesture, in accordance with the "new" anti-religious line of the Party. When the Council had before it a resolution congratulating the new Cardinal upon his elevation, the Red duo voted against the congratulatory message. And to the indignation of the rest of the Council members one of them—Benjamin Davis, Jr.—submitted a special statement assailing the Cardinal. His act was a product of the deliberate decision—ripening when I left the Communists in October to return to the Catholic Church—to work up an alliance of other national groups against the Irish. It is regrettable that my friend of long standing, Louis Adamic, fell a victim to this idea and went out of his way to malign the Irish and Catholics in his book, *A Nation of Nations*. Although not a Communist, Adamic has been serving their purposes for several years, largely as a result of my own zeal in getting him and them together. It is one of the many acts I deeply regret. Their influence has colored all his recent opinions.

Such "contradictions"—as the Communists would glibly have dubbed this anti-Irish anomaly in any other group— were the fruit of servility to the Soviet cause. The Irish did not throw their hats in the air every time the Red Army was mentioned; they were therefore to be listed among the politically damned. The Negro people were treated almost as cavalierly. The Communists were always vociferous in contending that they were the true defenders of the Negroes, and in 1940 they were doing double duty in their effort to influence the Negroes to oppose Roosevelt's anti-Hitler tendency. But when the Soviet Union was under fire a year later, the Negro rights were forgotten. Soviet Russia's interests came before those of any other people or nation.

It takes many experiences and much education to estimate these events in their proper light. In 1940 I was not yet ready for any anti-Communist conclusions. We were advancing toward the convention of June, the eleventh national convention of the Party. I was also preparing to take over the presidency of the new corporation that would be formed to control the *Daily Worker*. The exact character of that corporation was being worked out by the legal staff of the paper and the Party, and it was taking some little time. Browder had said quite plainly and publicly that the change was being made primarily for "defense." He told me privately it was also being made to assure a rise in the journalistic standards of the paper. There was a perpetual tug of war around the publication as to whether it should be "more popular" or "more educational"; the thought that it should be "more popular" was now uppermost.

The discussions preliminary to the convention began to wax hot and heavy. They were confined to the inner circles of the "top leadership"—a favorite Communist phrase—and the main question was how far to go in denunciation of Roosevelt. As a gesture toward "democracy" there was always supposed to be preconvention discussion open to all members who wanted to join in. Sometimes this was held and sometimes it was omitted. But no matter which course was pursued, the outcome was the same. The whole discussion was ignored anyway, and the report was prepared by Browder in accordance with the desires of Moscow. Long before the gavel fell for the opening of the convention on

Decoration Day, it was a foregone conclusion that it would be an orgy of Roosevelt-baiting. That's exactly what it turned out to be.

Because Roosevelt had dared to seek to curb Hitlerite aggression, he was assailed by Browder in his opening report as an imitator of Hitler. Tremendous applause broke out when the Red leader declared that "the Rooseveltism of the New Deal has capitulated to the reactionaries. . . . The new Roosevelt course is essentially for America the same direction which Hitler gave for Germany in 1933." It is ironic to remember that Browder denounced the President's modest plans to safeguard Greenland, Iceland and the Caribbean islands as part "of the great gamble of world redivision," when we note the Soviet Union's present insatiable thirst for Bulgaria, Poland, Romania, Yugoslavia—and all Europe and Asia.

But in this convention, as in all Communist party conventions, the Soviet Union was acclaimed as the only citadel of peace, the stronghold of democracy and the great source of free press, free speech and assemblage. These extravagant expressions were enthusiastically adopted in a special resolution on the Soviet Union. They were said of the country which today has a larger number of political prisoners than all the countries in the world combined, which ruthlessly suppresses any freedom of discussion and which has the most extensive secret police system ever known.

Where the allegiance of the Communists lay was confessed in two revealing declarations. One of them stated: "Amidst all the imperialist aggressions, the decisive thing is this: that the strongest power in Europe and Asia is not a capitalist state, but a socialist state." This was wishful thinking and not the truth, for it took the lend-lease of the despised United States to pull Soviet Russia out of the hole into which Hitlerite strength eventually put it. The second statement said: "By the measure of their hate of the great Union of Soviet Socialist Republics we can recognize the makers of war." Now, Hitlerite Germany was no longer engaged in hatred of the Soviet Union, and the burden of the war was accordingly placed at the door of Britain and President Roosevelt! The whole Communist yardstick of international morality—which was then my own—was whether an act was for or against the Soviet dictatorship.

In contrast to the harsh verbiage hurled at Roosevelt, a servility to Stalin was displayed, which is completely anti-American in its thinking. In one resolution he was acclaimed "the greatest thinker, leader and builder of our time . . . the great Stalin." Not content with that, in another resolution the convention hailed him once more as "the great Stalin." Such words were applied, mind you, to the head of another nation, while the leader of our own America was heaped with abuse. Was this sedition? That is precisely what it was, and one is lost in wonder at the long-suffering of a republic which permits such crimes against itself to continue within its own borders. Were many of those who agreed with these resolutions conscious of their sedition? I firmly believe that a number of them, at least, did not realize what they were doing. They were hypnotized by the "newness" of the Soviet Union and their belief that it represented the "future," and in some instances by a detestation of war. However, this did not make their anti-American act any the less dangerous.

Such considerations shaped my own thinking. To prevent the spread of the war seemed an admirable objective, and the Communists made the most of it. Their reports, resolutions and speeches were filled with that idea. Of course, they could and would shed the argument when Soviet interests required it. But in 1940 it furnished a powerful incentive to work hard against American aid to Britain. The whole history of British relations with Ireland and India had been repugnant to me—militantly so—and now Britain was facing an opponent mightier than Napoleon. The closer contact of the Soviet Union with the German people—and it was no secret that the Land of Socialism was furnishing the Land of National Socialism with oil and foodstuffs—meant the possibility of a tremendous Socialist force in Europe. Even though I thought the two nations would fall out eventually, I reasoned that because of their friendship the German people would be favorably inclined toward the Soviet Republics when the world at large was hostile. Those were my conclusions, after considering the whole historical setup. They turned out to be utterly wrong.

By March of 1940 the Finnish war was successfully completed by the Red Army. The leading comrades sighed a long sigh of relief—but not because of the unpopularity of the Party during this trying time. While American communities had looked askance at the Communists for this venture against Russia's small neighbor, the Party had weathered the storm very well by continuing underground. Many of our leading people were now completely in the shadow. They had vanished from Thirty-five East Twelveth Street and could not be found in any other public place. One by one, Jack Stachel, Gene Dennis, John Williamson and others disappeared, so that by the time Browder went to prison the following year, only a few were left around the building which housed the headquarters of most of the open Communist agencies.

The real reason for the relief over the successful ending of the Finnish war was the unexpected resistance Finland had put up. There had been no uprising among the Finnish people in favor of the Red Army. That provided Soviet Russia with a "new lesson," as someone close to the secret international apparatus informed me. I was told this at one of those hideout conferences which the Political Committee, the Trade Union Commission and every subcommittee of the National Committee then held. In order to attend, a few days in advance you would be notified that the meeting was scheduled to take place. Then, just before it came off, you would be told where to go—as a rule, some large apartment in central Manhattan. Some comrade would be glad to furnish the meeting place to the Committee, and the entire afternoon could be spent there in discussion. A few of those who were living underground could come quietly and on tiptoe to these apartment gatherings. They came one by one, spoke in whispers and left in the same manner.

One of these men of many aliases was present at such a meeting just after the Finnish war was concluded. It was the first time I had seen him for months and we had a pleasant chat. Communists always turn to current events, and he was frank in stating that the Soviet Union would "review the Finnish war in a new light. The inability to arouse any big section of the peasantry or workers to revolt on a big scale, plus the methods which Hitler was successfully using had combined to cause a new estimate to be made."

This was the first personal indication I had received of Soviet intentions to imitate Hitler's Blitzkrieg methods in dealing with small neighbors. The news was not entirely surprising. The No. 1 number of the *Communist International* for 1940 had cautiously hinted at it. It was in an issue exclusively devoted to singing the praise of Joseph Stalin, whose sixtieth birthday had occurred the preceding December. The old ritualistic notes were struck, as they had to be, in talk of the future of "the masses" and "the awakening protletariat." But as I studied the various articles I discovered a new tone. More than ever George Dimitrov was stressing the "iron discipline" that had to prevail in the Communist organization. This was a weather vane, and it pointed to the necessity for blind obedience in any new tack taken by the Kremlin.

However, it was D. Z. Manuilsky, still the chief annunciator of fundamental Soviet tactics—though no longer secretary of the Communist International—who made a few carefully phrased declarations that I considered of vital import. That they were made by this man to whom Communists everywhere listen almost as reverently as to Stalin and Molotov, was what gave them consequence. In an article on "The Great Theoretician of Marxism," Manuilsky had injected the warning that Stalin "sagaciously takes into account objective obstacles that stand in the way of the revolutionary will of the working class, of the will of the Socialist state." As I read this, I detected the suggestion that something new was about to be done, and putting the proverbial two and two together, I associated it with the hard struggle in Finland.

Leading Communists always decode official Communist documents in this manner. The "ideological" wrappings always contain practical instructions or cautions or represends. It's due to the fact that people of importance outside the Communist leadership—many American statesmen, for instance—never read the Communist documents in this light that so much ignorance concerning their tactics exists in high places in our country. In Manuilsky's extended remarks there was the added observation that Stalin "boldly sets revolutionary tasks designed to change the face of the world." This was a most pertinent tip to the comrades in all corners of the globe. It was telling them plainly—insofar as Communist verbiage is ever "plain"—that new tactics were being worked out. They would rely on Stalin and his Red Army's power and fifth-column sabotage more than in the past, and not wait for full-dressed revolutions in other countries.

There was to be a world-shaking sequel to this, and it is being enacted today in the continued commotion created everywhere by the Communist fifth columns for the benefit of the Red Army. It is evident in the current carefully planned "war of nerves" waged by the Soviet Union against Britain and the United States. And it is no chance coincidence, as we shall see, that it was Manuilsky who gave the first hint of today's Hitlerite tactics to the Communist Party of the United States when he appeared as chief delegate to the San Franciso Conference from the Ukrainian Soviet Republic.

To be sure, in "Lessons of the Finnish Events" in the No. 4 issue of the *Communist International* for 1940, the conclusion had been that "the ties between the working class of the capitalist countries and the Soviet Union will be strengthened despite all the efforts of the enemies to the contrary." But that had a certain defensive note in it which every alert Communist would detect. Furthermore, it is obvious that the Red fifth column would naturally operate among the working classes whenever possible as well as among soft-hearted "liberals" and in the apparatus of other governments.

These conclusions of mine were confirmed by the comments of the undercover comrade with whom I was talking at the meeting. And the overrunning of Latvia, Lithuania and Esthonia a short while later—despite the solemnly written pacts of nonaggression—merely bore them out. However, I looked at this situation from an entirely different angle in 1940 than I do today. The "new method of operations" not only did not alarm or affront me; it met with a warm response. In an old notebook in which I put down current thoughts or ideas for articles I find the justification for my response, as I expressed it at the time.

"The big job today is to save the nations which are on the brink of being pulled or pushed into the quicksands of the imperialist war," I wrote without hesitation. "Some of these nations will not be rescued from the war's world-wrecking orbit unless they are taken under the wing of the Soviet Union. The U.S.S.R. is the land above all determined to remain at peace. Any area or small country which has the good fortune to win the protection of the Soviet Union will be kept out of the blood bath, in so far as that is possible. The Mongolian People's Republic can testify eloquently to that. So will the tiny Baltic republics when this mammoth conflict has ended. There will be praise, appreciation and affection for the powerful and peaceful protector the Soviet Union has proved to be." Similar opinions can be found, in my flood of articles for the Communist press. The belief that the subjugation of the Baltic countries would move them into the path of progress, into the "future," was the casuistic defense I made for these Hitler-like acts.

Soviet-prepared news stories, which rained down upon the *Daily Worker* from Moscow, furnished other bright views of the Baltic invasion. The peasants and workers were represented as rushing out to greet the Red Army as "liberators." Touching tales were cabled across the Atlantic by Soviet correspondents, translated in Moscow for Anglo-American consumption from eye-witness accounts prepared for the Soviet press. When, later on, the 90-per-cent votes in each republic for incorporation into the U.S.S.R. were recorded, these overwhelmingly one-sided outcomes were cheered as the free will of the Baltic peoples. I did raise an eyebrow at this, but the bigger questions involved seemed to "overshadow objections," as I then put it. I can remember Jack Stachel's advice, sent in word from his hiding place, that we should think through a good explanation of such immense majorities.

"The *Daily Worker* should present these elections positively," Stachel suggested, "review the joy which the people

showed when the Red Army appeared and offset the demo-
gogy of the capitalist press, which will make out that this is
a Hitler '*Ja*' election." All the responsible comrades were
worried about the reaction in America to these election
results; they were greatly relieved when the whole business
was lost among larger world affairs. "They will forget all
about it now," said Foster jokingly, at a *Daily Worker* board
meeting which he attended. "That's one advantage of this
complicated world."

My notes for 1940 were as harsh against President
Roosevelt as they were enthusiastic for Soviet expansion. This
new estimate of F.D.R. was not so readily accepted as the
pro-Soviet conclusion had been. It seemed to me, still, that he
was the best qualified leader of the nation. And yet, I set
down these thoughts: "Is President Roosevelt callously leading the nation to the precipice to which Woodrow Wilson
brought us?" the yellowed pages read. "Regretfully, the
answer must be: 'Emphatically, yes!' Our present chief
executive is as enamoured of the British Empire as was the
man who devised 'the war to end war! He becomes increasingly belligerent in tone, and there can be no doubt that he
is set upon crushing Hitler Germany by military means.
Such an enterprise will now lead to the extension of the war,
to an impasse once again whereby the whole world will be
in flames." That sort of stuff crowded my articles in the
Daily Worker.

Other comrades were even more wild-eyed in their unlimited abuse of the President and resorted to every known
Communist cliché. In the course of an article entitled,
"Seven Years of Roosevelt," in March, 1940, Foster repeatedly accused the President of being "the chief warmonger,"
and charged him with promoting militaristic aggression to
win "world hegemony" for American imperialism. "Roosevelt, erstwhile liberal," he went on to say, "has now become

the world leader of the anti-Soviet crusade." Nothing was too evil to be said of the President. All these rash accusations were made against him because he was showing an inclination to halt the torrent of blood which Hitler had let loose upon Europe.

Had leisure and an examination of our consciences been allowed us, many of us might have been surprised into confessing that our motives for these tirades were exclusively pro-Soviet. The U.S.S.R. was lined up with Hitler, and we were ready to do anything that would strengthen its aims, whatever they might be. I had little leisure and, I must say, small desire for such soul searching. Since the big thing was settled in my mind, all other things followed. Then, there were imperative matters right at hand. One of these was the building up of "the defense" of the *Daily Worker*. The other concerned the difficulties to be overcome as a result of the conviction and imprisonment of Earl Browder.

For this next act—that of taking over the direction of the *Daily Worker*—you must go with me to an apartment in the outskirts of the Greenwich Village section of Manhattan. The time was immediately after the June, 1940, national convention; the apartment was that of Mrs. Susan Woodruff, an amiable elderly woman who went about doing good deeds for the Soviet cause. One of her favorite activities was to persuade public libraries to place the magazine, *Soviet Russia Today*, in their reading rooms, and she was singularly successful. Mrs. Woodruff had no conception, of course, of the undercover and espionage sections of the Party; her keen blue eyes expressed her kind but firm faithfulness to "internationalism." She was about to become one of the three "owners" of the stock of the Freedom of the Press Co., Inc., which sprang out of the ashes of the Compradaily Publishing Co. as the publisher of the *Daily Worker*.

The other "owners" were Mrs. Ferdinanda Reed and Mrs.

Carol Lloyd Strobell. They were as amiable and nearly as elderly as Mrs. Woodruff. Mrs. Reed's household was divided on the Soviet issue. Her husband and son were against her views and her daughters wholly with her. One of the latter was married to a Soviet citizen and their son was later to fall in the defense of Leningrad. Mrs. Strobell was an old Socialist and was to die within the year 1941. She was succeeded as an "owner" by Miss Anna Pennypacker—daughter of the former Governor of Pennsylvania—also genuinely devoted to Sovietism. By a form of trusteeship, the trio turned over the active control of the paper to three directors of whom I was president. The other two were Benjamin J. Davis, Jr., soon to become the Negro Communist councilman from Harlem, and Howard Boldt, a young man of German-English descent who had been city editor of the paper and was about to become Sunday editor.

The "owners" were, of course, only frontispieces. They came into the newspaper's office about four times a year, usually on the occasion of some big Party mass meeting, and they generally sat in the front row. I talked to them for half an hour on such occasions, gave them a bird's-eye view of what we were doing, and saw them no more for another quarter of a year. As one of them told me, they enjoyed "the thrill of being of service." They were classical examples of "nice people" who were used to conceal undercover skull-duggery against the nation—a conspiracy of which they were totally unaware.

Difficulties had piled up at the *Daily Worker*. I plunged into the job of doing away with them. For one thing, West-brook Pegler was working himself into a white-hot rage every other day or so over "the company union" of our editorial rooms. He could give color to his charges by citing the lack of any union agreement. My prompt contention was that the sole solution of that difficulty—and it was a headache of no small order—was to sign a closed-shop contract with the Newspaper Guild. The New York office of that union was in the pocket of the Party then, anyway. But the line I took was that there had to be the beginning of genuine collective bargaining. Fortunately, in this I was backed up by the business manager, William Browder.

Some influential comrades were either in opposition or in doubt, and it took quite a number of weary hours to convince them that a Communist daily paper had to have a union agreement for its editorial department. The wage scale was still far below those of other papers, but a start in the right direction had been made. During the course of this tussle, my old trade union loyalty came out strongly, and I asserted that it would be "impossible to operate the *Daily Worker* in this perilous period and provide for its adequate defense unless it was a union paper from top to bottom." That proved convincing.

Defects exist in every organization. It is not my purpose to dwell at length upon this reluctance of a Communist institution to install a union on its premises. But along with other and bigger incidents, it does illustrate the axiom that for Communists the Red cause is the chief consideration and labor unions are merely secondary. It was only the emphasis on the *Daily's* "defense" that won the day for the union.

Libel troubles were another sore spot with the paper. These I dissipated with dispatch. By the establishment of certain unbreakable rules, the possibility of any such action as had put Hathaway in jail for ninety days was ended. That was a record, because at that time the Communist organs and organizations were being raked by the fire of technical trials. Please note this, since it will be of some consequence in summing up at the end of the story.

Another bit of journalistic efficiency with which I busied myself has its elements of humor. From its beginning the

Daily Worker had been without a morgue. This led to sloppy journalism; dates and events had to be checked largely through the memory of members of the staff. Sender Garlin the pamphleteer, who had been with the paper eighteen years, was of special service in this connection and acted as a sort of walking index. This loose system was the height of inefficiency, though in the old days when the paper contented itself with the ready-made cries of "slanderer," "liar" and even more vivid terms for anyone who differed with it a morgue was not so imperative.

Those words were still hurled at anyone who questioned Soviet or Communist Party integrity, but there had to be more "body" to our writings than before. On joining the paper, the first thing I asked for was this "essential feature of any daily," the morgue, but was laughingly told that it was "too much of a luxury." For six years I kept urging its introduction and when I finally won the point I discovered that the orginal objection that had been raised was false. Many times 1 pondered why such an essential item should have been persistently neglected and even blocked. Only at the end of my Communist road did I see why. The Party bureaucrats are so absorbed in watching what *Pravda* says each day, checking the radio for Soviet statements and trying to decipher what messages are being conveyed, that they frequently lose sight of American technique. This is not what Stalin and other Soviet overlords want or expect, but it is almost inevitable in any such puppet like setup as the Party leadership. Very conveniently, they do not have to do any fundamental thinking—they just let Moscow do it for them. But the constant tension of trying to catch every hint and order sent from abroad is a man-size job in itself. And then they have to make sure that they are doing everything according to the specifications of the order.

For example, during the period we are now considering,

Foster was like one possessed in insisting that more strikes be called and more damage be done to the manufacture of goods for Britain. As mild as he is when relaxed, he can be irascible and unreasonable when the pressure to act comes from Moscow. He let loose every bit of his impatience on the trade union comrades for not doing more to cause confusion and commotion. And articles poured from his pen, in *The Communist* and *Daily Worker*, insisting on action and more action, faster and more furious. But when the smoke of battle had cleared away in Hitler's assault on the Soviet Union in July, 1941, Foster proceeded at once to criticize the North American strike and other similar walkouts as being mismanaged and too wildly conceived!

Naturally, we can take into consideration the fact that during a good portion of this period Earl Browder was in Atlanta penitentiary and for the first time in a long while Foster was able to "let go" and act the leader. He was making the most of his brief days on the stage. But the same phenomenon—of urging on and then condemning—had occurred over and over again. When the line changes, as one shrewd and outstanding comrade said in an unguarded moment, "We have to beat our breasts and pretend the last line was carried out badly in order to hide the fact that we act on word from across the sea." I might add that he immediately realized he had said too much. A look of fright passed over his features and, flushed and fidgety, he began to explain away his remark.

Though the bureaucratic concentration on "listening in" to the Kremlin's voice often hobbles the Communist leaders on technique, this must not be taken to mean that they are not very effective. As crude as many of their moves are, they have several huge advantages. One of these is that they win the most fanatical wing of opinion on any line adopted. They attract the people who will get out and plug and who will go to extremes to promote that particular line. Therefore, the orders they transmit get the maximum backing. To that must be added their greatest asset of all, from the standpoint of obtaining results—their continued and extensive practice of duplicity. This ability—if you wish to call it that—to deceive even one's closest friend in the interests of the cause is of inestimable value in moving thousands of people. These thousands do not know that it is Communists in disguise who are influencing others on a union's board or the executive of an innocents' organization or the directors of some civic group. What appear to the people to be responsible American agencies or individuals are in many instances Communists or those whom the Communists are using. Fortunately, there are ways and means of detecting these people and exposing their deceit. In 1940 and 1941, though, in the battle around Harry Bridges the Communists were able to enroll thousands of people who were completely ignorant of the Red manipulation of their thinking. Why do I know? Because I was very close to the publicity end of Bridges' defense, as the articles in the *Daily Worker* will testify.

In arousing sentiment for Earl Browder's release from prison, there were many more obstacles than in the Bridges case. Most responsible labor leaders refused point-blank to have anything to do with Browder's defense. The "why" of this was pretty obvious. Browder had been betrayed into confessing to the Committee on un-American Activities, then under the chairmanship of Martin Dies, that he had traveled abroad on false passports. It was finally revealed that he had made several trips overseas on such papers. His conviction followed speedily and the Supreme Court unanimously upheld the conviction. In March, 1941, he was sentenced to four years in a Federal prison.

Another illustration of my continued education in Communist morals, or lack of them, is the article written by William Z. Foster as the Party's General Secretary went to jail. "Earl Browder, Heroic Leader of the People" is the title of the eulogy. Said Foster then: "Earl Browder in jail is a vindication of the true fight which he has led, the fight for peace, security and Socialism. The masses whom Browder inspired with his insight and vision will make it [the end of the present economic and political system in America] a reality. For, what Earl Browder stands for is as big as the world. And there is no jailor, no matter how powerful, who can imprison the world." Finally he declared: "Earl Browder remains the heroic leader of the people. With him the people will be victorious." And yet, only four years later I was to sit for hours in a National Committee meeting and hear Foster state over and over again that Browder had been a "revisionist" and "a traitor to the working class" all his life.

The man in 1941 who repeatedly hailed Browder as "the representative of the best in America," declared in June, 1945, and thereafter, that Browder had *always* been unfaithful to his trust in the Communist party. Indeed, Foster was not content with making the assertion general, but went on to trace the depravity of Browder year by year. And that review included the years 1940 and 1941, when he was declaring Browder to be of heroic mold! What reason did he give to the sixty National Committeemen for his long silence on the degradation he now ascribed to the fallen chief? He said— and I was present to hear it—that fear of being expelled from the Party had sealed his lips all those years. In that scene (a close-up of which will shortly be presented for your edification) there flashed fully into my mind the mental and moral imprisonment which "Communist leadership" entails. The "leaders" are not so different from the labor camp politicals in Siberia.

But that was four years after this throbbing year of 1941.

The Browder case put a big new burden on the *Daily*—to whoop up the campaign for his release. We were filling pages with praise of his new book, *The Way Out*. It was an almost complete contradiction to his previous works on the People's Front, and was an exhibition of how flexible he could be. It was recommended as the open sesame to and understanding "of the teachings of Lenin and Stalin." Then Browder was hailed in all Communist organs as the "foremost foe of reformism"—that is, he was acclaimed as the chief enemy of the very "revisionism" which the Communist party now charges he imposed upon it and of which Foster says he was always guilty. But in June of 1941. Foster hailed Browder for "his true service" in leading the fight against "the American warmongers." He went on from praise to pan-egyric, cheering Browder's courage and intelligence, and the power with which he "distinguished himself" in the fight for a people's peace. These rhapsodies appeared both in Foster's articles in the *Daily Worker* and in the June issue of *The Communist*. His "fear of being expelled" moved him to a mighty eloquence.

How a leading Communist looked upon this serious business will be seen by referring again to the notes I indicted in those days. "The unfortunate feature of the Browder case," I wrote, "is the documented charge it makes to the effect that Browder is a foreign agent. That is most damaging to the movement, since it links up in the public eye the Party's leader and the Soviet undercover activities. We have done well to stress that his swearing to a false passport was in order to serve the Chinese people. That will not fully screen the fact, however, that some of these trips were to Moscow and that there has been uncontestable testimony of his being in the Soviet capital through his use of the false passports. This touches a tender nerve, the implied nearness of Browder to the secret police of the Soviet Union. The *Daily* will have to overcome this 'foreign agent' atmosphere by much greater emphasis on: 1. The animus of the Roosevelt administration in committing the Communist leader to prison, 2. Expanding the point made in the June number of *The Communist* on how much he has done 'to revitalize and activize the revolutionary traditions of the American people,' 3. Play up his book still more in stressing that he has shown 'the way out' of the imperialist war and that is why he is jailed."

The incredible feature of these observations, as I look over them now, is that there is no query as to whether Browder was in reality a foreign agent. My sole preoccupation was how to present Browder in the best light in a bad situation. The offense against the United States Government in swearing falsely to a passport, taking assumed names and pretending to be men who were later found to be Soviet agents, was apparently a small consideration to me. The very deceit which I had complained about in connection with the Communists before I joined the Party was then affecting me. The "objective" side of the struggle washed out the "subjective" sins.

What made this affair "the more embarrassing," the notes say, was the simultaneous revelation that the Atlantic City records had been doctored to make it appear that William Weiner, Party Treasurer, was born there. Actually, he was born in Russia and his orignial name was Welwel Warzover. Weiner was one of the pleasantest personalities in the powerful but shadowy inner circle leadership of the Party. Our regret at the ugly character of the case against him, and on which he was convicted, was personal as well as political. At the end of one ninth-floor conference on these cases, Robert Minor—who was then handling the "freedom" campaign with Gurley Flynn—was moved to exclaim: "We've just escaped much more serious harm, by an inch or less!" The relief in those words indicated that there were other false passport cases still undisclosed. We all turned to our tasks willingly, working to create sufficient furor over the Browder case to prevent further prosecutions or anti-Party revelations.

Rescue came in the shape of world-shaking occurences. The change was quickly reflected in our changed tune. On March 25, the National Committee had issued a statement entitled "Demand the Freedom of Earl Browder," and in the course of it said: "Demand that America get out and stay out of the war!" By June 28, the title of its new appeal for Browder read: "Free Earl Browder to Strengthen the United People's Struggle against Hitlerism!" Among its slogans now were: "Strengthen the fight for the military defeat of German fascism"; "Strengthen the unity of the people for the defeat of Hitler!" It's not necessary to explain the special pleading for Moscow in this case. America was of small concern to the Communists; our country should stay out or get into the war, according to whether it suited Moscow's plans or purposes.

In a footnote we should add that the Communist party leadership, which was to denounce Browder in 1945 as "an enemy of the working class" because he sought to maintain postwar peace between the Soviet Union and the U.S.A., hailed him in this 1941 document as "a brave champion of the workers' interests" because he opposed American national policy.

This manifesto was issued by the National Committee at a special "plenary session" eight days after the Hitlerite assault upon the Soviet Union. What a turnabout this involved for those working for Moscow can be seen on the contradictory views expressed in the July, 1941, number of *The Communist*. The chief article was by Foster who said, among many other similar things, "Assertions that either group of the warring powers is fighting for democracy and civilization are an insult to the people's intelligence." The same number carried a statement by the National Committee hurriedly interpolated, insisting upon the American people's participation in the war to the extent of backing up the Soviet Union. Within a month this was to be changed to a call to back up "the Soviet and British peoples." Whichever way Moscow went, there the Communists sought to drag the American nation.

During those first tense days of the Soviet-German war, when the Nazi war machine began to roll across the Ukraine, there were many anxious moments at Communist headquarters in New York. Everyone was uncertain about the quality of the Red Army. If a number of "experts" in the public press, who should have known better, made the mistake of underestimating Russian resistance, the Communists could scoff and sneer—but they were none too sure of themselves. I confess my own disturbance. For a long time I had known that there was something wrong with Soviet figures about the rises there in the wage scale and that made me suspicious of their figures about progress in other lines. I had estimated, as David J. Dallin does in his book, *The Real Soviet Russia*, that the figures given by both Stalin and Molotov on wage rises from the First Five Year Plan to 1938 would make an increase of 450 per cent. That would place the Russian wages at figures higher than those in the United States, whereas there was plenty of evidence that they did not even come up to those of France or England.

Conscious of these deficiencies while noting the retreats of the Soviet armies, we had to find some quick explanation. I and Gil Green, then the district organizer for New York, hit on the same "analysis" at the same time. It emphasized that Nazi Germany was hurling the "military might of all Europe, the munitions of the whole continent" against the Soviet Union. There was enough color to that contention to save the day, and to permit us later to cloud over the life-saving aid the United States war materials provided.

From then on, throughout the war, we wove back and forth this way and that. The nod of Moscow to the Right sent us spinning in that direction; if it was to the Left, we stumbled after. When at the end of 1941 the Japanese dropped their bombs on Pearl Harbor, the outcry went up from the National Committee of the Party (meeting on December 7 just as the assault came): "Everything for Victory over World-wide Fascist Slavery!" The line-up of the powers that I had foreseen in 1934 was now a reality—seven years later. The Communists began to hurrah for the war, to hail the Anglo-Soviet-American alliance, to acclaim Roosevelt a hero, and to fill the air with shouts for the Second Front— all according to the tone set by the chiefs of the U.S.S.R. The acclaim for Mr. Roosevelt was contained in such sentences as the following which appeared in an article by myself in the February, 1943, issue of *The Communist:* "The outstanding merit of President Roosevelt's address on January 7 is that it raised the banner of the offensive on all fronts— and reaffirmed the Government's policy and intent to be the carrying through of the land attack on Europe. In tone it was a fighting war speech, such as the country wanted to hear from its Commander-in-Chief."

Thus did we Reds throw up our hats for the Roosevelt whom we had hissed as a "warmonger" only two years before. Essentially it was the same Roosevelt—but the Soviet Union had changed sides and the Communists here obediently turned their coats with it.

In the same way we were to cheer the Teheran meeting in December, 1943, at which Roosevelt, Stalin and Churchill swore to peace for years to come. And Earl Browder was to state solemnly that the Declaration of Teheran was "the political guarantee of a stable peace which will banish the scourge of war for generations to come." Stalin joined in writing the same thing into that document, though unfortunately the Soviet officials didn't believe in it for a minute. That was to be learned later from Jacques Duclos—to Browder's sad though temporary undoing.

The Reds went on shouting for the Anglo-Soviet-American alliance until the atom bomb erased Nagasaki and Hiroshima. Then they were to make another turn-about-face as Moscow showed its teeth to the United States and threw the unholy shadow of World War III across the riddled world.

By then I was still "of them but not with them." For two years I had been resolved to return to the Catholic Church and was looking upon Communist antics in the third person. It is strange that during the time the Communist party was endangered and Browder was in jail and the *Daily Worker* was jeopardized, I thought little of Catholic matters as they related to myself. I was intent on discharging my responsibility to the Party—and it was a grave one. If we could carry the Party press through without interruption, we could consider that a decided moral victory. I watched libel with hawklike diligence. My standard question was: "It may be logical but is it legal?" The entire defense of the paper was successful. There were no serious attacks upon it until after all danger was over and a new period had been entered. By then the Party was basking in the sunshine of being on the right side of the war. At that late date, Rep. Martin Dies did try to assail me for a telegram of instructions sent to our Washington correspondent, Adam Lapin. But I was able to make a reply which Alexander Trachtenberg, long a member of the Central Committee and a Red veteran in studying such tussles, stated was "dignified and devastating." At any rate, the episode closed there.

With the Communists again in the majority camp, through the Soviet-American collaboration against the Axis, I returned to my thinking of several years before. "What about my relations to the Catholic Church?" I abruptly asked myself, shortly after Pearl Harbor.

It was as though I had performed my assignment from the Party and was now intent upon putting my own personal house in order. Logically, there was no other reason why that question should come up at that particular moment. Perhaps the stifling air of bureaucracy was strangling me and I was seeking to free my soul. One thing I can note as having been of some consequence. That was the general morbidity of so many of my comrades, their furtive unhappiness with life and the unendurable aspect of the years stretching ahead of them. In my capacity as managing editor of the paper, many avowals of moral weariness were given me—and they came to pain as well as to enlighten. Only the other day I read in a Chicago paper the oft-repeated tale of the "fanaticism and boundless energy" of the Communists—and those qualities were highly commended. Doubtless, others might learn from them in zeal, but I happen to know that in countless cases this endless activity arises from a feverish desire to get away from the deep challenges of life. There was a balm for such moral illness, I knew—and it lay in the Catholic Church and its Sacraments.

Whatever may have prompted the action, on a wintry afternoon in late December, 1941, I entered St. Patrick's Cathedral. While taking a walk after talking to some political figure in an uptown hotel, on my way back to the *Daily Worker* office, I found myself in front of the Cathedral. Suddenly, I had a tremendous desire to be at peace with myself and to be benignant in a Christian spirit in my dealings with all men. I went into the church, sat in a back pew and breathed, "I will be as the publican." And I prayed—with a fervor drawn from the dim past—for Catholic-Communist reconciliation. I had intended to be there only five minutes;

I stayed for an hour. Looking at myself frankly for the first time in years, I went further and pledged that if the grace were given me to return to the Church, I would do so at all costs. "To Thee, O Sacred Heart of Jesus in the Blessed Sacrament and to Mary the Immaculate, I pledge that if this comes about I shall be a daily communicant for the rest of my life, to make amendment for my years of sin."

That was an enormously difficult undertaking. "How can I with honesty leave Communism, which opposes Catholicism, and once more fully embrace Catholicism which combats atheistic Communism?" It was a soul-rending query, for one who still thought that the "future" lay with the Soviet form of government but that individual and social peace could come only through the Catholic Church. Even after all the goose-stepping I had witnessed in the Red camp, the idea that "Socialism is inevitable" still had a powerful effect. There was gnawing pain in the conflict, and so I prayed for light and the strength to follow it.

In my notes for 1941, the last item reads: "Press for Catholic-Communist co-operation. It can be demonstrated that this will help change sentiment in Ireland to the Allies and will insure the rallying of the 300,000,000 Catholics of Europe in the anti-fascist fight." I was still in the fog—as much as was Augustine when he went to the heretic Faustus to get intellectual aid against the Catholics. And yet, in my small way, I was as much on the road to Rome as the African saint and doctor had been approaching his mighty, historic conversion.

EIGHT

The Red Strait Jacket

NOWHERE HAS a true-to-life description been presented of the mental concentration camp in America known as the Communist Party. Several people have essayed it with indifferent success. They have never hit upon the wizardry of words which can convey to Mr. and Mrs. Average American a reproduction of the barrack-brain existence imposed upon professional Communists. This is not necessarily due to the writers' deficiencies. Mr. and Mrs. Average American simply live so far from mental imprisonment like that of the Reds that they cannot conceive of its existence here.

If I now attempt to depict this strange phenomenon, it is because as an editor for an official Communist publication I had a vantage point from which to study intensively the whole Communist scene. Such an editor has to be aware of the links with Moscow, and of the orders coming in from secret agents and the impact of those orders on the Party and its functioning. He has to be well versed in "the Communist code" by which to unravel and interpret rapidly the practical instructions sent by Moscow through a covering of ideological and involved language. Day by day he has to do this unraveling; night after night he has to study the various articles written and speeches by Communist leaders both here and in Moscow to know the lights and shades within the line. He has to know, too, what comrades are suspect and what comrades are to be played up in the Red press and why.

Before I present to you the various episodes by which I

came to know and, in part, to live this grim, lock-step life, there are one or two matters on which you should be informed. They have to do with the MUSTS for the professional Communists. These regulations will serve as an introduction to an appreciation of the tightness of the Red strait jacket.

The first requisite for a Communist is to understand that he is serving Soviet Russia and no other nation or interest. Never will he be permitted to express one word of reservation or criticism of the Soviet Government, its leaders or their decisions. Whatever they say or do is always 100 per cent right, and America can be right only by being in complete agreement with the Soviet Union. Never, during the twenty-five years of its existence, has the *Daily Worker* deviated from that rule; never has it ceased to prostrate itself before the Soviet leadership.

The professional Communist can't be like the average American and say: "This may be good but there are features of it that are deficient." If it is Soviet-spawned he must say in effect: "This is infallibly correct. There are no flaws in it whatsoever. Anyone even hinting at a flaw is to be denounced as a liar and a slanderer of the Soviet Union." The Communist has to think through a method by which he can defend every act of the Soviet leadership and blacken the reputation of everyone daring to whisper that it may be wrong. By that device, the Communists frequently have been successful in politically blackmailing a number of "liberals" who fear to be out of step with Soviet Russia, but whom the Communists secretly despise. This I can state confidently, for I have met with Soviet secret police on American soil, and at their request have gone over certain "lives and careers" of Party members with them. Whenever such information is wanted it can readily be obtained by the NKVD police or any other Soviet agency by reason of the check maintained here on active Party members and officials.

The professional Red must next recognize that his life and career may be secretly and repeatedly studied by Soviet agents. Records are kept of each member in any kind of key post, just as they would be for those engaged by any other espionage system. When a member takes up a new post, he must file a complete new biography. This is checked for new data and also to observe if it differs from the ones previously filed. In his biography he is required to list his relatives, where they were born and now live, their occupation, and his relations with them. His entire personal and labor history must be given—previous marriages if any, his children and his arrests in labor disputes. He must also give a complete accounting of his financial resources, the average salary he has received throughout his working life, any bonds or other property he ever owned, and what he now owns, if anything. He is expected to record his motives for doing certain things if they are deemed important and must list any organizations he has joined throughout his life. His Party record must be given in detail. There is nothing left uncovered by these biographies.

The secret Control Commission is supposed to keep all these records. Every Communist party in the world has this Commission, and its function is supposedly to discipline recalcitrant members. The Commission personnel is hidden in the sense that it is never made public, and sometimes members of the National Committee vote for it without knowing the individuals. Often the membership of the Control Commission is composed of people whose names even the active National Committee members have not heard. From experience, I learned that one of the chief functions of this Commission is to keep undercover contact with Moscow agents. Therefore, in addition to information that will help certain Party work here, the records have one specific purpose. They are convenient card indexes to check sources of information for Soviet ends. There can be no better key to a knowledge of where to go for certain data than from the "clean-breasted" story of who the comrades are and what their origins have been.

During the latter part of the Browder regime, these records were not asked for with such frequency, but they were more than compensated for by a speed-up of the "information" system. The Communist must know, beside filing his life history, that he is being informed on constantly. Each comrade is supposed to report anything that seems at all questionable in another. Especially does this duty devolve on anyone particularly active or in a position of importance or responsibility within the Party. A huge whisper machine is constantly at work, keeping tab on the comrades. Phrases have to be carefully considered before they are uttered; every clouded comment that is carelessly dropped in conversation— if it is on any sensitive subject—must immediately be "covered up" by a report twisting what was said. "What defense can I make?" is what the Communist must frequently say to himself when he speaks an unguarded word to another.

This consciousness of cover-up and of being watched has been brought to my attention on numerous occasions. On one of these a member of the Political Committee, gleeful over "good work done," began to explain in some detail the use of certain Protestant missionaries in South America as Communist agents. He referred in particular to an Episcopal minister in Haiti, whose name he mentioned, and laughingly said that he was both a zealous Episcopalian and a hard-working Communist. Then, fearful that someone would report his indiscretion, he skillfully tacked around and added that this information had come to him as gossip and that he doubted its validity. The two people listening to his comments understood at once that the whole matter was to be forgotten.

Since an editor supposedly gives a review of his "political health" in every article he writes, and since I was ex officio in close touch with the ninth floor, I was almost immune from such espionage. But even I did not escape. In 1944 I was conscious that letters about *Daily Worker* matters that I had received from certain comrades through the country were known to Dennis, who was then quietly building up a personal machine. This could have occurred had the correspondents sent copies to the ninth floor, but I found that was not the case. The information could get to Dennis, then, in only one way, and that was through one of my chief assistants. He was reporting on my correspondence—largely inconsequential, incidentally—through that peculiar fear which on occasion grips Communists. This could have been his sole motive, for the young man admired me very much; I had had evidence of that. I had also been in a position to give great aid to him and his family, and knew they appreciated it. Incidentally and ironically, Dennis could have had the letters by asking me for them: politically they were beyond reproach!

To test fully whether my suspicions were correct, I took advantage of a message that came along concerning Dr. Ivan Subasitch, who was about to go to Yugoslavia. The London *Daily Worker* rashly cabled a query as to how Subasitch stood. When I took the cable to Avram Landy, who was in charge of the Slav work, he was very much perturbed indeed.

"We want to say that Subasitch is OK now," said Landy, "but let them know that Tito will isolate and eliminate him as soon as he has consolidated certain forces through Subasitch's aid. It's not easy to do."

Landy knew more than the London Reds through having concentrated on the Subasitch case while the worthy doctor was in America. And a way was found to give the tip-off to

London in a cable, in which certain "Slav organizations" were given as the source of our information.

When I got back to the *Daily Worker* office, I told the suspected assistant what had occurred and said: "It looks like the People's Front is being shot to pieces."

Two weeks later, little, red-headed Jacob Golos of the World Tourists, who did much undercover work for the Soviet agents before his death, came into my office for a secret discussion. In the course of talking about other matters —in particular an American secret service agent who had gone to Europe and whom Golos was anxious to learn about— the World Tourist man looked up at me with a smile and said, "Maybe we should be careful where we give opinions of Subasitch."

Since he and I were on very good terms, and had been for years, I shook my finger at him and said laughingly, "Somebody has been telling!" Still smiling in a pallid way, he retorted, "Well, it would be good to see Earl about those things once in a while." In other words, I was supposed to offset any reporting on me by counter-reporting to Browder. When I quietly let the assistant know that I was aware he was reporting, he was very chagrined and even terrified. But I told him to "forget it," since he considered that "his duty."

When a violent new turn takes place in the Party, there is a complete ransacking of the reputation and record of every member of any consequence. It is a miniature imitation of the Russian purges. But for the persons involved it may mean social ostracism from certain groups, continued abuse, or even occasional physical violence. An extraordinary Control Commission is appointed for the Party and one is functioning now. Since the work of this Commission has to be somewhat public in some of its announcements in the Red press, it is a different body from the mysterious sub-cellar permanent Control Commission. Native Americans are not wanted on the permanent Commission, but on the extraordinary Commission, they are necessary as a blind.

Just before I departed, I was asked to present to the extraordinary Commission all the data I had on Arnold Johnson, district organizer in Ohio. Although I had refused to have anything to do with the Trotskyites and had fought them without quarter, Johnson had pursued another course. He had actually joined them for a while, against my advice. It was I who had persuaded him, after two weeks of nightly discussions, to give up the Trotskyites, denounce them and become a Stalinite Communist. Now the Control Commission was suspicious of his loyalty. It was raising many questions as to why he had taken so long to make up his mind, and whom he had been associated with in the past. Step by step, I had to give all the measures I had taken to induce Johnson to change his mind and record his reactions to each suggestion. His status was still doubtful when I left the Party a few days after, though my statements had visibly impressed the Commission as to his good intentions.

Properly disciplined, the professional Communist must always be ready to be at the command of any one of the men of the mist who may present himself. Out of nowhere, as though he became visible through a heavy fog, one of these men will suddenly float into the life of a comrade, introduced by some superior Party member. Then will begin furtive meetings, and the comrade will be required to get certain information in the special field or community or group in which he lives and labors. Occasionally he may be given a vague hint of why the information is necessary, if that will expedite his getting it, but often he hasn't the slightest notion, unless he can guess for himself.

The men of the mist themselves fall into at least five categories. There are the actual members of the Soviet secret police, operating on American soil. They are "business men," or "experts" or, as during the war, military men. Practically all of them are Russian-born, here ostensibly for trade commission purposes or some other legitimate end. They stay far away from any Party office and also avoid the vicinity of the Russian consulate or embassy. Then, there are the "alias men" functioning in or around the Party apparatus. They may have positions of an executive character (dealing with funds or fund raising). They are quiet-moving, quiet-speaking people, as a rule, and frequently have strong Russian accents. Sometimes they turn up in the role of supervisors of the Party's "political health," and examine or edit its publications from a background position. Their posts vary from semipublic places within the Party to more shady and secretive assignments. Since their roles change, within the space of a few months one might run into them in one capacity or the other.

The "representatives of the CI" (Communist International)—or their later equivalents after the CI was supposedly abolished—comprise a third category. Their function is generally filled by one man at a time, and during that period he is in a rather powerful position. He is the link, chain or transmission belt between the general policies of the Soviet Union and its agent here, the Communist party. One of the men formerly functioning in this capacity was the notorious "John Pepper," a Hungarian whose correct name was Pogany. Another was "Williams," who is reportedly now a radio commentator in Moscow. In earlier days, when the Party could be more indiscreet, the representative worked in the national offices and was known to many of the comrades. Such was the case with "Edwards," who was in that post when I first joined the Party in 1935. Just before my departure in 1945, the man performing this duty was the mysterious "Hans Berger." As a rule, he wrote about the German scene for the *Daily Worker*, but practically no one of the *Daily's* editorial staff was privileged to see him. Even the remuneration for his articles was sent him through the ninth floor so that contact with him would be strictly limited to one or two persons. "Berger" is, in reality, Gerhard Eisler, long a Stalin agent in Germany and other countries, and reputed to be the brother of Ruth Fischer, the noted German anti-Stalinist refugee. It is she who sends out information bulletins from New York exposing the connivings of the Soviet dictatorship.

In October, 1946, the identity of Berger-Eisler became a matter of national interest. When in a radio address from Detroit I charged that "the equivalent of a representative of the Communist International" still functioned in America, Frederick Woltman of the *New York World Telegram* quickly identified him as Berger-Eisler. At first, Eisler sought to contend that he had never heard of "Berger" and then was forced to confess that he was the man using that pseudonym. Further he admitted that he had entered this country on a perjured statement. Even then he continued to play the part of a poor German refugee. But it was soon shown that this "poor refugee" had written some of the most vital articles in *The Communist* in 1942, 1943 and 1944. The first of these was a contribution on "Twenty Five Years of Soviet Power," in which he joined with Earl Browder, then head of the Communist Party here, in discussing that matter.

The other two groups of mystery men work in the open Party itself. One of these is made up of a core of a few men, all Russian-born, so far as I know, who remain in key posts no matter who heads the Party. Whatever changes occur in more public positions, these men quietly remain in about the same capacities and deal with such vital Party institutions as finances, defense of the Party and the like. They are tied in with the secret Control Commission. In addition to these are Party executives, large or small, who are normally public but who may suddenly appear in the office of another comrade in a "confidential capacity." The managing editor of the *Daily Worker* may be working with Comrade A, district organizer of the Detroit area, let us say, when suddenly that comrade shows up in the New York office en route to some "secret mission." The public explanation may be that he is ill and has to go to a sanitarium or some rest resort. The comrade asks in a low voice that a "very confidential conference be held for a few minutes," and I always had a very private sanctum for such hush-hush talks. Browder also moved into another room than his own office for such discussions for, as he told me, he feared constantly that a dictaphone might be placed in his regular workroom.

Settled in the private room, the erstwhile district organizer in Detroit (or whatever the place might be) then states that he is on his way to Mexico (or it may be the Philippines or Paris). If we like, he will be glad to take a message to our correspondent in whichever city or country it is. This is, of course, appreciated, though it is quickly divined that that is not the chief reason for the conference. Possibly, Comrade A adds significantly, a New York business man or writer returning from Mexico (or the Philippines or Paris) may drop in to see me or may phone me and want to lunch with me. It will be helpful if I will meet him, as he may carry a report of some value to the Party. The report, he states, will have to be passed from hand to hand and I will be expected to give it to a certain leading comrade on the ninth floor who is concentrating on the Mexican or Philippine or Parisian matter. Through this device a ready and reliable source of communication has been set up, while Comrade A is away on his "mission." He will, beyond that, establish mailing drops with other comrades—in particular with a woman secretary whose name is virtually unknown to the newspapers or the public in general. A letter to this Miss X or Miss Y or Mrs. Z from Mexico would not be suspect.

A number of the *sub rosa* comings and goings noted from the *Daily Worker* sanctum had to do with Latin America and Canada. The American party has been assigned the job of keeping Latin America in ferment against the United States. Many of the quiet visits to my offices were in connection with trips and secret messages back and forth into Mexico, South America and Cuba. One of Foster's first public letters after unhorsing Browder (it was published in *Public Affairs* of October, 1945) was a communication to Luis Carlos Prestes, head of the Brazilian Communists. In that letter, in the usual involved Communist jargon, Foster assured Prestes that he should go to town in anti-American work and disruption. Prestes shortly thereafter issued a declaration that he would fight for the Soviet Union and against Brazil in any war of the Americas upon the USSR. This defiant threat was likewise uttered publicly by Diego Rivera, the mural painter, who has now returned to the Stalinist camp in Mexico.

Communist shadows are constantly flitting back and forth across the Rio Grande, carrying messages harmful to the United States. It is not for nothing that Latin America was once characterized by "Berger" as "the soft under-belly of the U.S.A. which can be opened up through a progressive Spain"—by which, of course, is meant a Red Spain.

There is a marked "division of labor" in conscripting people for work in this undercover world. Sometimes one person is pressed into the service, sometimes another. This may be because of his particular knowledge or previous experiences with certain groups, or it may be because of his field of operations at a given moment. But not letting the right hand know what the left hand is doing within the Party leadership provides a big cushion to conspiratorial work. It diffuses the possibilities of disclosure, "confessions" or tips to anti-Red governmental agencies. It also makes for the maximum safeguarding of secret infoimation and protects the movements of the mystery men. With the Soviet secret police, or their equivalents, this rule was even more scrupulously applied. Any Communist, even though he was a leader, would be permitted to have only part of the mosaic of conspiracy and conspiratorial contracts in his hands.

It was rather early in my Party career that I was summoned to meet members of the Soviet secret police working on American soil. I was still labor editor of the *Daily Worker* and had not yet gone to Chicago as editor of the *Record*. One evening in December, 1936, I was sweating on a pro-CIO editorial, trying to finish it before attending a meeting at which I was to speak. The telephone on my desk rang imperatively. The call was from Jack Stachel on the ninth floor. I was wanted at "a conference" there.

Up I went, to find a member of the Control Committee and a lean, wiry man whom I had known as Michaels in Stachel's office. "You are wanted to meet some friends of importance," said Stachel. "Do they want to see me now?" I asked, nettled at the thought of the engagement I had. "Immediately," replied Stachel, with a knowing smile. "But I have an important meeting tonight," I answered. "Nothing could be more important than this," he replied, and the member of the Control Commission confirmed his statement.

Accordingly I went along, to a restaurant not so far away—Topps on East Fourteenth Street. In a quiet corner a well-built individual of about 40 was seated. His large blue eyes were conspicious, and one of them was slightly astigmatic. We went directly to his table and he was promptly introduced to me as "Friend Richards." His Russian accent proclaimed his name fictitious, but I was well aware by then of the many men with this type of cognomen.

As we ate together, Richards quietly told me his purpose in seeing me. His commission was to investigate the condition of the Social Democrats, and to determine who among them and what Trotskyites and "fascists" were making organized efforts to enter the Soviet Union. He intimated skillfully that he and his colleagues were on the lookout for men who might try to sneak across the borders to assassinate Soviet officials or commit acts of subversion in Soviet Russia.

The prevention of these misdeeds was highly laudable in my opinion, and I said as much. The conviction of the defendants in the first trial of the Trotskyite-Zinovievite Terrorist Center, as it was dubbed, had convinced me of the existence of "the sinister plots" of such groups against Soviet Russia. That trial was still fresh in my memory, as it had occurred only a few months before. That the Trotskyites had enough bitter hatred of Stalin and his ruling clique to employ any method against them had been impressed upon me in my study of Trotskyite theories and tactics. Early in 1936, by bringing out information given by Arnold Johnson, I had publicly exposed Trotsky's plans to create uprisings and other violence in the Soviet Union. This objective of the exiled hero of the Russian Revolution had been conveyed to the inner circle of the Trotskyite bureaucracy here in America by Maurice Specter of Canada, who was one of their number. He had heard it from Trotsky himself when on a trip to the former Soviet leader's place of exile in Oslo, Norway.

Richards nodded approval when I expressed my opinion, and laughed heartily when I said "the Trotskyites would not halt at anything." But where did I fit into an enterprise for the protection of the Soviet Union from plotters? I was readily told. I was to collect all the data I had on enemies of the Soviet Union within the Left or labor ranks, and specifically the Trotskyites. Their names were to be given and everything else about them that might be pertinent to this inquiry.

Particular attention was to be paid those who did much traveling, especially abroad. If I could learn how long they were gone and where they went or were reputed to have gone, so much the better. Could my report be ready by the following Monday, three days hence?

The answer was "yes," and it was thereupon agreed that we meet at Childs Restaurant at 86th Street and Broadway at three o'clock that Monday afternoon. To provide against any sudden change on my part, Richards would phone me late Monday morning. We would confirm or change the time, but the place, under any circumstances, would remain the same. We also agreed that the place of each future meeting would always be arranged at the preceding meeting. It would never be mentioned over the telephone; only the time could be referred to, since that occasionally had to be amended because of the pressure of my editorial labors.

Thereafter for many months I was to move back and forth across Manhattan, consorting with gentlemen who changed from time to time but to whom I was never to mention the place of meeting over the phone and only the day and hour if need be. Our meetings, in various restaurants, never lasted longer than an hour and were sometimes shorter. They were held in the midst of busy days, crowded with heavy editorial work and many speeches at night gatherings. Sometimes the information which I furnished was so trivial I expressed doubt as to its value, and even suggested I might slow down the inquiry for a while. To this they demurred, insisting that everything was most helpful to them.

The first shift in the personnel of my mystery men came in March, 1937. The rain had fallen in torrents all that morning and was still heavy when I finally got over to the Union Square subway station, late for my appointment farther uptown. There was many a headache in trying to live a brisk, business like open existence and then make it dovetail with

undercover associations. All too often some person of consequence or someone who fancied his mission was vitally
important would pop up just as I was about to go to meet
my unknown friend. I would be obliged to give my opinion
on this pressing matter or that, thoroughly and thoughtfully,
while itching to be on my way to the Russian rendezvous.

As luck would have it, in the crowded, dripping subway
that day a man whom I had not seen for years attached himself to me. Apparently he had no particular place to go and
was quite willing to lunch with me and go over "old times."
It took generalship and the promise of a pleasant party
within a week to get rid of him. After changing trains I
finally got to 111th Street and Broadway where Richards
was awaiting me. To my surprise "our friend" was at ease
in the rear of the restaurant, although I was more than a
half hour late and punctuality was one of his chief requests.
Several times he had said: "Remember it is not advisable for
me to stay too long in one eating place. I can give a full
accounting of myself," he would add with a low laugh, "but
it isn't good to arouse any suspicions." He always spoke as
though he were being trailed by other secret agents and was
treading on dangerous ground in a city full of spies and
counter-spies. His super-caution seemed grotesque to me as
an American who lived out in the open air of freedom—
especially since I believed that the objective of his searchings
and seekings would help our Republic, too.

This occasion was an exception to his ordinary alert, it
seemed. His near-carelessness arose from causes which I was
to learn later. He was very satisfied at the lift he had given
to the prosecution in the recently concluded Moscow trials
of the second Anti-Soviet Trotskyite Center and pleased
that he could now leave New York for a short period. I
noticed as I walked to his corner of the restaurant that a
lanky man was with him. "This is Michaels," Richards said

promptly, as I reached his table. "Another Michaels," he added, smiling, referring to the man who had originally introduced us. "Our friend here will take up my duties for a little while." Michaels, who seemed younger than Richards, despite his thinning hair, had a whimsical smile and a lackadaisical air which seemed strange for the labors to which he was dedicated. He was well versed, though, in all that I had been doing and referred once to "records" that he had consulted before our meeting. Once or twice after that I heard that generally avoided word, but where these "records" were or what they contained remained as much a mystery as the actual names and addresses of these men who drifted in and out of my existence at least once a week.

For three weeks in March it was Michaels whom I had to pursue from point to point in mid-Manhattan. He remained as indifferent at every secret session as he had been at the first. Once or twice he missed engagements, which I discovered was a forbidden breach of rules for the Soviet secret police. Apparently he often slept late and found it impossible to make his rounds. His nonchalance led to a new bit of education for me, on the continued close connection between Soviet agents and the undercover Communist party apparatus in America.

One early afternoon, during the time I was dashing around keeping track of Michaels, I had occasion to go upstairs to see Roberts-Peters (the semi-open secret man in the national office) on business connected with the paper. When our immediate business was transacted, he volunteered in that quiet, monotonous tone of voice which he knew how to assume when demanding alertness: "That man Michaels is not so hot, eh?"

I started inwardly, but long experience in the labor movement had taught me how to maintain exterior composure. "He is pretty jaunty for the work he is doing," I agreed, adding quickly, "That is, if you are talking about the same man I am." With a wry smile, he said dryly, "We are thinking of the same man."

To the "not so hot" secret agent I was indebted for one other item of educational advancement. It was he who boot-legged to me the first inkling I had that there are men who long to escape from whatever it is that rules in the Soviet Union. Often during our brief three weeks of conferences I would catch a wistful, almost dreamlike expression in his eyes. One day when we were to go over my "report" at 47th Street and Lexington Avenue, he went, by mistake, to a Lexington Avenue tavern farther uptown. It was a locale in which he had another appointment that night. Discovering his error, he rushed down to 47th Street. With some haste and many apologies, he arrived late. just as I was wondering how much longer I could remain away from my duties at the *Daily Worker*. When we got settled down, he exclaimed: "To you as an American it does not really matter whether a date is missed; every restaurant is the same. You have an infant-like innocence of political or other discipline."

"There is something to be said for freedom," I rejoined with some pride.

"A lot," he agreed with a fervor that made me stop eating and look earnestly at him. He blushed, fumbled his fork and added hurriedly, "Americans can have such a good time. Isn't there some way I could have a good time, a little fun?" It was uttered in imitation mockery.

"He is reaching out to get your aid," something said to me. It was the voice of experience, that voice which had made me understand the political palavering of certain "on-the-fence" governors in strike situations. The man is feeling out how to confess his desire to stay in America, to be of America. The man doesn't want "a little fun"; he wants the reality of "freedom." A wave of pity for him swept over me, such pity as I had occasionally felt for some leading Communists when I detected the reality behind the mask they tried to keep on. What can a man do when he recognizes that those who pretend to be leaders are mere pawns, shoved around on a board by a master hand? He can't help them; he can only hope they will work their way through the maze around them. He can only be sad, especially if he does not recognize the force of the fury from which they seek to flee. After all, I was then a conscientious Communist.

Michaels knew how hopeless it was. He made one more effort to outline carefully what was gnawing at his inner being, but gave it up in the middle of a sentence with a sardonic laugh. "Never say I wanted to be an American," he said with assumed archness. It put a period to that phase of our companionship. The next week Richards returned and Michaels disappeared forever into the Soviet fog.

Always inclined to bluster on the slightest provocation, Richards came back in surly, sullen spirits. All the high good humor with which he had left three weeks before had been lost somewhere on the road. He spluttered for a few minutes at "these people" and "that person"—all perfectly meaningless to me—until suddenly he asked : "What do you know about the national executive board of the Socialist party?" That was the "Party" headed by Norman Thomas, more or less—not the Social Democratic Federation connected with the *New Leader*. (Never throughout our association did these agents ever query me about this latter group.)

To the best of my ability I proceeded to sketch each of the personalities on that board as I knew them from newspaper experience. "Fine," he said, rubbing his hands together. "That's the best view of these gentlemen I have yet obtained." Then in a heated manner, directed at anonymous individuals, he added: "Those who have been in charge of this work ought to be thrown out the window. They know nothing about these things. They should be tossed out of the ninth floor. They should be deposed."

After a number of other redundant sentences flaying persons unknown, to my consternation he said: "We'll have to put you on the ninth floor at once. You know this whole Socialist Party machine, and those handling it know nothing. We'll move you to the ninth floor tomorrow."

"Excuse me," I retored with mock humor but with decided firmness. "This is not my line. I am a journalist and wish to remain so. The man who is charged with supervision of this work in the Socialist Party is an efficient comrade." It was, indeed, none other than Jack Stachel, who had weathered many storms and was considered to be "the power behind Browder."

"The results do not conform to your estimate of this person," responded Richards, the blood mounting to his neck and face. But that was all he said on the matter.

My uneasiness at this conversation was due to more than the possibility of a distasteful assignment. For the first time I was face to face with a concrete case of control of the American Party by agents of the Soviet Government. Was it a reality I was striving to run away from intellectually? Was it something I did not want to acknowledge?

There were a thousand proofs of such control—tens of thousands if I wanted to dig them up. They could be evaded, though, by a mental trapeze act. But not this direct issuing of commands in my very presence. A man like "Edwards," I could tell myself, with some straining at casuistry, was a representative of the Communist International—and by repeating that over and over again, I could convince myself that the CI and the Soviet Government were different entities. The confidence with which Richards, an NKVD Secret Police Agent, was prepared to depose a leading member of the Political Committee of the American party was too definite to be treated in this cavalier fashion.

Nor was the episode ended with his assertion. The next morning, when I arrived at the *Daily Worker*, a note was awaiting me from Browder. He wanted to see me immediately; I was not to delay "on any account." Accordingly, I hurried up to the general secretary's office, where he and Stachel were sitting crouched over the desk. They were speaking in whispers, and their faces wore expressions that were a combination of worry, fear and general alarm. Before I could guess the cause of this atmosphere of gloom, Browder said in hushed accents: "Our friends say that they have planned with you to take over the work in the Socialist party We will do whatever is necessary, but we would like to know what is desired."

"Desired!" I exclaimed. "There is nothing desired by me. This is a mistake. Our friend asked me to relate and review what I knew of the Socialist party leadership and upon my doing so he did want to put me in control. But that, I am convinced, is undersirable."

Both of them gazed at me as though I were some strange kind of piscatorial specimen. For a man to speak out against being appointed to a high post was an anomaly. I learned more of all that later, but such an attitude was not considered healthy when the nod came from across the seas. Not having been trained "for foreign work" in the Marxist-Leninist Institute at Moscow (as all the other leading comrades had been) I had all along a certain innocence about such subjects that made me both bolder and more naïve than was normal among the Reds.

We had a lengthy discussion on the whole affair, which ended by my making it more than plain that under no circumstances would I accept a post of this character. What made the conversation much more protracted than it should have been was the almost panicky (and certainly painful) assurances by the Party leaders that they were doing all that was possible to spread dissension and division amongv the Socialist party leadership. "Of that I have no doubt," was my final declaration.

Walking down the familiar stairway from the ninth floor, I was in more of a daze than its dim light warranted. I had been given a glimpse of such subserviency to an opinion presumably mine, but which I knew came from the powers in the shadow, as to startle me.

I had just beheld Browder, "the leading Marxist in the Western Hemisphere," shot through with fright, he whom the Party leaders rose to cheer for thirty minutes every time he walked into the National Committee session to make his report. And Stachel the ever-alert, who barked at so many other trembling comrades, had been shriveled up physically in the nearest approach to panic that I had ever witnessed in a man vested with responsibility. And who had caused this? One whose real name none of us knew, one who had no connections with the American nation and no relations with the American people.

From that instance forward—and that was in 1937—I began to think more frequently in the "third person" about the Communist movement, to examine it more critically. And yet, the sweep of events seemed so strong, the urgency for "the democratic nations, including the Soviet Union," to stand together seemed so great, that I did not flinch from my fealty to the Red cause. I was thankful, just the same, that I had relations with "the outside world"—with the America of free speech and free press—which made my status different from that of most of the comrades.

When a man denies his soul God's sunlight and faith, he substitutes a pride in his intellect which he dubs "conviction." That was my fatal error. I had become "convinced"

that the "future" was so well mapped out through my
"analyses of the world situation" that this served as an
anchor in every stage of doubt about the Marxist theory or
tactics. I was sold on the idea that I thought as "a scientist":
that with Hitlerism dead, the country to which I was so
devoted—the Soviet Union—would become more democratic
and would join with the United States to save the world from
wreckage.

"You didn't stand up for me," said Richards, with reproach
in his voice, when next I met him. He was not as irascible
as I had thought he would be. The reason was evident from
his next sentence: "They began to jump right away," was
his comment with sly laughter in his eyes.

"Please, remember," I said, "that I am a journalist and
not a weaver of schemes in other organizations." "You under-
estimate yourself," he said, with a frown, and then added:
"But I forget—you are American-trained!" That was
standard explanation of certain differences of views and
tactics that I had heard from the mystery men before and
was to hear again.

The full implications of the incident were largely erased by
"the surprise" Richards had for me at the second meeting
that followed. It was then that I met Roberts, who proved
to be quite a contrast to the previous "contacts."

For this meeting Richards had asked that I be at the
Childs Restaurant at 103rd Street near Broadway, but that
I remain outside if possible, "as we may have to go some-
place else." He showed up promptly at the appointed hour
and said: "Let's catch a taxi." We went to 111th Street and
Broadway and there met a man who was inconspicuously
looking into a shop window. He turned at Richards' "hello"
and revealed himself as a fatherly man of middle size and
middle age and foreign aspect. There was a sadness but also
an intelligence in his deep brown eyes that immediately

impressed me. His excellently tailored but conservative clothes enhanced his appearance of stability and solidity. He might easily be some recently arrived European business man—and that was supposedly his role, I was afterwards informed.

A pallor in the closely shaved blue-black beard of his upper lip told me that he had recently done away with a mustache. Richards soon alluded to "the operation." "You want to look like an American," he jested, "and so you take off your whiskers since you think them Russian. It's too apparent. You should put the mustache back on again."

Roberts listened to this admonition solemnly and without the semblance of a smile. Beneath his paternal appearance, he was alert and fanatically eager to note everything down mentally and do something about it. We finally sat down in the restaurant near by, and there Roberts' initial remark to me was one that would win anyone to co-operation with him. "I have been studying English away from everything for six months. Is my accent too bad, and if it is will you give me—" he hesitated, searching for the colloquialism—"a lift?"

I agreed that I would, and we plunged into the first of scores of conversations we were to have together. Richards, my original NKVD acquaintance, left us after he made the introduction, and save for a two-week period a short time later when Roberts was away on a long trip and Richards served as "relief man," I have never laid eyes on the blustery fellow since. He went back into the twilight land of Moscovite-Marxist conspiracy, unlawful existence and espionage.

With Roberts, who was as persistent in his pursuit as he was quiet in demeanor, my own life became more and more tense. Whereas the other "friends" had wanted a question or two answered at each session, Roberts began to urge three or four or five—and on infinitely larger topics. He had a much wider knowledge of the Trotskyite machine than had his colleagues, and a much keener scent for key information and key personnel. This undercover life of mine began to encroach on my public activities in a serious way; day after day it was most difficult to give plausible reasons for absences from the office when I had said I would be there. The finesse required to account for the unaccountable was all the greater since all Communists watch the conduct of their comrades, ready to report on them at the slightest hint of nonconformity or secretive associations.

The data Roberts desired was not so hard to obtain. "Americans know nothing about conspiracy," he had explained in a philosophical moment; and the ease with which "secret and confidential" material can be unearthed is one of the wonders of a democracy. Mine was not a menial task, such as looking in keyholes or examining mailboxes. It was to obtain information about persons, dates and addresses which Roberts requested; and I went out into the highways and byways of New York and picked them up in casual conversations. Not that the items gathered for Roberts' predecessors were all small stuff. For instance, one day I noticed from the news wires that "Romm" was mentioned in connection with the accusations in the Moscow trials. Later on I ran down someone who I remembered had known Romm well in Washington, I inquired about his travels and was shown some of his post cards from Europe. So I asked to have the opportunity to look them over for a while, and brought them to Richards. He purred like a cat and sent them with all dispatch to the authorities in Moscow. A few days afterward, I was pleased, though surprised too, to have Browder hand over to me without comment a number of other post cards from Romm to another friend here. Neither he nor I asked how they had been obtained or how he knew I was collecting them. They, like the others, went via the same hands to the same goal.

In breadth and depth the inquiry was greatly expanded by Roberts. Addresses were one of his specialities. "Can you tell me," he would begin in his Russian-English," who lives at this number?" And he would then hand me a slip of paper with number and street on it. In one case it turned out to be a place ("a Trotskyite passport place," he had called it in giving it to me) which soon became internationally famous as the starting point for the Rubens couple on their mysterious voyage to the Soviet Union. Weeks after I had found the address, I was interested, though not surprised, to find the same number and street mentioned in the papers in connection with the passport of Mr. and Mrs. Rubens. They came into the limelight with the arrest of Mr. Rubens in Soviet Russia as "a Trotskyite saboteur," while his wife was apparently an agent of the Soviet secret police. Her American citizenship brought the case into the public prints on a larger scale, but when the mystery went unsolved, the papers gradually lapsed into silence.

To find that particular address I had gone to a well-known writer who lived in the neighborhood, and in the course of conversation on many other subjects, got from him the names and number of the occupants of the nearby apartment. Sometimes the section organizer or branch organizer of a particular area could give me the desired address, though without knowing the reason why.

"Can you tell me where the Trotskyites here get their mail from Trotsky in Mexico City?" was another query of Roberts. It was not so difficult to answer, although the number was kept secret. I ran into the newly noticed newspaper correspondent, Leigh White, who was then connected with the publishing house handling the Trotsky manuscripts, and in the midst of a conversation I said casually: "It must be a problem to keep track of the copy from Mexico City." And lo, he told me that it came first to the home of Trotsky's old secretary, a woman who was one of the centers of Trotskyite international intrigue. She was a lady of mystery, too—on the other side of the Communist fence—just as much a Communist as any of the Stalinites and just as unscrupulous in her methods as they were. Her husband was an architect in Newark but had a home address in Manhattan for the purpose of the international plots and counterplots to which they had devoted their lives. Outside the half-darkened world that lies below the surface, they were known to very few persons as having any connections with anti-Stalinist maneuvers.

A newspaperman can make inquiries and get information much more easily than most people. Seldom did I make an engagement for secretive purposes only. I would conveniently comoine my private business with such topics as a proposed article, or the source material for a series of features, or the address of a proposed correspondent. It was the hour or so consumed by Roberts in the early afternoon—a most difficult part of the day—that caused most of my harassment. But there was no other hour to meet him, since at night he had engagements with people who worked in the daytime at more exacting jobs than mine. "How can I meet a government clerk any other time than in the evening?" he asked me innocently one day, when we were discussing our schedule.

Photographs, too, came into his field of inquiry. He began to bring me a number, one after another, and ask, "Do you know this man? Or that?" For the most part they seemed to be men and women seeking Soviet visas. Then he inquired about certain names on lists, which he said were "Trotskyite couriers." One of these was an inconspicuous newspaperman working in and out of China, who later, I believe, became associated with Reuters. Another was Sylvia Ageloff, whose name became widely known as the woman who brought Leon Trotsky's assassin, "Frank Jacson," into Mexico.

Afterward, he guardedly, presented a few persons, "seriatim," so to speak. Generally he asked me first about their Party records and then how they would fit into further underground work among the Trotskyites or other groups. Then he would take me to dinner—these meetings were generally in the evening—and the person under scrutiny would be with us. It required no special powers of divination to know that Roberts was "raiding" the Party's undercover apparatus and taking over some of its workers or operatives for his own purposes. After getting the individual's record, my job was to size him or her up according to their attitudes and associations (if I knew them) in the past.

A young man who said he had formerly worked for the FBI was accepted. Another, who was in a most strategic position to supply information, was rejected because he was too stupid. And so the winnowing went on. One day Roberts startled me by asking that I bring Miss Y, a young woman who he had learned was a friend of Sylvia Ageloff, "the Trotskyite courier." I had known Miss Y in the CPLA (Conference for Progressive Labor Action) and had been aware that she seemed to know both certain Trotskyites and certain Stalinists. I was not sure about her fealty, but Roberts had apparently checked and seemed assured that she was "loyal," though she had never done undercover work before. That was why he wanted me to introduce her to him. I complied with his request.

As 1937 went into the summer, the prospect of going to Chicago to head the *Midwest Daily Record* became more definite. That was more than welcomed, despite my old affection for Gotham. It would get me away from this dual personality, which was entirely too tiring for a long-term occupation. At first Roberts was inclined to oppose the move, but I persuaded him that it was advisable not to raise any obstacles. It would look strange if I suddenly retired from

something I had always been so intent upon—the "education" of the Middle West.

Scarcely was I settled in the Windy City, however, when
my friend's voice followed me. A long-distance call came into
our crowded office and in his well-known accent Roberts
suggested that I take a trip to New York "on important
business connected with your paper." I was up to my neck
in the difficult undertaking of trying to make the *Record* go,
and this was disturbing. I said it was impossible to come
when he wanted me to on such short notice. He agreed, but
in a few days I did have to go to Manhattan on *Record*
business, and no sooner had I arrived than l got word Roberts
would like to see me. Thereafter when I went to New York
on newspaper business (which was frequently) or to a
National Committee meeting, he always found ways and
means to send word he would like to check with me. Several
times I had to take special trips East on his account. This
was compounding suspicions against me in Chicago, of
course. In the midst of our many problems on the *Record*, it
took some mental agility to think up good reasons why I
should go off to New York for a day or two. Generally I
avoided too much explanation by leaving on Saturday night
and returning Sunday night—or preferably Sunday afternoon. I always went by train, since that gave me time to get
a little rest en route.

In these hurried expeditions, whether for the *Record* or at
Roberts' own request, several more individuals were brought
to me "for inspection," as I began to label this process. As
1938 drew toward a close I thought the pressure would be
dissipated as Roberts had not checked on me during my past
two visits to New York. But my anticipation was premature,
for on the very next occasion he advised me (after sending
word that he would like to see me) that he was about to visit
Chicago for several days. He needed my co-operation in re-

gard to certain persons there. Accordingly one fine day he arrived at the Hotel Stevens—registered as "Rabinovitz," a leisured business man—and phoned me that he was in the city. A couple of people out of the Chicago Red undercover apparatus dined with us, their records were furnished Roberts through my rapid queries, I gave him my impressions and he departed after three days. It was not long before our dinner companions left Chicago and were absorbed into "work" that was as misty as the men directing it.

In the early summer of 1939 I got a long-distance phone call from Roberts, asking me to add two days to my stay in New York when I attended my next conference there. The date was set, and for two days I was involved in conferences with him about some of the individuals he had presented to me. Finally he asked me to meet him in some apartment far up in the Bronx. He told me then that he was about to leave for Europe for good. In the apartment I met one of the young men I had seen before; he was using that place surreptitiously to meet his wife, who was working among the Trotskyites. Roberts and I took a long walk, in the course of which he said that he was leaving for the Soviet Union, and that his wife and son were going along. He mentioned the funny papers he had to collect for his little son, who wanted American "funnies" very much for the voyage. It all sounded pretty genuine, and I had heard of this small son several times before. Roberts had always claimed vaguely that he and his family lived in Brooklyn.

As the evening sun was hitting the roofs and walls of the brick buildings of the Bronx, Roberts shook hands with me for the last time. "Tomorrow I'll be on the boat for the Soviet Union," he said, half in regret but also half in satisfaction. "If you ever get to Moscow, I may see you there." And we parted—I to get the train for Chicago, he to go into Nowhere, so far as I was concerned. It was not until 1941 that

I learned that this quiet-voiced, grave-faced, intelligent man had arranged the preliminaries for one of the greatest political assassinations of recent years. He had served his Soviet masters well, using many innocent people in the process and calmly abusing their confidence. It was a first-class instance of the ruthlessness with which the Soviet machine will use people for its ends and then leave them shattered and uncertain to face as they may the consequences of Soviet plots and ganster acts. So far as I could piece that plot together, several unsuspecting persons were left high and dry in this very fashion. Even I did not dream that this mild-mannered man, so preoccupied with "defending the Soviet Union," was engaged in such a fantastic fatality as was to be staged in Mexico City.

And yet that is the story of the killing of Leon Trotsky. In 1940 and 1941 the Miss Y whom I had brought to Roberts (I keep her name anonymous as I have made a religious pledge not to injure innocent people) was severely ill with tuberculosis and confined to various convalescent homes. I had not seen her for many months, but before going away she had looked me up and hurriedly told me part of the story. I did not fully believe it then. When she came back from hospitalization, we had a longer talk. From that talk I learned that Roberts gradually got her to establish close connections with the Trotskyites, including a trip to Paris to attend a Trotskyite "congress."

I had known vaguely of this trip, since I saw her before she left and knew she was troubled. Both she and I thought, though, that she would be setting up a better means of checking up on those who stole passage into the Soviet Union and how they did it. With that in her mind, she was persuaded by NKVD people in Paris (if I remember correctly, the agent then was another woman) to introduce "Frank Jacson," as a Belgian count, to Sylvia Ageloff "the Trotskyite courier," who promptly fell in love with him. It was later disclosed that through her he became accepted by the Trotskyites and was smuggled into Mexico, where he gained admission to the Trotsky household. He was the man who murdered the former Soviet leader.

"Liquidation" of bothersome members of the undercover apparatus had been whispered pretty loudly on occasion among leading Party comrades. I simply gave no credence to such rumors. "The Marxist can never yield to the anarchistic acts of individual terrorism," was an old adage that everybody, including myself, seemed to believe. It was a member of the Political Committee who first disabused me of some of these fantasies. He was slipping in his position, and for some unaccountable reason, tried to take me into his confidence. But he could go only so far and then something seemed to stick in his throat. Once, in the rear of a National Committee meeting, he had suddenly whispered: "Even such wise men as Browder and Stachel get their orders how to think from abroad. Their 'lines' are not self-starting." When I looked up quizzically, he laughed rather vacously and became stone silent. His was a case history of the mental concentration camp, and by way of escape, he went deeper and deeper into the bog of alcoholism. But he did acquaint me with some notable phenomena.

One of these incidents had to do with Julia Stuart Poyntz, the American schoolteacher who walked into Nowhere one day on the streets of New York. In the early days she had been a prominent member of the Communist party and was a part of the conspiratorial apparatus, but just before her disappearance, she had begun to differ with that group. The member of the Political Committee, whom we will call Comrade H, advised me, almost in so many words, that she had been "liquidated" by the Soviet secret police. In the course of the Rubens case a dispatch that was very favorable to the Soviet stand had been played up on the front page of the *Midwest Daily Record*, and I was surprised to find that several of the leading comrades were bothered about it.

When I saw Comrade H in New York I said, "It was a big surprise to learn that some comrades were disturbed by a news story which strongly supported what the Soviet authorities had said." "Oh," he replied immediately—and it was clear he had intended to speak about the matter of his own accord—"some were a little taken aback. That is one of the subjects we do not want to mention at all in our pages. It might lead too closely to the Poyntz case."

"What in the world can it have to do with that?" I exclaimed. "Well," he drawled, "that is hot cargo, that case. We never want to allude to it in our press or touch on anything that might lead to a discussion of it. It's hot cargo, mind you, and it could cause serious trouble in the undercover." Then he caught himself up short, and quickly cracked some meaningless joke. And a year or two later when we were discussing a further development of this case, he was even more emphatic.

On another occasion Comrade H made some interesting comments or confessions regarding Ignatz Maria Reiss. That faithful Red and member of the conspiratorial apparatus for the Communist International had suddenly gone sour on his CI work, disillusioned by the cruelty of the gangster apparatus. He was kidnaped and liquidated in France, and the evidence pointed overwhelmingly to the Soviet secret police. The *New Republic* chose to say as much and to make a bitter assault on Soviet assassination methods. Here was subversion against the Soviet Republics in a field the Reds considered their particular stamping ground. Although we heaped scorn upon the *New Republic* from time to time, we considered the editors soft-headed enough to "come back, always come back" to the Soviet line after certain meanderings. This rude talk in its pages was highly displeasing, and I suggested that we reply to it.

Comrade H said this was "impossible" and he stressed the word. But since the Reds are so quick to call anyone who criticizes them "a slanderer" and "a liar," it seemed to me that they could answer such a serious accusation. I was stubborn and persisted in raising the question in our board meeting, although in a properly disciplined manner.

Comrade H took me aside then, and said, "Don't you know what you're doing? You are raising a question which we will not deal with under any circumstances. This Reiss case is closed so far as we are concerned. We have received definite instructions not to mention it, no matter what happens. The facts won't stand discussion."

Even then, I said, being somewhat chastened, "Frame-up, eh?" And he replied, "That's it," but very unconvincingly. The Reiss case was dropped.

Every leading Red is conscious of these shadows of the undercover apparatus floating across his path or in the background of his labors. They begin to mold for him a strange double life, one that has to be furtive and false. He has to be ready to lie at the drop of a hat if such is necessary to conceal some shadowed person or cover up some unlawful act.

Gradually his personality is warped by other unnatural demands upon him, not the least of which is the dictate that he follow the line. And if he is in a leading position he must do more than follow—he must be prepared to decipher "the Communist code" and translate it accurately for the Red adherents. This becomes almost second nature, and one gets fairly facile at it as the years roll by. I cannot help repeating that it is a technique that should be better grasped by men in high posts in the American Republic.

There is something fascinating in the way the "Communist code" operates, both in the transmittal from the Kremlin here and from the Communist party headquarters in New York to the Reds throughout the land. One of the chief ways of conveying the line and the tactics to be used is through the speeches and "reports" of the Soviet officials. These are given on every gala occasion and also at the various Parry Congresses. They are then faithfully and fervidly echoed in the "reports" and speeches of the Red leaders here.

These Communist reports are almost always involved and long-winded. They begin by reviewing the scene in which the report is being made, and then proceed to consider the "relation of forces—what can be expected from various circles, how "the people" will react, and how different groups can direct their activities. Then the specific activities are enlarged upon with many embellishments in "ideological phraseology." The involved language is a splendid cover-up for orders about new propaganda and new agitation on the part of Reds in countries other than Soviet Russia. For one thing, it permits the transmission of instructions for warfare against a specified country without appearing to do so, and is therefore most handy for conspiratorial purposes. It also gives the illusion of "scientific" analyses of social, economic and political problems—the great alleged cornerstone of Marxism.

Naturally the Kremlin cannot announce by an open order to the American Communists that Soviet Russia intends to wage unrelenting war on the United States. Instead, the Soviet Communist documents will declare that "the United States is one of the leading aggressive imperialist nations, lighting the fires of a new world war." They will assail "the reactionaries in the United States who are inciting a new vendetta against the Soviet Union, which amounts to treason to the building of the peace." And by similar prolix phraseology they will give definite instructions to American Reds to create division in the ranks of the American people.

The editor of an official Communist publication must be

more than adept at reading these hidden and delicate meanings in official statements, articles and interviews. Not so long ago I had the privilege of looking over a study of the Communist press made by a private association hostile to the Red movement. I was impressed by the number of my own articles referred to. And how had these articles been written? Many of them had been composed after consultation with a member of the Political Committee from whom I had learned the latest data received from various parts of America or Europe. And all of them had been written after reading and studying the usual publications from Moscow and the latest declarations of Soviet leaders. From them I had taken the cue to the tempo and temper of the articles and had simply expanded on the line and explained it.

In 1940 a study by Eugene Varga, the Soviet economist, appeared in the *Communist International* magazine (No. 4 of that year) entitled "Monopoly Capitalism in the Second Imperialist War." It was a purported analysis of the war economy of various countries at that time—when the Soviet Union was lined up with Hitlerite Germany. The piece came to a couple of definite conclusions. One of these was "The United States will emerge from the war with enhanced economic power." The other was "The most decisive fact is that in the struggle between the two systems—capitalism and socialism—the superiority of socialism will be considerably and rapidly increased." To buttress these conclusions a third was drawn from the prophecies of Lenin that "the proletarian revolution" matures in war.

To the active Communist the Soviet leadership was hinting, as it so frequently did in the years before 1940, that war between the United States and the USSR was "inevitable." In that war, so the message in Varga's lines read, the Soviet Union would "inevitably" be victorious, and "the superiority of Socialism" would be established.

Such prophecies of the destruction of the United States were but a rehash of the resolution adopted in 1928 at the Sixth Congress of the Communist International which denounced the United States as "the Dollar Republic" and the "exploiter of all other nations." However, Varga's words were more frequently quoted here because they were more conservative and sounded more like a "scientific analysis" than many of the others.

Those American Communists who, like myself, hoped for a long period of friendly relations between the USSR and the USA, realized upon reading Varga's piece that they could not raise such ideas just yet. They lived in the expectation of doing so, and hoped that the Soviet overlords would regard genuine friendship with the United States as Soviet interest. But for the year 1940, they knew from Varga's article, and others like it, that they were to block American international policy. Editorials in the *Daily Worker* would criticize the measures being taken by President Roosevelt, and the *Communist International's* slant would dictate the day-by-day judgment of problems that arose in Chicago and San Francisco, or anywhere else in the country.

Through these articles and the editorial utterances in *Pravda, Izvestia* and the like, the possibilities of new attitudes are also hinted. On May Day, 1941, there was a striking case in point. Up to that "holiday," the Soviet Union's policy had consistently been to hold on to Hitler and not to break with him. But the Nazi invasion of Greece and Yugoslavia thrust a spear into territory which the Soviet Union considered within its orbit. The German armies were uncomfortably near the strategic Dardanelles. Through the May Day message of George Dimitrov, general secretary of the Communist International, the USSR let the Communists of the world know that it was dissatisfied with Hitlerism. The message was signed with an unfamiliar name, but those skilled in international intrigue recognized it as the name of a street in Berlin where Red publications had been issued. We all knew that it was the substitute for the regular May Day message Dimitrov generally sent out. It was therefore treated as such, studied carefully, and used as the foundation for many Communist editorials. It condemned the invasion of Greece and hailed the resistance by the Yugoslavs in particular as a splendid contribution to the liberation of small nations. It was a broad hint, indeed, that the Soviet Union's hitherto idyllic relations with Nazi Germany were approaching a breaking point, and it was flashed to the Communist world, in this covert manner, almost two months before the "surprise" Hitlerite assault on the Soviet borders. This coded message can be read in the 1941 May Day issue of the *Daily Worker*.

Though sensitivity to the fine points of "the line" is a solemn obligation for the leading Communist, it should be apparent from the above illustrations that he has considerable aid from his source material. He has to think through a method, however, by which to conform completely and to defend every act of the Soviet leadership, and that is not always so easy. This he does blindfolded, so to speak, without any real knowledge as to "who is who" in the trends and tendencies within the Soviet Union. In this country people know that Herbert Hoover stands for this viewpoint and Henry A. Wallace for that one. They know that Joseph E. Davies believes it is perfectly all right for Soviet agents to carry on espionage against the United States, for he has said so. But the Communists here, for all their air of omniscience, cannot have a comparable knowledge of any Soviet leader. They can only guess, and they cannot afford to guess wrong.

Where does Zhdanov stand in regard to future foreign relationships? And the chief figure in the Red Army? How did they vote on the new decision to out-Hitler Hitler and to carry on incessant warfare against the United States? Nobody knows. Publicly the Soviet leaders all vote alike and thus maintain the fiction that they are all scientists and always think exactly alike. Consequently, the Communists here have to act on the theory that the Soviet dictatorship is absolutely infallible, and that everyone who disagrees with it is a knave and a scoundrel. The morbid mentality which this produces can be only faintly imagined; to see it in reality, one has actually to live this jailed life.

An apt illustration of the resulting stunted intellectual integrity can be found in what I call the "Strange Case of Comrade Dennis." The hero of this episode is Gene or Eugene Dennis, who in July, 1946, was made General Secretary of the Party. I cite his particular case only because he was one of the loudest in adulation of Browder when the latter was in power and then, next to Foster, became the loudest in denunciation when Browder bit the dust. Dennis emerged into a leading position in the Party out of a nebulous background. His origins are unknown, some saying he came from Utah and some from Nevada. At one time he told me one state, at another time he referred to the other. He had had no career in the labor movement—although that is supposed to be the testing ground for Communist leadership—and there was a strict rule against publishing his picture in the *Daily Worker*. This rule persisted even though he is a prepossessing, tall fellow, whose photograph would not be unattractive.*

When Ruth McKenney, a tearful type of Red and the author of *My Sister Eileen*, wrote *Jake Home*, Dennis volunteered a decree about Browder that was astounding indeed.

---

* During the past year, this rule has been relaxed and Dennis' picture now appears in the paper's columns. Probably the circumstances which caused the rule have been nullified by the statute of limitations.

I had written and published a review of the novel, speaking rather well of its central theme but panning certain features. Dennis was not content with that, but had his wife, under the fictitious name of "Peggy," write a review lambasting the book on other scores. One of the chief objections to the novel, according to this review, was that it had not made Browder a principal character. I pointed out to Dennis that this would have been difficult because during the period depicted in *Jake Home* Browder was not conspicuous. "Nevertheless," he rejoined, "no work of ours can go out without Browder's being prominently mentioned."

Had I been an astute Red politician I would have realized that he was hitting at Foster, but I merely went on to insist: "Do you mean to tell me that we must bring Browder into every book, willy-nilly, even though he doesn't fit in at all?" "Decidedly," said he, with asperity, "for Browder is our great leader, who has brought solidarity and clarity to the Party. That must be shown over and over again." And so it was decided that Israel Amter should add his shrill voice to the condemnation of *Jake Home*—which killed the novel for good as a Red production.

When the program of liquidating the Communist party as such, in order to work through the Communist Political Association, was put through, all the Political Committee members suddenly evinced a desire to become "journalists." They loaded the *Daily Worker* pay roll as "associate editors," although several could not even write coherent English. This would permit them to function, even though the "association" or Party became a shell. Dennis initiated a big movement to make Browder editor in chief.

For years I had urged that some responsible member of the Political Committee be made editor or put in a similar capacity so that we could have the benefit of a close relationship with that committee. But I had successfully opposed the nomination of Foster as editor in chief several months before because he could not give full time to the undertaking. And I was opposed to Browder on the same ground, since, as I maintained, "an absentee editor will be a joke." Dennis insisted, nonetheless, and I knew his motive was to give the Political Committee members a better excuse to attach themselves to the *Daily* as "associates."

Dennis was impatient and insisted upon a meeting on the matter. When he had gotten three Political Committee members and myself together, Dennis immediately launched into the most fulsome praises of Browder. I made notes of the phrases at the time, so impossible did they seem. Remember that this was the man who in a few months was to be the loudest in demanding that Browder be deposed and driven from the Party. But in the *Daily Worker* conference he hailed the Communist chief as a man "of enormous prestige," and spoke of his "incomparable grasp of Marxism," "his sterling integrity," his "conspicuous modesty," his "guidance of groups outside the Party," his "genius," "the respect which statesmen have for his high mental attainments," his "unbending adherence to Bolshevism," his "unending opposition to any deviation," and so on and on. Ironically, the nomination of Browder to this post was one of the indictments later made against him—"his grasping for power"—and one of the chief hounds bayings at his heels was Eugene Dennis.

In the last National Committee meeting at which Browder appeared in all his glory—not so long before his degradation —Dennis began his own report on the national scene with salute after salute to the chief. His first words were that he "identified" himself "with every word uttered by Comrade Browder, in this most magnificent report he has ever made throughout his brilliant career." And he went on from eulogy to eulogy, and reminded us that Browder was even under-

mining his health in the Red cause. (Symbolic of the world
of falsehood in which Communists live, in July, 1946, Foster
represented Dennis as having been early in his opposition to
Browder.)

In a comparatively short while I was sitting in the Hank
Forbes Auditorium at Communist headquarters, at the
National Committee meeting of June, 1945, listening to
Dennis insist upon the "liquidation of Browderism." He
made every indictment he could think of. What made these
mental and moral acrobatics the more repulsive was the
secret which lay back of them. Browder had orginally been
raised on high because he was Stalin's man and was supposed
to embody the sacred gift of "fuehrership" handed down by
the master minds of Moscow. But he was discarded and
degraded when word came through the French Communist
Duclos that the masters had no further use for this man who
had gone to jail for them and had twisted and turned as
they ordered. Dennis' trapeze act was repeated by about
sixty other members of the National Committee in double-
quick order. Only men and women who worship the "*Fuehrer
Prinzip*" with fervor equal to the Nazis could be guilty of sueh
lack of integrity. The Red voices had the same timbre as the
"Sieg Heils" that were heard at Nuremberg.

Such subservience cannot fail to effect all measurements
of personalities and principles. They are all blotted out in
the complete surrender of will to Moscow's dictates. One
illustration—of the thousands that could be given—will
suffice. I choose it because the man involved has considerable
education, prides himself on being a music critic of extensive
knowledge and in general is acquainted with culture. He is
Milton Howard (draft name, Halpern) and he was a member
of the editorial staff of the *Daily Worker*. When he was con-
scripted in 1943 and a farewell party was held in the garden at
432 West 18th Street in Manhattan, Howard-Halpern

declared to the assembled party that writers on the paper should consider themselves as "valets to such leaders as Stachel, Browder and Foster, whose feet they are not worthy to embrace." Though I was chairman of the affair, as an American I could not but feel deeply shamed by this servility, which any common man in the Middle West would view with contempt. But that was not the chief offense against human dignity in this declaration which, incidentally, almost everyone present applauded. Howard now assails the same Browder as "a traitor to the working class," by which he means to the dictatorship of Soviet Russia. And he looks askance upon Stachel, who has been forced to admit that he "yielded too much to Browderism." Those whose feet Howard was unworthy of embracing a few months before are now crushed under his feet, insofar as is possible. And simply because the Kremlin has so decreed.

The extreme intellectual degradation to which Communists must submit is illustrated by the latest chapter in the Browder story (up to November, 1946). Consider the mental acrobatics which are required of a Red, first to cheer Browder to the echo on every and all occasions, then to consider him as an "enemy of the working class, the Soviet Union and the Communist movement," and finally to accord him distinguished attention as the representative of the three big Soviet book trusts. This last position he obtained, as is generally known, by his trip to Moscow and his plea to Stalin and Molotov. This resuscitation of Browder as a trusted Communist figure is in line with the Soviet dictatorship's set policy of keeping alive a conciliatory leader and a belligerent leader in every country. Each one, on occasion, can then be pulled out of obscurity like a marionette on a string whenever Soviet policy requires the emergence of one puppet leader or the other.

After all, the resultant abandonment of standards is to be

expected in the agency of a country in which incense to Stalin is so thick as to equal or exceed that to the "Fuehrer of the Nazi Reich." It is the product of the system that caused the German Communist writer Peter Weiden, though a rather clever fellow, to exclaim of the Soviet Union: " . . . from out of its midst arises and is constantly arising anew the incomparable type of man, the Bolshevik. . . . All the boldness and wisdom, the profundity of thought and the greatness of achievement inherent in the working class, merged and raised to singular perfection, is embodied in the person of Comrade Stalin." To which he added, in a sort of orgy of ecstasy: "To become like Stalin!" (Taken from *The Communist International*, 1940, No. 1.)

It was this same abandonment of all moral political standards that in 1935 led Karl Radek, the noted Soviet writer, to hail Stalin as "Commander in Chief of the Proletariat," while he privately scoffed at the Marxism under Stalin and was himself about to suffer the death sentence. It was the sense of terror-stricken imprisonment that led Christian Rakovski, anti-Stalin Soviet leader, to denounce the defendants in the first "purge" trial at Moscow and to express his "feeling of boundless and warmest sympathy, for the beloved teacher and leader of the working masses, Stalin." By his declaration Rakovski was then paving the way to his own future trial, for all in opposition to Stalin were to be wiped out.

All groups, movements and countries have their leaders and heroes. But totalitarianism, whether red or brown, elevates the chief leader into something even more autocratic and all-knowing than the ancient Asiatic potentates. It produces a servility which stifles and stultifies. The Communist Party in the United States aped the Communist Party of the Soviet Union and elsewhere in following the Fuehrer principle to the point of idolatry. After the fateful National

Committee meeting which dethroned Browder, I asked two old-time members of the Party: "How in the world did it happen that one man became so powerful as you say Earl was?" Their answers—one of which was given by Charles Krumbein, C.P. National Treasurer, who has been jailed here for going to China for the Red conspiratorial apparatus on a false American passport—were enlightening. Both confessed: "We bowed and made obeisance to Browder because of what he represented. In our servility to him, we thought we were honoring the leader of the proletariat, Comrade Stalin, because Browder was supposed to convey Stalin's ideas and his magnificent judgment to us comrades here." No confession could be franker and none could be more damning to the Red strait jacket which turns men of courage into Russian robots.

NINE

Communist Confessions

O<small>N A</small> May night in 1945 I arrived home in Crestwood, where we then lived, and tossed a copy of the *New York World-Telegram* onto the kitchen table. It contained the story by Fred Woltman of an article in the French Communist party's theoretical organ, *Cahiers du Communisme*, assailing Earl Browder for "revisionism." Pointing to the paper, I said, "There it is written: The line has drastically changed. We are to witness still another zigzag, with the old 'sectarianism' riding high."

There had been no hint of this article around the *Daily Worker* and the Political Committee had kept me ignorant of its existance. Nonetheless, my Communist training came to my assistance, and for almost an hour in between bites in my late evening meal I outlined for Margaret exactly what would happen within the Party and in international Soviet maneuvers. During this past year all the predictions made in our kitchen that night have been fulfilled.

"Why, you are forecasting next year's history and its ugly prospect," exclaimed Margaret, who had entertained some hopes from the Teheran agreement. "More than a year," I replied with the assurance of my knowledge of the Communist code. "This is the beginning of a Soviet war of nerves against the other Allies, and specifically against the U.S.A."

"Revisionism" was an offense from the Right that was as criminal as "Trotskyism" from the Left. Both were convenient terms for any Red leader in a non-Soviet country who had permitted himself to become so closely identified with the preceding line as to sign his political death warrant when the next turn came. Jacques Duclos, the general secretary of the French Communist party who authored the above-mentioned article, would never have hurled such a gratuitous accusation at the head of the American Communist organization unless prompted by Moscow. Only a few years before, the Kremlin had dispatched Browder to Mexico City to unseat the entire leadership of the Mexican Communist party on the grounds of "Trotskyism and corruption." Now he was being made to walk the plank on his own account and Duclos was declaring the Teheran pact, Browder's great foundation stone, to be merely a "diplomatic" document Stalin had never meant to pledge peace there!

To a very inner group there had been a hint, of course, that the Soviet views were about to change. The most sensational by-product of the San Francisco Conference was never published: the whispered orders of D. Z. Manuilsky, boss of the Communist International, to the American party via the French comrades. We got wind of this at the *Daily Worker* through a long letter from Joseph Starobin, foreign editor of the paper, sent post haste from the conference scene in California. Manuilsky's indirect command did not censor Browder in any way, but it did bluntly order that Stettinius must be fought. However, this was supposedly in order to forward the pledge of Teheran—and so it was conveyed to us. There was not the slightest indication that Manuilsky intended any such drastic operation within the Party as Browder's political execution, though sharpshooting against the United States officials was not exactly the way Browder had talked. Naturally, the *Daily Worker* leaped to follow the Manuilsky command and increased its slurs and shouts against the Secretary of State.

Why was the chief of the American Communist outfit so publicly humiliated? That was another thing my wife and I discussed that night, and our decision was in accord with the facts as we later learned them. Browder had always done everything that Stalin and his councils had ordered; he had even accepted prison for them. Why should he be so cruelly held up to international ridicule, scorn and damnation? Those who know the totalitarian mind will appreciate the "why" of this abnormal procedure. Browder's humiliation furnished a dramatic vehicle by which the Kremlin could tell all communist agencies and agents that the United States was the enemy at which its chief barbs were directed—even when they shot through the British Empire to hit Uncle Sam. With unusual zeal, Browder had relied upon Stalin's pledge of "generations of peace" made at Teheran in December, 1943. To castigate Browder for advocating a course that followed logically from Stalin's statement would be tantamount to a declaration that the Teheran agreement was scrapped. It would advise every intelligent Communist, guided by the Communist code, that the Soviet Government was about to embark on a long period of aggression and antagonism to its late allies, and specifically to the United States. Were Soviet Russia to make any such bold and brazen assertion it would soon alienate the "softheaded liberals and simple-minded American statesmen" whom it hoped to lead around by a leash of sentiment and "peace-loving" ways.

As to "the quiet man from Kansas"—as the Red-tinted song writer Earl Robinson had soulfully saluted the Communist chief—he was expected to "take the rap." For the good of the Red cause he must acknowledge that he had been in grievous error, even though he had done only what Stalin in effect had ordered him to do. His duty was to comply forthwith, to assert publicly with strokes upon his breast that he had sinned. That is the common Communist custom, under such circumstances. "Everything for the leader; everything for the Fuehrer," is the rule. Life, reputation, and personal self-respect must be sacrificed for the all-powerful, all-perfect state of the steppes.

That is precisely what Sam Carr, or Kogan, well-known member of the National Committee of the Communist organization in Canada, is doing at this moment. Caught red-handed in deals to turn over the atom bomb and other military secrets to Soviet Russia, in conjunction with the Soviet secret police, Carr has disappeared. The Communist organization in Canada has stated that it has disciplined him through its National Committee because of this disappearance. In that way they keep their own skirts clean, and Sam Carr, with the aid of an extensive espionage system lies low until it is safe for him to reappear. Then, he can publicly be taken back into the National Committee. Meanwhile, his running away makes it more difficult for the prosecuting authorities legally to establish the connection between the Soviet espionage apparatus and the Canadian Communist organization.

But why did Browder refuse to accept this assignment, an act of rebellion so foreign to his entire career? That is a question we could not discuss that evening in Crestwood, since we did not know what the head of the American Communists would do. However, it was no surprise when he did finally show signs of revolt. He counted on Stalin to pull him through—and that can be said with assurance. This was more than just an ephemeral hope. It did leak across the Atlantic to the Communist headquarters in New York that Stalin was actually not in full agreement with the Vishinsky-created crusade of aggression. For weeks there were whispers around the Communist corridors (as I had learned confidentially after I had left the Red camp) that Stalin's trip to Soochi, his refusal to speak on the Bolshevik anniversary program, and his long silence in 1945 were signs of his displeasure at the turn of events. Even a dictator is subject to palace pressures and has to bend to some of them, as Hitler also learned. Many comrades cynically stressed, too, that Stalin could not appear effectively as a war god so soon after cooing as a dove of peace at Teheran. He would have to pretend to be against a war policy. Nor did Browder experience the final ignominy of expulsion from the Party until Stalin had made his warlike speech upon his return from the Soochi vacation. That was interpreted as the signal of Stalin's surrender to those who wanted quick and insolent expansion, even at the expense of the Americans' displeasure. The Foster puppet leadership here immediately took it as license to go ahead and throw Browder out. Their procrastination is significant, since for weeks Browder had flagrantly violated the rules of the Party and, from a Communist viewpoint, should have been expelled at the very beginning of his revolt.

The morning after the publication of the *World-Telegram* story I arrived in the office early, as was the rule when anything unusual might be required in the day's work. Phoning Stachel, I asked him if anything was to be done about the Woltman tale. His reply was "No, we're ignoring that." I understood that reply very well. It said, in effect: "We're on the spot. We who make such raucous charges of self-interest and corruption against anyone who disagrees with us are struck dumb because we are again caught in a bad position." The cold, hard fact is that the entire leadership was in a pale-faced panic. Two hours later, when I went up to see if anything else was to be done, three or four members of the Political Committee were in a hushed huddle in which the "Duclos article" was being mentioned with horror. One of them, either John Williamson or Roy Hudson, called me aside and asked if I had seen Foster during the morning. They were afraid that he was making the rounds, which he frequently did, trying to find out surreptitiously what was afoot and working up complaints against the Browder regime. That had been one of his major occupations during the past few months, or, indeed, years.

I came to the immediate conclusion that they were trying to discover a formula that would pull Browder out of the depths into which he had been thrust, before Foster could begin the blast that they knew was coming. That was the answer to their not advising the journalistic end of the "Communist Political Associaton" that the Duclos article was in existence. They were playing for time in which to work out a defense against Foster. For several weeks thereafter, Browder veered first to the Left and then to the Right and back again, and there was no consistency in his columns in the *Sunday Worker*. His frantic efforts to locate some point at which his amended line would conform to the Duclos decree were pitiful to behold. Meanwhile, the frenzied consultations about what could be done to save something from the wreckage of Browderism went on and on.

I now looked on all these convulsions and convolutions with a certain detachment. That is, two years ago I had decided to return to the Catholic Church at all costs, and we had then moved to Crestwood—out of the Communist milieu —for that specific purpose. Earlier in that very month in which the Duclos article was published in the *World-Telegram*, Margaret and I had agreed that the move to the Church would be made during my vacation the following August. Of this I shall write in greater detail in a following chapter. I mention it now to emphasize that it is in this third-person capacity—as a visitor at the Communist conferences and conventions—that I record the unusual scenes which transpired.

We are about to behold the spectacle of Browder's debasement being rivaled by a series of Communist confessions that indict every leading Red of servility to an extreme degree.

Were they not embodied largely in official documents they might be considered as fictitious, the work of someone's imagination. If every alert American could have accompanied me during June and July of 1945 to my office every day, and to the meeting of the National Committee which "acted" on the Duclos article, each one would have been nonplused at the open acknowledgment by leading Communists that they were political playthings of the Kremlin bosses. Those acknowledgments you can examine with me at any rate in this account.

The net that was to entangle Browder was woven in the last month of 1943. Then it was that President Roosevelt, Prime Minister Churchill and Premier Stalin met at Teheran and announced their complete agreement on the conduct of the war. "Our military staffs have joined in the round-table discussions," said their official declaration, "and we have concerted our plans for the destruction of the German forces." What electrified the world, though, was the promise of a peace that would last "for many generations." That pledge was specific, direct and without equivocation. It was a solemn covenant of the three Allied heads with "all nations, large and small" for co-operation to assure "a peace which will command the good will from the overwhelming masses of the peoples of the world and banish the scourge and terror of war for many generations."

Browder received the nod from international Red headquarters to sponsor this viewpoint to the utmost in America. In his book, which he named *Teheran*, Browder declared with enthusiasm: "For or against Teheran—that is the touchstone of American and world politics for the next period, until the principles of Teheran are realized in life to their full extent." To which he added: "The Teheran concord furnishes the platform upon which can and must be gathered all forward-looking men and women of all classes and political ideologies, subordinating all other considerations to the single purpose of welding a firm and effective majority of the people and directing the nation and the world along the Teheran path."

From these statements certain very definite conclusions followed. Among them was that Marxists would have to appreciate that the postwar United States would be a "capitalist United States"—and he underlined the word "capitalist." The American people, he said, were in no way prepared to accept Socialism, and any large-scale attempt to make them do so would only split up the "progressive camp" and prevent the co-operation which would lead to peace. He also implied that European peoples were not ready to accept Communism, and that no Red wave was likely to sweep that continent after the war.

In one of the several lunches I had with him during this period, he let me know that he too had learned something from the Finnish war. "The difficulty in forming a Communist Finnish government under Otto Kuusinen would be increased a hundredfold in Austria, Hungary, Bulgaria and other countries west of the Soviet Union," he volunteered. "Governments halfway between Socialism and capitalism in character will undoubtedly be worked out in many of these regions." He also told me that this was the view of "the international Communist forces," by which I knew he meant Stalin. Strong credence was given to this belief in May, 1944, when "Hans Berger," the mysterious representative of the international Communist apparatus here, came out in defense of Browder in *The Communist* of that month. When Berger assailed Max Lerner of the newspaper *PM* for saying that Browder had "betrayed" the liberals by the "national unity" proposals contained in his report to the National Comittee on January 7, I could not forbear from smiling sardonically at the thought that a man whom even the staff of the *Daily Worker* could not see in person was dictating American attitudes—and rapping Foster!

All through the Communist ranks the chant of "Teheran," was uttered as though it were a talisman and not an idea, until the word became meaningless. Only a few Communists—among them myself—attempted to expound Browder's views intelligently. In the May, 1944, *Communist*—the same in which Berger's piece appeared—the chief article was written by me. Its title was "May Day for Victory and the Teheran Goal." In it I wrote: "American labor's duty and that of the people as a whole is bound up, too, in the mammoth national election contest around the Presidential election. The fate of the war, as well as the pattern of the peace, is involved in its outcome. It is the triumph of the Teheran agreement that is at issue with the promise of enduring peace."

It was almost the swan song of my hope for a Communist movement that would think in terms of America and would bring about understanding between Communism and the Catholic Church as the foundation for the future. By now I was a Catholic in thought mistakenly seeking to convince the Communists, rather than a Communist striving to reach the Catholics. My words no longer rang out as they had in the Chicago days, when success in getting Communists and Catholics together seemed so near. I was testing the Communist movement now, and no longer testing the possibilities of Communist-Catholic coalition. I was not writing as an all-out champion of Browder, but rather as one who, though leaving the Communist camp, was taking one more stab at my old idea of Catholic-Communist co-operation.

The "Teheran" perspective caused plenty of grumbling within the Red ranks. Browder had to turn from his warm endorsement of postwar national unity to reply to the snarling at his heels. Referring to the unhappiness of some Communists at the long-term peace pledge of the Teheran pact, he exclaimed: "Imagine the joy in Hitler's propaganda office in Berlin if it could truthfully broadcast to Europe that Americans, and American Communists in particular, have no confidence in the Teheran agreement—not in its military phase, its political phase, or its postwar perspective!"

Aware of the belief of some Communists that the Teheran pact was merely a trick on Stalin's part (as in truth it turned out to be), Browder hit hard at them. "It is sad but true that even some Communists—not many—have fallen into the trap of a cynical evaluation of Teheran," he wrote. "Of course they give it a special slant. They boast what a 'smart guy' Stalin is, and how he put it over on Roosevelt and Churchill." Such persons, he contended, are "but repeating the Trotskyites in reverse," and both, he alleged, were copying Hitler.

Chief among those who held this "cynical evalution" of Teheran was William Z. Foster (draft name William Edward Foster), who was just being removed as National Chairman of the Party as the Communist party became the Communist Political Association. He refrained, of course, from expressing his conclusions in a crude way. (He did not say: "Soviet Russia will sabotage the Teheran agreement by seizing as much land as it can and by following a Hitlerite policy in the states adjoining it." Instead he blamed the failure to achieve postwar peace on "American imperialist expansion."

After Browder had presented his "Teheran" views to the National Committee meeting in January, 1944, Foster wrote a letter to the National Committee objecting to them. He said that Browder had too "rosy" an outlook on American capitalism. Actually, there could be no expectation of internal peace here nor international peace after the war, since "American finance capital," which was "strong, greedy and aggressive," would not permit it.

Everyone familiar with the Communist code could interpret that thinking without too much effort. What Foster was saying was that World War III was inevitable and that Stalin's commitments to peace at Teheran were so much window dressing to deceive America. The Reds should therefore be prepared to undermine "American finance capital"; and since even he admitted that America was a long-time capitalist country that meant military action. When on February 8, 1944, a special enlarged meeting of the Political Committee was called, the forty comrades who attended all understood Foster's intent. With the exception of himself and Sam Darcy, the firebrand who always saw anti-American warfare as the Communist objective, the group voted his letter down.

This assemblage was a most dramatic one, with the trade union Comrades led by "Blackie" Myers of the Maritime Union, pleading with Foster to refrain from pressing his view. I was in the Middle West on urgent business for the *Daily Worker* and was unable to attend, but immediately upon my return I heard the sizzling details.

"The one hope left for Foster," said Ben Davis, the Negro Councilman from Harlem, "is to appeal to a higher court." He was giving me a confidential lowdown on the debate and decision. The location of this "higher court" was not mentioned, but we both knew its name was Moscow. The Negro councilman, who was also vice-president of the corporation that published the paper, was elated at Foster's rebuff. He was sure the "higher court" would vindicate Browder as vigorously as the special meeting had. A year and a half later, in the same office, Davis was expressing glee at the "shellacking Duclos has given Earl."

Pressed on all sides to retreat, Foster submitted sullenly. He withdrew the rejected letter and agreed not to submit it to the 1944 national convention of the Communist Political

Association. Those members of the National Committee who were not present on February 8 did not even see the epistle. I was permitted one short survey of it, so that the managing editor of the *Daily Worker* would know what was current in the movement. But none of the members had a copy of it. It was totally suppressed. And yet, more than a year later it turned up in the possession of Jacques Duclos, general secretary of the French Communist party. More than that, it had been submitted to all "other leading European Marxists," for Browder had to admit publicly that they agreed with Duclos. It indeed had gone to "the higher court."

The day after my talk with Davis, Browder asked me to lunch with him over "the extraordinary session discussion." We went to a quiet place where we could chat at some length without interruption. Browder expressed his contempt of Foster's mental processes. "W.Z.F. quit thinking a long time ago," he said dryly. "Everyone who considers well what the Teheran concord says and who said it, knows that it is an avowal of peaceful relations, until Soviet strength is enhanced and enlarged. When it comes time to face those issues of future friction out of Soviet growth, we shall do so, and the Soviet Union will not be the loser."

I stated that it would cause grave misunderstanding if Stalin put his signature to a pact and the American people later found out he was insincere in signing it. Browder went even further than that. "The world will go into chaos unless we work out Teheran's objectives, and chaos will bring on a conflict with which the Soviet Union may not be strong enough to cope. The United States is the most powerful country in the world today." And it was clear that in Browder's view, which he emphasized a number of times in his conversation as Stalin's view, the objective was to nurture Soviet strength "until it could compete on an equal or superior footing with all other countries."

It is little wonder that Browder, in speaking to me that day, threatened those Communists who opposed him with the prophecy that "the alternative of Teheran" is "chaos and anarchy in a very large part of the world." He feared that any break between the Soviet Union and the United States would break the Soviet Union, and boldly assailed Foster's views as "predicated on war between the two countries." Later, he was to repeat this latter charge in the Political Committee, thus divulging the real aim of Moscow in the new view expressed by the Duclos epistle.

Both contestants for the Kremlin's accolade were concerned primarily, then, with the will and welfare of the Soviet Union. Browder prudently promised that peace between that country and the United States would benefit the "land of Socialism" until it could get on a more solid footing. Foster saw armed conflict between the two countries as the big hope of the U.S.S.R., to be preceded by a war of nerves such as the world has lately witnessed. Even with some difficulties in postwar America, Browder thought capitalism would be too strong to be challenged by the Soviet Government either from within or without. Foster, on the other hand, frankly anticipated that American differences and dissensions would give the Stalin dictatorship its chance for world domination. This was the conclusion I drew that day from my talk with Browder, and it has been confirmed by what has followed.

It was certainly confirmed by the Duclos article. After three weeks of perturbation and vacillation, that piece was finally acknowledged as authentic by the ninth floor. I can distinctly remember the day on which the copy of the French article came down for publication in the *Daily Worker*, with an introduction by Browder to run with it. Two copies were furnished me, one for the composing room and one for my personal study. It was not until the next day that I received the copy sent me as a member of the National Committee. So little were the members of that body considered that they did not get the copy until after it had appeared in the paper.

The "worthlessness" of Browder's Teheran theory was immediately apparent to all the National Committee members. Almost the only one who hesitated before joining the general stampede to become "Fosterized," as I dubbed the process, was Elizabeth Gurley Flynn, whose Irish flared up in defense of Browder for a few hours and then died like a snuffed-out candle. Then there was Roy Hudson, a slow-thinking person who went around hinting that Browder would be "vindicated" but in a way known only to himself. In Cleveland, where he and I spoke on the same platform, he said as much to the Ohio comrades. Elizabeth Flynn's slowness in catching on to Moscow's voice was "due to the tragic fact that she has not been educated at the Marxist-Leninist Institute at Moscow." So a veteran member in the Party assured me solemnly one night as we were putting the paper to bed. He had been a prominent member of the staff of that institute for a number of years and ought to have known what he was talking about. He also volunteered that Roy Hudson's difficulty was due to "a blight on his thinking apparatus."

However that may be, the audience assembled for the "trial of Browder" at the specially called meeting of the National Committee in June, 1945, was a completely hostile one. Sixty members of that body and about twenty specially invited trade union leaders met for a three-day session at the Hank Forbes Auditorium in the headquarters building.

"This time," I resolved, "I will attend a National Committee meeting all the way through and really see just what makes these people tick." I made special arrangements to be present every hour and every minute of the proceedings. I wanted to get a final view of the Communist party before my departure, which I had by now firmly resolved upon.

The meeting was scheduled for ten o'clock in the morning and was to open with a report—this time, of course, by Foster. Browder, for whom meetings had waited breathlessly in the past, arrived early and took a chair at the front of the hall. Of the eighty persons who entered the hall, only three greeted Browder with the traditional "Good morning." I was one of them, and the other two were Doxey A. Wilkerson, the Negro professor from Howard University whom the Communists had put in the managing editorship of Adam Powell's Harlem weekly, *The People's Voice*, and a trade unionist who was not supposed to be Red-tinted. The other seventy-seven, who had formerly stood up for half an hour on all occasions in the past to applaud, to cheer and shout for Browder, now contemptuously ignored him.

With a rage-contorted face, Foster arose to point out the slough of error into which all the Communists except himself and Darcy had fallen. The assembled eighty again heard the long-forgotten words: "blood-wrung profits." Again they were reminded of Bernstein, Legien and Gompers, whom the Bolsheviks had branded as "notorious revisionists." And so they still were, said Foster, but Browder was "more shamelessly bourgeois" than any one of them. That was casting him into the nethermost Communist hell, since no one could be lower than Bernstein, Legien and Gompers.

Not content to condemn the fallen Communist chief for recent "errors," Foster tried to trace his guilt far back in his leadership. He was charging that Browder's revisionism could be seen in the original withdrawal of the Communist party from the Communist International, when Stachel interrupted.

"We had better leave the C.I. alone," Stachel said dryly. "The decision to leave was for protective and political purposes agreeable to all parties concerned."

Thus reminded that in his Leftist fanticism he had begun to trample on the toes of the Moscow masters, Foster dropped that subject like a hot iron. But he continued to denounce Browder's "enervating revisionism," his "dictatorship," his "chronic tailism," and his "magic reverence for the spoken word" which made him "a talker, not a mass fighter." Warming to his subject, Foster went on to condemn Browder's nursing of "corroding bureaucratism," his "lowering of the Party's prestige," his play for "infallibility," his "deep intoxication with unseemly adulation," his "opportunist practice of supporting Roosevelt without self-criticism," his "corrosive effects" on the Party and his "line which dovetails with the big capitalists' plan of imperialist expansion and world domination."

The entire utterance was one long tirade against the man whom Foster had hailed in 1941 as the "great tribune of the people," as one who had "distinguished himself" in all phases of the antiwar struggle. In 1941 it was Foster's opinion that "it is quite impossible to do justice to the work of Comrade Browder in the historic fight of the American people to keep the United States out of the war." But in the special National Committee meeting of June, 1945, he asserted: "Browder's policies have been a detriment to our Party for years." These contradictory views can be examined at leisure in such articles as "Earl Browder and the Fight for Peace," written by Foster for *The Communist* of June, 1941, and "The Struggle against Revisionism" by the same Foster for *Political Affairs* (successor to *The Communist*) for September, 1945. The latter article on revisionism is a watered-down version of the speech made at the National Committee meeting. But even the restrained version contains all the phrases quoted above.

In his eagerness to damn Browder forever, Foster gave the Red game away. The following was part of his speech and was published in the September, 1945, issue of *Political Affairs:* "How far Browder was prepared to go to prevent political discussion was shown by the way he suppressed my letter of January, 1944, to the National Committee. The only way I could have gotten this letter to the membership was by facing expulsion and a sure split in the Party." In his speech that June morning Foster was even more emphatic, saying that Browder was angling for his expulsion and would have acted on the slightest provocation.

When Foster sat down, up rose Gene Dennis to upbraid Browder still more. He who had hailed the man from Kansas as "the genius of American Communism" now berated him as having led everyone down a crooked path. As was seemly, Dennis mentioned his own "errors" a couple of times, but most of his blows were aimed at the bowed head of Browder. Then it was announced that "Comrade Browder will be given unlimited time" to state his case—a gesture at allowing free discussion before a jury that knew its verdict in advance.

When he stood up to speak, absolute silence greeted him. But there was a buzz among the auditors and a straining forward to hear what the "defense" would be. In his first talk to the Political Committee before this meeting was called, Browder had already charged that Foster's line was "predicated upon war between the United States and the Soviet Union." A watered-down but enlightening version of this view is indicated in his printed statement in the *Daily Worker* of June 10, 1945. In effect, it accused the Duclos-Foster leaders of promoting Soviet warfare against the United States. Trained as they were, the audience knew what these charges entailed and they were concerned about how far Browder would go.

While he again injected this thought into his remarks, he did so obliquely. Instead of a vigorous defense, for an hour and a half in a singsong voice—interlarded with occasional sarcastic digs at his auditors—he read extracts from his various writings. These were intended to prove that he did not advocate "signing away" the revolution to American big business. Since everyone present had read, studied and repeated these words at countless meetings, there was a form of insult in this method. So a number of subsequent speakers indignantly charged when they got the rostrum.

There was no madness in this method. An hour or two after Browder had finished we had a recess, and I was chatting with William L. Patterson, the Negro who had been associated with the *Midwest Daily Record* when I was editor. "Why do you think Earl resorted to such a peculiar tactic?" I asked. "It didn't give much hope to anyone who wanted to defend him." Patterson, it turned out, had a fine case of anger against his former chief. Shaking his head, he declared that "Earl has made no case at all; it has been a bankrupt performance." Then, answering my question, he said, "It's clear he is preparing an appeal to the East."*

On one vital matter Browder was adamant. As he closed his monotonous talk he suggested that he would go along with the draft resolution before the National Committee if one addition were made. He had told me some days before that it was the key to the whole preservation of "the Teheran policy." That was a pledge to "support the development of American markets in the world scene." And he repeated it several times so that it would sink in.

The more he insisted upon the insertion of that phrase in the report, the clearer it became that the Foster-Dennis clique would reject it. Their pretensions of concern over

* Of course, since this was written Browder has gone to "the East" in person, after having been expelled from the Party here. He has come back a "nonpolitical person"—something absolutely forbidden by the Communist rules—and a "friend of the Soviet Union," despite his expulsion from the Party. Now the representative of the Soviet book trust in America, it is obvious that he will be of great value to Soviet Russia. It is also obvious that it was the hand of his old master, Stalin, that saved him from complete annihilation. This strikingly confirms my analysis.

possible unemployment were thereby demonstrated as
bankrupt, for the expansion of American markets is essential
to hold off joblessness. But to that inconsistency they paid
not the slightest heed. And why? Because the adoption of
such a pledge would have been a signal that the Soviet Union
genuinely intended to co-operate with the United States
instead of sabotaging and undermining it, as the new line
intended. That is why Browder chose "American markets"
as his battleground and why his opponents sought to cancel
the real issue in a fog of "revisionism" charges.

Three days and nights (until midnight) of breast beating
and bizarre confessions followed. Never in all my varied
experiences have I beheld anything so like an Arabian Nights
scene. Each member of the Committee seemed to outdo the
others in striving to demonstrate that he was a dolt and a
dupe of a "higher power."

Samples will suffice. Roy Hudson, who had long been
dubbed "the Commissar of Labor," affirmed that he had "an
inadequate grasp of Marxism" and that he had always
surrendered to what he thought were "Browder's greater
ability, superior experience and mastery of Marxism." Tall,
rawboned and awkward in manner when speaking, Hudson
made a ludicrous figure as he declared: "For years every
instinct in me rebelled at certain methods of leadership,"
which he admitted, had been bureaucratic and autocratic.
But, he said, his relation to Browder had been as "an employee to an employer," and the former chief had ordered
him around as "though I were his employee." This last
confession caused a gasp even among that crowd. However,
when Hudson's speech was printed in the *Political Affairs* of
July, 1945, these damning words were carefully deleted. The
rank-and-file comrades were still to be deprived of knowledge
of the full depths to which the "leaders" had sunk by their
own admissions.

What made Hudson's words the more absurd was the statement to me a few days before by a person well known in the C.I.O. He had said, "Whenever I come to report to Hudson I quake in my boots, I fear so much his grim correctness and his grasp of Marxism."

Particularly pathetic was the case of the former famous cartoonist, Robert Minor, who "had been flaying around in all directions," as several comrades reported. Minor had been Browder's closest confidant, was Assistant Secretary of the Party and had prominently carried the ball for Browder in the *Daily Worker's* pages after the C.P.A. was formed. But overnight he somersaulted from out-Browdering Browder to uttering the most savage, extreme and ultra-revolutionary echoes of Foster and Duclos.

Groans of protest rose in the hall when Minor said that he had "waged a continual struggle" against Browder. He was to be reminded that he had, in fact, used Browder's "approval" as a bludgeon over everyone else. With a sickly and scared look on his face, he persisted in trying to prove that he had been wrestling against Browder's revisionist errors all along. He who had traveled jauntily to Spain as a sort of commissar in the civil war was now shakingly reporting that Browder "had gone to several Senators in Washington— or was about to go—to get their advice as to whether even the C.P.A. should be closed down."

There was a hum of anger at this revelation. Voices shouted: "Who are they? Name the Senators." Then Jack Stachel's harsh accents again cut in. "We have no reason to discuss this matter here in this semipublic way," he declared. "Drop it!" And dropped it—so much so that the Party members have never officially heard of the incident, even though it occurred in a session of their "own" National Committee.

Shortly afterward Elizabeth Gurley Flynn scathingly scored Minor for always having been "fastened to Comrade

Browder's mental apron strings." Then she made some confessions on her own account. While everyone again gasped
with surprise, she said that she had been "afraid of our own
National Board and National Committee." She asserted that
whenever she wanted to raise a question, she was hampered
by being made to feel she knew nothing about "theory."
Although a member of the Political Committee, by the grace
of Browder, and therefore one of six people in the inner circle,
she broke down and admitted that this "inferiority complex"
had prevented her from doing anything about anything.

The drama moved from confession to confession. Comrade
after comrade agreed that many speeches were written in
approval of Browder's reports before anyone knew what was
in them. Others said sarcastically that much had been made
in the past of the "unanimous votes in the committees and
other organs of the Party, but these had all been the fruits
of hothouse forced unity." (Another "unanimous" or "*Ja*"
vote of the National Committee was recorded in the May
24, 1946, issue of the *Daily Worker* for a Foster statement
which said: "Any attempt to spread Browderism within
the Party will be ruthlessly combatted." That meant, of
course, that any show of real democracy would be wiped
out.)

One small voice was heard for practical action in favor of
a democratic regime within the organization. That came from
me, who had resolved to make "the need for democracy"
one of my final tests of the organization. When it was my
time to talk I stressed the "lack of democracy" which the
reports all demonstrated. I then presented a motion that
"a special commission be created to forward the extension of
democracy within the organization, such a commission to be
permanent in character." The proposal was immediately
seconded by the Negro educator and editor Doxey A. Wilkerson. But the indifferent faces before me as I made the

motion and the lack of response to Wilkerson's second, gave a forewarning of the motion's fate. Quite visible on the countenances of my colleagues was the bored expression which said: "Another American-trained bit of nonsense." Democracy was no more wanted under Foster than it had been under Browder.

The motion, I may add, was never put. In the evening session of the last day, when motions were acted upon, I went to Charlie Krumbein who was the chairman. "Is my motion for a commission on democracy on the agenda?" I asked. "It is not," he replied, "and we can't get it on." Time was his excuse, but when I spoke to John Williamson, Party secretary in charge of the agenda, he said wearily that the motion was "implied in the other things we are doing." So all mention of the motion was suppressed and the Party members had no knowledge that it was ever put. And in Wilkerson's remarks, which were subsequently published in *Political Affairs*, that section is completely expunged.

While the speech making was waxing warm, Browder let it be known that he was actually appealing to "a higher court" by being conspicuously absent from the sessions. The second half of the first day and all the second day, he did not appear. But he was in the building, supposedly busy in his office on the ninth floor. When Committee members met him in the elevators only one or two exchanged greetings with him. The ancient stigma of "enemy of the working class" was already upon him. It was precisely the title he was to receive from the Foster-Dennis leadership and the *Daily Worker* later on.

Again "Blackie" Myers of the National Maritime Union tried to rescue "unity" by announcing to the second-day session that he had appealed to Browder to return. On the third day Browder heeded the appeal. Not only did he appear, but he made another and rather brief speech. He began by saying that he "apologized to anyone who felt insulted by his method of presenting his case." Some had thought him "arrogant" for staying away from the meeting, but he pleaded his health, which he had to guard carefully. He hesitated before continuing, and then once more made a short statement favoring the inclusion of "support of American markets" in the draft resolution, but his voice was not so firm as it had been.

For the remainder of the third day the former chief listened to a torrent of abusive oratory directed at himself. Slumped far down in his chair, he sometimes put his head between his hands as the flood of criticism poured out. It ended with Foster's "summary," in which denunciation of Browder was again the theme. Foster noted that some comrades had thought him too severe on Browder, but nothing could be too severe for the fallen chief. The high light of the "summary"—though it was hastily suppressed afterward— was Foster's slip in mentioning that he had refrained from expressing his opinion in 1944 because, as he said, "I had been told there were tips from abroad that we should stand by Browder's line." That was raising the iron curtain a little too far, and it was quickly pulled down again.

At the night session of the third day, the National Committee voted to hold a special convention the following month—July, 1945. Then the Communist party would again emerge from the ashes of the "Communist Political Association." The accompanying resolution breathed the up-and-doing spirit for "the revolutionary cause" which Foster wanted. Only one ballot—Browder's—was against the resolution. And the Browder amendment for the inclusion of "American markets" was voted down. As a parting guest, I considered myself a spectator and took no part in the voting. When my resolution for a "commission on democracy" was

presented and defeated, I felt that my work there was
finished.

At these sessions, there was the customary but ever-
strange sensation of hearing a subject discussed in surface
terms when a deeper meaning was intended. Nothing could
better illustrate the Communist method of discussion and
the need for the Communist code in understanding it, than
this meeting's debate and the resolution adopted. The subject of the debate—the perspective for postwar America—
was one in which everybody—including all Americans—was
concerned. And the temper and tone of the proposals made
by Browder on the one hand and Foster on the other were
astoundingly alike. Browder was prepared to accept everything in the Foster-Dennis document if it would include the
"American markets" matter. And Foster adopted the entire
immediate political program of the Communist Political
Association previously prepared by Browder, with only one
or two exceptions.

But that was not all. Browder was willing to agree to the
bitter blast in the resolution against the "big capitalists,"
because he had always said enough on that subject to give
himself a loophole for this turn of events. And despite his
excoriation of Browder for favoritism to the "big capitalists,"
Foster had created a loophole of his own on this point. This
was in his promise to "co-operate" with certain "capitalist
groupings"—of course, only when Soviet aims required
such a course.

Even on the prophecies regarding the immediate future,
which seemed for a time to be the point of cleavage, there was
substantial agreement in wordage. If Foster saw confusion
and conflict in "capitalist America"—and his resolution
dwelt long on its sins and shortcomings—he did not count on
these for the adoption of Socialism in the near future. Far
from that, he acknowledged, as Browder had done, that this

would not take place soon. If Foster saw the sky red with strikes, that had also been a possibility in the war period when John L. Lewis and others were persuading the workers to lay down their tools. Then, however, the Communists had looked upon these walkouts with abhorrence; now they were, in effect, huzzahing for any stoppage in postwar production. What, then, was the point of the bitter debate?

The key to the whole business was in the first part of the resolution, in which "American capital" was damned for not having done its utmost in the war. Since "capital" rules America, according to the Communist formula, this was a rebuke to the American nation for not having played as big a part in the victory as had "the decisive blows of the Red Army." The resolution then continued: "The reactionaries, the dominant forces in America, are trying "to organize a new *cordon sanitaire* against the Soviet Union, which bore the brunt of the war against the Nazis and which is the stanchest champion of national freedom, democracy and world peace."

We can afford for a moment to analyze that sentence, since it is the clue to the document. Where was there any evidence of plots for a *cordon sanitaire* against the Soviet Union? There was none. On the contrary, impressed by the value of business relations with Russia, the "dominant" interests in this country had actually rushed to co-operate with the land of Socialism. And our well-meaning Secretary of State had hastened to Moscow with almost as much avidity as Mr. Chamberlain had to Munich. Meanwhile, the Soviet Union had annexed lands to the extent of 300,000 square miles with a population of 25,000,000. It had taken control of thirteen nations with 175,000,000 population. It was forming puppet armies against America—from Albania to Manchuria.

How could any truly American organization proclaim a

government that had so recently and ruthlessly trodden down the liberties of the people of Poland, Yugoslavia, Romania and Bulgaria "the stanchest champion of national freedom"?

And how could any American group term "the stanchest champion of democracy" a government that exists on elections, in which 95 per cent of the vote is for Stalin and his satellites? There is no such unanimity among human beings on political events. To which could be added the undemocratic fact that the Soviet trade unions—which are supposedly among the chief depositories of this "democracy"—*have often not met in actual national conventions for ten or fifteen years.*

The long lapse in real trade-union meetings in Soviet Russia was a painful piece of knowledge to me. As a newspaperman, I had tried repeatedly to obtain accounts of the conventions of such union bodies for the edification of American workers. They were not to be had. Finally, a former Moscow representative of the *Daily Worker*, who is three-fourths cynic and one-fourth Communist, asked me sardonically what I was looking for. "Those conventions you want—do not exist," he said wryly one day when we were alone. A few minutes later, fearful at what he had said, he returned to my office to ask me not to misinterpret it.

I assured him he need not worry, but I realized that he had given me a hint of the truth. In 1945, when it was decided that I should go to London to the first meeting of the proposed international labor federation, I remembered this incident. While making arrangements for my trip, I said to some of the members of the Political Committee, "I will be able, too, to obtain good stories of the conventions of the Russian or other Soviet trade unions. I would like to get your aid in assuring I meet the right people for that."

My remark met with silence and thereafter the zeal with

which they had been promoting my trip noticeably diminished. When it was found that transportation difficulties would prevent my going in time, there was audible relief among certain of these comrades. Only recently I read (in the *New Leader* of May 18, 1946) that Solomon Schwartz, supposedly well informed on Soviet affairs, specifically charged that the Russian trade unions have not met since 1932.

After the acclamation of Soviet Russia as the outstanding champion of all things democratic, the Foster-Dennis resolution warned President Truman that he must "carry forward the policies of the Roosevelt-labor-democratic coalition for American-Soviet friendship." By "friendship," of course, is meant "subservience to the Soviet aims." The irony in this admonition can be better appreciated by knowing that the special "Roosevelt Room," which had been planned for the *Daily Worker* for general use of the Party in forwarding the memory of the late President, was scrapped overnight when the Duclos article was received. In the discussion at this very National Committee meeting, Stachel and others had brought out that "we had been too lenient in our judgments of Roosevelt, and made opportunistic mistakes of establishing too close relationships with Roosevelt." That was the tenor of the whole gathering, and it was specifically pointed out that Duclos had written his article *before the death of the war President*. He had, therefore, intended to include Mr. Roosevelt in his general denunciation of those too friendly to "reaction." Even a dotard, if familiar with the Communist code, knew that thundering the name "Roosevelt" at Truman was, in effect, political blackmail in the effort to make him toe the line of Soviet ambitions.

This observation is reenforced by the Communist estimate of President Truman. When he came into the White House, the ninth floor sent me a report on how he stood. It stated that when a Senator he had often played cards with Senator

Harvey Kilgore of West Virginia and Senator (afterward Governor) Walgren of Washington. Both of these men were considered "friends of the Soviet Union." And the note added that Congressman Hugh DeLacey, who "always is right," could be counted on to influence Walgren in the "right, pro-Soviet direction." After the Duclos article, this hopeful attitude toward Truman began to change, and then I received a memo stating that Truman is "uncertain, wishy-washy and can only be frightened into pro-Soviet action by charging that he is not doing what Roosevelt would have done."

In the resolution, the entire responsibility for "future aggressions and wars" was placed upon "American capital." Every Communist knew that this phrasing was an advance cover-up for any and every rude act of aggression on the part of the Soviet Union. The very fact that the resolution denouncing Browder's revisionism had adopted much of Browder's immediate program, signified a great deal. It implied continuous warfare upon the United States from that moment on, but not to the point of open conflict until Soviet resources were strong enough to batter down the U.S.A.

As five or six members of the National Committee walked down the hallway, during the recess of the final night session on June 20, one of them said: "The Third World War is on." The others agreed in subdued voices—most of them glumly, one or two with glee.

The convention of July 28 to 30, which was called by the National Committee, adopted the Foster-Dennis resolution with some additional amendments. Earl Browder was sacrificed on the altar of the Moscow Moloch, though he made one last stand. On July 30, at the Federated Clubhouse in New York, Browder appeared before the convention to plead his case. Again he charged that the dominant resolution was "based on war between the Soviet Union and the United

States." Some of the delegates shouted "Shame"; others cried, "It is provocation!" Later on Browder apologized for his statement and said that he had been "misunderstood." It did him no good; he stood condemned. The last I saw of Browder was the former chief of the Communists half-slinking down the street after the convention, with his faithful attendant Harold Smith at his side.

Meanwhile, the drastic intent of the new line was illumined by another and somewhat accidental circumstance. It was the unscheduled debate which broke out in the staff of the *Daily Worker*. For three hours of three mornings each week, over a period of more than three weeks, the battle continued. The storm was not over the new line—everybody obediently denounced "Browderism"; the conflict raged round the question of the goal and tactics involved in that line, particularly with reference to the United States.

Into the crowded, cramped room in which the discussion was held, a number of leading figures in the Party managed to squeeze themselves. They were there simply as auditors—a tribute to the important character of the quarrel. Among these who came for this purpose was V. J. Jerome, who in reality is editor of *The Communist*, now *Political Affairs*, even though Dennis has lately been given official credit as such. Another was Alexander Trachtenberg, head of all the Party's national and Moscow-obtained literature. A third was John Williamson, then known as Secretary of the Party. Informal bulletins as to what was transpiring were issued from the ninth floor—for the lid was off as it had not been since the earlier "sectarian" days when the real intent of the Communist movement was more frankly and furiously stated.

This energetic argument arose from what was the normal procedure whenever the line was changing so violently. Discussions were ordered throughout the Red organization— supposedly to settle policy, but in reality to ferret out any political laggards or discontents with the new turn. As the official organ of the Communist movement, *the Daily Worker* was naturally most responsive to the order. Its talk fest began at the earliest possible moment.

At first the talk was largely denunications of the falling chief. Several staff members even went so far as to intimate that Browder had been an espionage agent for Big Business from the very beginning. Though this is a favorite Communist accusation, it didn't go here. I called those speakers promptly to time. "If Browder was a spy, how can anyone believe in anyone?" was my argument. This met with general approval, because they realized that such chatter would only cause more uneasiness in the already disquieted Party.

Very shortly the theme of the discussion became: "Is the United States a hopelessly capitalist country?" Interest in the debate ran high. Picture a room in which only twenty persons can comfortably be seated jammed with about sixty, all listening intently to a torrent of verbiage. An outside observer would have been at a loss to understand the fury expended on the subject. He would have thought it rather abstruse and abstract. It was, in fact, the very opposite. The question was whether the Soviet Union had as its goal the complete destruction of the American nation.

And everybody in the room knew that. "If the affirmative is the correct answer—if America is devoid of any possibility of being converted to Socialism—then the only reply of the Soviet Union must be the destruction of American power by fire and sword." That's the way one astute comrade put it after one of these sessions, and he was putting it bluntly but well. In the coming historical period "a hopelessly capitalist country must get the same dose as the hopelessly fascist country, Germany, got from the Red Army." An educator-comrade who had watched the course of the discussion with pain and concern interpreted it in these equally eloquent words: "The question back of the question is: 'Can Socialism be achieved in America with the assent of the people or on the banners of the victorious Red Army?' It's a desperate game we are now called upon to play."

Jumpy, ever-busy Jack Stachel knew the desperation involved, and made giant efforts to put the brake on it. As soon as the question came up, he tried to stall it off. He told me that's what he was doing. Why he did not say, but it was evident that he hoped secretly, as Browder did openly, that in time the sentence against the departing leader would be moderated. Over and over again Stachel had expressed the "shame" he felt at the accusation of "revisionism." Beyond that he did not go, but some suspected, and even said that he didn't see any criminality in "Browderism" at all.

It was James Allen (draft name Sol Auerbach), just returned from short service in the Army down South, who forced the issue to the fore. Everyone pricked up his ears at Allen's presentation. He had been foreign editor of the *Daily Worker* before being drafted, but returned as foreign editor of the Sunday edition alone, so that he would have plenty of time to write a treatise on Marxism. His audience knew that he had inside information on Moscow's mind, as those engaged in foreign news work always had. They were in touch with the most sensitive nerve centers of the underground apparatus, and frequently made incognito trips to Mexico and, in the old days, even to Paris and other European or Asiatic centers. Allen had been secret agent for the Communist movement in the Philippines, and not so long before the eruption over the new line had been on a highly confidential journey to Mexico City.

Allen impressed the assemblage by the professional assurance with which he presented ideas that only recently would have been considered rash and immoderate. He spoke concisely and precisely as he expounded a plan for America's perdition.   He had no hope that the American people would embrace Socialism willingly, and argued that the "American bourgeoisie" will never let up in their "warfare upon the Soviet Union." The only way to establish the proletarian dictatorship in America would be through "international intervention," so that the "present capitalist encirclement of the Soviet Union" will become a "Socialist encirclement of the United States."

In a quiet voice, which contrasted oddly with the hair-raising message he was conveying, Allen followed the "plots and schemes" of "odious and oppressive American imperialism" throughout the world. As I watched him, I began to wonder if he were talking of "American" or Soviet imperialism. It was certainly not the United States which was seizing the lands of its neighbors right and left.

Nonetheless, Allen waxed warm over the "danger menacing the Chinese people from the American imperialists." I remembered then that eighteen years before the "International Workers Delegation to China" had made the very same predictions about the United States, in its reports to the Soviet leadership. That delegation had been composed of Tom Mann of Britain, now dead, Jacques Doriot of France, since shot as a "renegade" and "fascist," and Earl Browder of America, under censure even as Allen spoke. The purpose of that delegation in 1927 had been to gain support for "revolutionary and class-conscious" movements among the Chinese, and against America. The cry from the Red ranks then had been "Hands off China!"—but under that slogan the Soviet Government had built up a Chinese Red Army and had established a force in China that kept the country in turmoil. America's aim, in contrast, had been "the Open Door."

Expanding his theme, Allen spoke of the "two outstanding

and opposing forces in the world today—the United States and the Soviet Union." He saw them in bitter combat for domination of the globe. Again as a student of Marxism, I was reminded of all the similar declarations which for years have been drummed into Marxist heads by the Soviet educational agencies.

What Allen said was almost word for word what can be found written by Eugene Varga, the Soviet economist, in *International Press Correspondence* for May 30, 1927. Read it and you can hear Allen speaking:

> The most significant tendency in international politics at the present time is the separation of the world into two great camps: the capitalist, conservative and counter-revolutionary camps on the one hand and the revolutionary camp on the other. The center of the latter is the Soviet Union, while the United States are more and more pronouncedly constituting themselves the center of the counter-revolutionary camp. . . . This concentration of the world's forces into two rival camps is certainly the most important political factor of modern times. The development as such is veiled by the fact that relations between the United States and the Soviet Union are relatively good, while the lead in the struggle against the Soviet Union lies rather in the hands of Great Britain.

Allen's words, however, were much more ominous because the United States and the Soviet Union are much closer now than they were when Calvin Coolidge was President of the United States and Nicholas Lenin had been dead only three years.

Before the clatter of the *Daily Worker's* three-week oratorical marathon had died down, these conclusions had been reached:

1. The Soviet Union was about to launch a "war of nerves" against the United States. (This prediction was made in June and July, 1945, when the world scene was comparatively serene.)

2. The United Nations would be used as a sounding board to "expose American imperialism"—hitting at it through "British imperialism."

3. Soviet expansion was to continue on a Hitlerite basis, *i.e.*, by winning elections where possible for the Communist puppet parties, but by force against other nations when that was feasible. Even Stachel admitted that there were "expansive tendencies in the Soviet Union" and hinted that they came from the Red Army.

4. A Red Spain (to be carved quickly out of a "Republican Spain") would be used as a jumping-off place for alliances in Latin America by which to weaken the United States.

5. The Soviet Union appreciated that its present economic strength and military equipment were not comparable to those of the United States. It counted, though, on the desire of the American people for peace, the repugnance to anything like a permanent draft here, and the Administration's desire to maintain the United Nations at, apparently, all costs. It also counted on "friends of Soviet-American friendship" within our borders to keep this country in such a state of doubt as to weaken America's will and therefore America's defense.

6. There would be gradual, step-by-step encroachment across Europe and Asia, to gather strength from those continents to turn against the United States when the proper time came.

There were many additional proposals and observations, including the plan to discredit General Douglas MacArthur and his control of Japan.

As Allen and others proceeded to present this prospect of assaults upon the United States, I asked myself why he was not disciplined for such extreme views. What he was saying, it is true, was no more anti-American than the expressions of Varga in 1927, or than Foster's announcement of allegiance to the Soviet Union during that period. Nor was it more hostile than Nicholas Bukharin's speech to the Fifteenth Congress of the Communist Party of the Soviet Union eighteen years before, when he used the term "Americanism" as one of contempt and hatred.

Allen's plan, however, was more concrete and definite. And it was voiced at a moment when the Soviet Union was supposedly about to co-operate with the United States in the United Nations. Only six months before, Allen had been rebuked by the Political Committee for making similar statements prematurely. And the threat of expulsion from the Party for "provocative views" had been in the backgound of the decision against him. His new assurance, then, could mean only one thing—that he was actually representing the International line and was giving to the Communist writers in an unadulterated form which even Foster would not dare to employ. This was the Soviet position, beyond doubt. Confirmation of my opinion was soon to come from Berger himself the C.I. representative.

Allen then produced a document attacking General MacArthur. It had come to him through secret channels and was originated by Red agents in the Philippines. He insisted that it should be published in the *Daily Worker*. Although I now considered myself an "onlooker," I was still responsible for the conduct of the paper, and Allen's stand put me and the other members of the editorial board in a difficult position. When Jack Stachel got wind of what Allen was up to, he again demurred and did everything in his power to prevent the publication of the document. But the Foster-Dennis hand was behind Allen, and the anti-MacArthur piece was published. It was the opening gun here in the general Soviet campaign to drive him out of Japan.

Even more vital than the Foster-Dennis decision for the

anti-American "plan" was the stand of the international representative of the "demobilized" Communist International. "Hans Berger," who had previously rushed into print in *The Communist* of May, 1944, to uphold Browder, now agreed with Allen to splattering MacArthur with Soviet-made mud. And to clinch the matter, Stachel was later compelled to acknowledge that he had too frequently "yielded to Browderism."*

Out of the Allen episode I collected another piece of evidence of the eternal watch the Communists keep upon each other. For months certain members of the editorial board of the *Daily Worker* had been secretly reporting to Stachel on the "political health" of certain staff members. Now, scenting the new line, these same people ran "up the backstairs" to the ninth floor to report on Stachel to Dennis and Foster. They even spread the rumor, discreetly, that the man to whom they formerly reported was to be expelled for "Browderism" and thus belittled his standing.

All these Communist conferences and confessions can be summed up by quoting John Williamson, the dull-spoken man who was formerly Secretary of the Party. In the September, 1945, issue of *Political Affairs*, he wrote on "The Reconstruction of the Communist Party," and said, "Our mistake was *not* in trying to streamline or Americanize our organizational form. The decisive thing is the political content of our organization, and that is precisely where our

---

* Since this was written, the Soviet Government has actually acknowledged its animus toward the United States. As part of the flood of vituperation against our country in the Soviet-controlled press in 1946, there appeared an article by Eugene Tarlé, historian and one of the present favorite "line-conveyors" for the Kremlin. In July he charged that America was "fascist" and compared it to "fascist Germany," which Anne O'Hare McCormick criticized in the *New York Times*. Since in Communist jargon the word "fascist" means something that has to be wiped out, the United States is obviously scheduled for future Soviet destruction. Shortly afterward, the National Committee of the British Communist Party denounced America as "fascist."

revisitionist line had its foundations." In other words, the "mistake" was not in being American in form but in making gestures at being American in substance. What we should be, Williamson's words say clearly, "is American in appearance but Russian in reality."

That is what the Communist membership and officials were reminded sharply by the upheavals around the Duclos article: That you are, comrades, first of all agents of the Soviet state, which now is engaged in a deadly war of nerves against the American nation.

TEN

In Two Camps

IT WAS in October, 1943, that I finally made up my mind to return to the Catholic Church, no matter what the cost. If that entailed a break with the Communist organization, then I would. The pledge I had made in St. Patrick's Cathedral two years before was merely an aspiration, but the 1943 resolve was an actual decision.

"The Lord has written wisdom into my heart," I said to myself—for as yet there was no one to whom I ventured to talk about my trend of thought. "An appropriate moment has been chosen, too," was my added mental comment. In the Catholic calendar, October is the month of the Holy Rosary, and in view of the daily rosary of my parents for over thirty years it seemed an appropriate time.

Even at this hour of my spiritual advance, my outlook was tempered by the hope (now dimming rapidly) that Communism and Catholicism could be brought together. And two more years of agonizing over that hope were still to follow before the promise which I made to myself in 1941 and repeated in 1943 was fulfilled. "Why all this dallying and delaying?" many will ask—and with good cause. Indeed, many of them have asked me or Margaret why I lingered so long in the camp of Communism. Unfortunately, it is a question more readily asked than answered. Again I can only resort to St. Augustine, in whose *Confessions*, as he spoke to God I read: "These things went through my mind, and the wind blew one way and another, and tossed my heart this way and that. Time was passing and I delayed to return to the Lord. From day to day I postponed life in You." And again, farther on in his journey, "I indeed was in both camps, but more in that which I approved for myself than in that which I disapproved. For in a sense it was no longer I that was in this second camp, because in large part I rather suffered it unwillingly than did it with my will. Yet habit had grown stronger against me by my own act, since I had come willingly where I did not now will to be. Who can justly complain when just punishment overtakes the sinner?"

Since I had clouded my vision with materialism, was it any wonder that I should grope and grasp for shadows, straining to see the right way and yet not perceiving it? As a Communist I had striven to persuade the Catholics that the battle against anti-Catholic totalitarianism and Ku Klux Klanism lay in alliance with the Communists. Now, as a Catholic, I would say to the Communists, while remaining in their ranks, that understanding with the three hundred million Catholics of Europe and the twenty-five million Catholics in America was vital to their cause. So I reasoned with myself like a man in a dream. Augustine put it well when he compared such a man "of both camps" to one awakened from his sleep. He knows that he must get up, and yet wants to linger a little longer on his couch.

One providential fruit came from such halting and hesitation: I examined the Communist position and Communist methods of treachery and deceit fully and critically. And thereby learned the truth concerning the Communist conspiracy against America and Catholicism. I was enabled to grasp the realities of the Soviet Union's concerted and unrelenting determination to crush both religion and our nation and to pursue a study of these objectives to the bitter end.

In 1943 there were plenty of disquieting signs pointing to the existence of that conspiracy. Those who look back to the sequence of events may express surprise at such a statement.

Was this period not the honeymoon of the "Anglo-Soviet-American alliance," as the Communists liked to toll out that expression in countless meetings? Was this not the very moment when the Communist International was "dissolved"? Were not the Allied leaders about to confer at Teheran and promise the world "generations of peace"? All very true. But to anyone inside the Communist camp who interpreted what was actually transpiring, the farce of much of it was quickly apparent.

Though the Communist International was supposedly dissolved, I knew from the discussions that the representative in America of that very body would write the article in *The Communist* explaining it. This was arranged so that all active Communists would be at ease on the proposal and would recognize the "dissolution" as merely a formal affair. The C.I. representative, "Hans Berger," not only wrote the article in the November, 1943, issue of *The Communist*, but calmly continued to function in America even more actively than before. For who would think of deporting or disturbing him, when the body he represented no longer existed? And so he went on giving orders and making decisions, right down to the day when he decided in effect in favor of Allen and the theory that America was "a hopelessly capitalist country."

The whole key to Berger's article was that the dissolution of the C.I. was not to be put on a par with the "collapse of the Second International." Through that device he was able to convey to every alert Communist that while International links with the Soviet state could be more carefully forged, they were still as strong as ever. Each wide-awake Red knew well that the Soviet Union's interconnections in every land would not end as had the "collapsed" Second International. In other words, the C.I. would not die!

Browder signaled the same idea with his carefully worked-out phrase that Communists would be more international by being more national. This was a nice thought designed to tip off the "faithful" as to what was really afoot while befuddling the confiding "friends" in Washington. Berger recommended Browder's utterances as being characterized by unusual "brilliance."

As managing editor of the official Communist organ, I sat in on several meetings of the Political Committee at which these feints at ending the C.I. were discussed and arrangements to handle them were made. No one present was under any illusion about what was involved in the alleged "dissolution." As Robert Minor put it, "Mr. Roosevelt will swallow it and find it sweet." The chief concern was that the comrades know the precise nature of the action. Quite a few had become too patriotic four years before, when Browder had popularized the phrase, "Communism is twentieth-century Americanism." They were quickly reminded in the usual Communist "ideological" language that their first allegiance was to the Soviet service. So the members of the Political Committee wanted to make sure in 1943 that no worth-while Communist suffered any fairy-tale vision that the C.I. was actually disappearing. To make doubly sure, it was agreed that an article by Dmitri Manuilsky on "The Glorious Victories of the Red Army" should be run in an early issue of *The Communist*. It appeared in the same November number in which the Berger piece on the C.I. was published.

Why were Manuilsky's name and article chosen for this purpose? If you know that, you get again an interesting illustration of how the Communist leadership transmits its conspiratorial thoughts to its key people and particularly to those who have been trained at the Marx-Lenin Institute in Moscow. Each knew that Manuilsky was and had always been Stalin's right hand in handling the International apparatus. He had been made secretary of the Communist International when Stalin wanted most to clear it of all his opponents. And he had led the big crusade against the United States, caricaturing it as the chief enemy of the peoples of the world, right up to Hitler's rise to power. Even when a new frontispiece was needed because of Hitlerite victory in Germany and George Dimitrov was made secretary of the C.I., Manuilsky continued to be known as its real boss. As Foster said to me one day when discussing the question, "Dimitrov is the head, but Dmitri (*i.e.* Manuilsky) will always be the heart of the C.I."

It may have been that Manuilsky's article was ordered printed by the Communist International itself—I do not remember that fully—but the decision by the Political Committee to publish it was definitely based on what Manuilsky's name would convey. And that would be that the C.I. still lived, though it might not appear in the open daylight of the world.

The contents of Manuilsky's article were designed to prove that it was the Red Army alone which was winning the war, and that the efforts of the other Allies amounted to almost nothing. According to his effusion, the American dead on the beaches of Africa and Anzio were of small consequence, and the tons of American lend-lease of little value. Without detracting one iota from the "glory of the Red Army" it can safely be said that the picture was overdrawn. But the Manuilsky piece was the foundation for the contemptuous attitude toward our fighting men which the Communists employed as the war went on.

To this double-dealing around the C.I. were added other deceptions. At the same time, I learned of the plan for a Red Poland—anti-British and anti-American. It was to be the base for a Red belt of Slav states, "a battering ram for the Communist conquest of Europe," as A. Landy put it. Landy, *the man in charge* of the "national minority group work" in the United States—also closely connected with all Soviet plans in Europe—had given me a sketch of this scheme. He had urged that the *Daily Worker* look sharp for any opportunity to "expose" Stanislaw Mikolajczyk, the head of the powerful Polish Peasant party. Various ninth-floor, memorandums, from Landy in particular, had stressed the value of the article on "the Polish reactionaries" by the C.I. representative "Hans Berger," which appeared in the June, 1943, issue of *The Communist.* We at the *Daily* were asked to keep that piece in mind when writing our stories and features.

"But that article aims its guns at the Sikorski group and Colonel Matuszewski," I said, for I had read it carefully a number of times. "There is nothing in it injurious to Mikolajczyk, whom we have called a 'liberal' at times."

"We must link him up with the Sikorski government in exile, with which he is co-operating," was Landy's reply. "At one swoop we will get rid of the 'liberal' wing in Poland and open the way for a completely friendly government." "That will be an all-Communist government?" I inquired, in order to get my bearings.

"To all intents and purposes, yes" was the reply. "We must proceed cautiously so as not to disturb the placidity of Washington. Our goal will be the elimination of all but the pro-Soviet elements, just as we are doing in Yugoslavia and are planning in Bulgaria, with the liquidation of men like the Agrarian George Dimitrov."

Although I knew it well, he went to pains to explain the difference between the Agrarian Dimitrov—marked for slaughter so that there would be a Red Bulgaria—and Dimitrov of the Communist International. "The only genuine anti-fascist leaders left in Europe," he ended dryly, "are pro-Soviet leaders." This was one of the fantasies carefully cultivated by the Communists, who even took credit for the Catholic revolts against Nazism as being Red-inspired.

"If this deluge of deceit is being poured out in the midst of coalition warfare," I inquired of myself, "what will be the state of affairs when that war has come to an end?" It did not presage peace. Even on the eve of the meeting of the Allied chiefs, the scuttling of any terms agreed upon was already arranged by the Soviet Union and its agents. Why should such a disruptive attitude be maintained by the Soviet Government?

It was not hard to find the answer. The basis of Communism is the denial of the moral law. While presenting itself as a remedy for the evils of extreme economic liberalism, it contains the same poison within its system as the philosophy it condemns. They both reject genuine order and morality. While loudly claiming that it will halt social disintegration, Communism speeds that disintegration, for deceit as the basis of "morality" and slavery as the height of "freedom" are the benighted outcomes of materialism. There would be no peace if that sort of conduct continued. That's what my knowledge of Soviet aims taught me in 1943, and I was profoundly disturbed. The thing to do was to return to the moral foundations from which I had fled—to the Church, which calmly presents the moral law as essential for man and the sole course for real peace.

My dissatisfaction with what was afoot in the Communist camp was heightened by the instructions we were getting from the representative of the "dissolved" Comintern. In several messages, Berger urged that the *Daily Worker* level its guns at those who were talking about "war aims" and the "pattern of the peace." We held a special meeting of the editorial board on the matter sometime in September, 1943, and decided to label such proposals the creation of the "fascist-minded" and the "isolationists." Berger's insistence was such that we were all pretty well convinced that the Soviet Government wanted to keep the peace terms a matter of suspense. There could be only one reason for such coyness. The Russian dictatorship hoped to keep the world in turmoil and make the peace impossible. It was during this discussion of the editorial board that I first recognized the inner necessity for totalitarianism. For its own preservation it must create disorder in other lands in order to keep at bay the unrest in its own.

As soon as I got the chance, I raised the question with Browder: "Would it not help morals here to give some indication of what should be America's outlook for the postwar world? To stress that it will be different from the debacle of 1920?" But Browder, looking up with that half-fearful, half-professional look which so often haunted his face when he was handing down decisions, declared with such finality that it ended the discussion: "Our sole task now is to cement the bonds between the United States and the Soviet Union." And I understood at once that Berger's position was the Soviet position—and consequently "our position."

The creation in Moscow of the National Committee of Free Germany followed the same pattern of trickery against the anti-Axis coalition. On July twelfth and thirteenth of 1943 this committee was born at a conference of German prisoners in the Soviet capital. With its central slogan of " *Unser Zeil: Ein Freies Deutschland*," it had a certain propaganda value within Germany against Hitler. But its chief reason for existence, we soon learned through our reliable channels, was to "beat the other Allies to the draw," as one member of the Political Committee expressed it. It was designed to carry Soviet propaganda into Germany before American or British influences could be at work.

There was still enough of the Communist in me to wish for the extension of Communism. But to extend it through Hitlerite tactics and power politics seemed to me to poison any hope of "genuine Socialism" arising from the people.

What seemed to me particularly offensive and fatal to the expansion of real democracy was the organized deceit planned against the American people. If the Soviet Union could think in these terms, when its land was freshly ravaged and the Nazis were not yet conquered, what might be on its agenda when the uneasy peace came? The catastrophe of 1920 would again be ours, but on a more gigantic, more terrible scale. My strong belief in the greater democracy of the Soviet Union after the destruction of Hitlerism was crumbling.

During those late 1943 days I found a memorandum on my desk which gave me another severe jolt. It came from the ninth floor, was signed "A. Landy," and read: "Ignore all news stories on treason or disaffection by small Republics in U.S.S.R. Advise foreign department only." In this negative way I frequently received ill-wind information of a serious character—and this, of course, was very serious. There had been such a world-wide build-up of the solidarity in the "defense of the Socialist fatherland" that this was an eye-opener. Nor did the memo say that "Trotskyite agents" or "reactionary remnants" among the population had been guilty of this treason to Soviet Russia. It spoke of "Republics"—and while these were stressed as "small," that involved whole peoples in the treason.

When I got hold of Landy he mentioned "extensive trouble in two republics," but hinted that several other republics might be in similar bad odor. Since 1941 the whole world had known that the "republic" of the Volga Germans had been extirpated and the entire population moved to Siberia. That had been secretly justified on the ground of "protection for the population" as well as of disaffection. But this time there was no such trimming to the blunt declaration that whole populations of "self-determined republics" had revolted and been crushed by the Red Army. Such was Landy's information, which I was asked to suppress.

The grave reflection on any "democracy" in Soviet Russia which this Soviet-admitted news. contained was not lost on me. "The votes of these republics have been more than 90 per cent for Stalin right along," I commented with misgiving. "And the information we have points to a revolt of at least 90 per cent of the people *against* Stalin. This cries out that the elections were as much *'Ja'* elections in those divisions of the U.S.S.R. as were the Hitlerite ballotings in Germany. Furthermore, there must be many other peoples—great masses of them—who would not go to the extent of treason but are also opposed to the dictatorship." It was a disturbing recognition of a reality that I had long wanted to evade.

The resemblance between Hitlerism and the Soviet regime was too close for comfort or for confidence in the latter's service to the people. Over the ticker tape across my desk came effusive statements by gentlemen who called themselves "liberal"—and who in many respects deserved the name—acclaiming the "democracy" of Soviet Russia and often implying that it was ahead of our own freedoms. I became increasingly astounded at their positive declarations on matters of which they understood so little. In my own hands were data that demonstrated how ill-founded were their assertions. I felt keenly the conspiracy of which I was a part—to drug the American people with opium dreams of a world that did not exist. The drug, I began to see, would be fatal to our national existence. Was it therefore not my duty to drop my odious role, and cease injuring my country?

During those evenings at the *Daily Worker*, as we put the paper to bed, I worked out the connection between Hitlerism and Soviet totalitarianism. They were both founded on hate. And no such materialist doctrine could ever save the world. Instead, it was leading the world into another conflict before World War II was even completed. There must be a return to the belief in human brotherhood—to the religion of

Augustine, Loyola and Francis of Assisi. The dignity of man could be safeguarded only through a full understanding of his relation to Divinity. This was essential for America too, for some of our own national defects were the results of moral shortcomings, of the rejection of the gospel of love.

Such reasonings brought me to the portals of the Catholic Church once more. They were not powerful enough to make me enter; for that something more was required. This additional impetus came from within myself, from the "must" within me that would not rest until I enjoyed again the Sacraments of the Church.

Never long absent from my thoughts in that fall of 1943 were these words of Psalm 85, *Quam dilecta:* "How lovely are thy tabernacles, Oh Lord of Hosts! my "soul longeth and fainteth for the courts of the Lord." This charming inheritance of the New Dispensation from the Old expressed the stirrings in my own soul. To obtain the moral fiber which I needed, to lead the life of inward peace for which I longed, the Holy Eucharist on the Catholic altar was imperative for me.

There could be no rest, I understood, until I had through Penance and the reception of Christ in the Sacrament of the Altar made myself whole again. Men of differing opinions may explain this longing, this quest, in many ways, I am aware. For me the explanation is simple, and it is the true explanation. The prayers of my good parents which had long stormed Heaven on my behalf, the remembrance of me by many priests at many Masses and not the least at Monsignor Sheen's through these years, the grace which followed from all this intercession for this erring son of the Church had their fruits. They hammered at my soul. They left me no respite. I was aware of that even while I fought the battle out within my heart and mind.

Those who wish to measure the longing that was mine—

and the anguish—can turn to no more illuminating pages than those of Thomas à Kempis, in the fourth part of his *Imitation of Christ*. That section, dealing with the Holy Eucharist, was a favorite of my youth, and I now returned to it for solace and courage. Dwelling on Christ's exhortation, "Come unto me," Thomas exclaims, as I did, too, "They arouse me, those most gracious words, so full of sweetness and of love; but mine own offenses do dishearten me." But there was hope as well in these pages. In an earlier chapter, "Of attaining true freedom of heart," à Kempis knocked at the door of my conscience with the words, "Forsake thyself, resign thyself and thou shalt enjoy much inward peace." But it was long before I could clear away the clouds from my befogged vision and come to know what this counsel meant.

Late into the night in the early winter of 1943, I read and thought much, looking out on the lights of the Astoria elevated lines—for we were living in Long Island then, and had been since we came back from Chicago. Always that spiritual struggle will be associated in my mind with the green and red glitter of the elevated structure and the firefly gleam of automobiles as they flashed into Grand Central Concourse from the Triborough Bridge.

I call it "struggle" advisedly, for that is the proper term. Communism and Catholicism are not halfway houses; they represent views of the whole man and of the whole of life. The attraction of the materialist conception of history with its "logic" about the "inevitability of Socialism" was fighting me against the necessity which I felt to return to the code of morality taught by the Catholic Church. However, the question was no longer: "Shall I return to the bosom of Catholicism?" It was now rather: "Shall I continue to seek the reconciliation of Communism and Catholicism, with the understanding that if I fail I shall return to Catholicism immediately?"

In such a quandry a man not only reads and thinks but also resorts to prayer. It was in the quiet of a visit to the Blessed Sacrament, again at St. Patrick's Cathedral, that I had made up my mind in October to become a Catholic once more. There, too, I solemnly pledged to the Mother of God that my conversion would not occasion hatred for individual Communists. Many of them were as they were because they had not received the grace that had come to me. It was the evils in the Communist system at which I would aim my blows, and through the display of brotherly love strive to influence those who remained in the Communist camp. After I had made this vow I experienced a sense of peace such as I had not enjoyed for three stormy decades. But there still remained the question of a final attempt at Catholic-Communist reconciliation. It was that which harried me, late into the night.

At that time I wrote of Catholicism: "For him who wants internal peace and spiritual sanity, his sanctuary must be the Catholic Church. Magnificently does it live over and over its function as the representative of Christ. To His perfection and to the immaculate character of His Mother, the Church adds His affection for the sinner. That love throbs through every hour in Catholic life. How humble but happy does it make us all to know that the Church's first head, St. Peter, wiped out his sins of denial in rivers of tears, just as must each sinner everywhere. The genius who brought the Christian message to the Gentiles was he who previously had held the cloak of those who stoned the first martyr Stephen to death. The light on the road to Damascus led him to this repentance in Arabia and then on to his mighty mission. And at the head of the 'virgins and widows,' in the Litany of the Saints is the former woman of sin, Mary of Magdala, dramatizing that no one who repents is lost. This religion of true brotherly love, this brotherhood in Christ, is the solace for the world, individually and in its social sickness."

To me—recognizing my guilt in having deserted the truth—such considerations were overwhelming. They bowed me with sorrow even as they raised me up with hope. When I considered my daughters' future, the appeal was even greater. After I had left the Communist party, the comrades accused me of having done so for "the security of my family." That was the truth, but it was not for the kind of "security" the Reds were thinking of. It was spiritual security, in a world that was casting aside all moral values, that I had in mind. I wanted my daughters to enjoy the pleasures of true Christian culture and the inner peace and benignity of the Christian personality; and the only promise of such security lay within the fold of Catholic Church.

In such cogitations another query came to the fore: "What would Margaret say or do about any such proposals?" I could not forget that she had no links at all with Catholicism, and that her early life and all her training had been away from the Church. She had once said to me in a casual but firm way: "I could never become a member of the Catholic Church." And our life together had been so uninterruptedly happy that I felt it would be folly to disturb that relationship with any heedless word or deed. Little did I know then that when she spoke of the Catholic Church, she had in mind something very different from the reality. Afterward, I blamed myself for having been so shy in speaking my thoughts to her.

Her solid knowledge of the Catholic world view and the essence of Catholic worship, gained later under the tutelage of Monsignor Sheen, was a thing of beauty in the turbulent time ahead. That understanding might have been hers long before had I pressed the subject. And yet I did write my mother: "Within five years, I can tell you confidentially, my whole family will be in the Catholic Church."

It was Margaret, though, who furnished the opportunity to prepare for re-entering the church for which I had been waiting. She insisted that we move into the Westchester County hills and I gratefully grasped at the suggestion. This would remove us from the Communist milieu, which was so necessary in order to work out entrance into the Church. Living in a community where Communists were active, we would never be able to attend Mass regularly or take any other measures that might be essential. The constant intrusion into the Communist leader's private life and the reporting system which went with it would preclude any effective steps toward Rome in a place like Astoria.

When Margaret announced that she was bent upon the Westchester expedition I applauded vigorously. Her determination had orginally been caused by the doctor's insistence that my eldest daughter and I escape from the dust and dampness of Long Island. Every week end Margaret took the commutation trains beyond Mount Vernon, looking for possible houses. At last one sunny day in December she arrived with the news that she had found just the place in Crestwood.

It was then that she let me know that there had been still another reason for the lure of Bronx River country, so far as she was concerned. What she said seemed to be an answer to my prayers, though in a surprisingly oblique direction. "When we go out there," she announced, "I want to attend the Episcopal church and have the girls attend, too. It's a ritualistic church, but near enough in its general attitude to the Unitarian so that I shall feel at home. Then, too, we know the Whites and that will make it easier."

She watched eagerly for my reaction. Her announcement certainly was not expected. Personally, I was totally immune to Episcopalianism and realized that this new development within my family was odd and might even be difficult. But I said, quite honestly: "Do the thing the way you want. It will be agreeable."

The Whites did make things easier for Margaret, as she had suggested. Eliot White was an Episcopal clergyman and we had much affection for him and his wife Mabel. Some months before, I had recruited both of them into the Communist organization. Though I had had some misgivings about it at the time, since I was troubled about the Red movement, I felt that their admittance would tend to broaden the Communist organization. White was a man of culture and good will. He was white-haired and dignified in appearance and always wore a flower in his buttonhole. When we launched the big campaign for the organization of the Brooklyn Edison Company in the early Thirties, I had called on him to man the picket lines after the goons had attacked the organizers. He had gone gladly and courageously and the goons had knocked out a number of his front teeth. In a few months he was to baptize my children in the little and ancient Episcopal church of St. John's at Tuckahoe, and to give Margaret stimulus for attending the services regularly. I looked upon these proceedings without approval but I abided by my agreement with Margaret—praying for her meanwhile, and asking Our Lady's aid in her regard.

On the frigid morning of December 17, we moved to Crestwood only to discover that the coal we had been led to believe was ours in reality belonged to our nearest neighbor. But with good grace these neighbors agreed to "lend" us coal until we could order our own. It was the winter of the coal famine and we were to battle for fuel throughout that season.

In the midst of the confusion of moving, I received word that my father was dying. This fell like an oppressive weight upon my soul. He who had been so gentle and so Christian was leaving this life, and I could not yet tell him that my house was in order. I recalled the walks we had taken together so long before in which we had discussed Shakespeare and many other intellectual topics, and how, above all, he had brought to my youth the fragant breath of Catholicism and had stressed its beauty.

I spent the two days that we were getting settled in our new abode trying to get a train reservation to Indianapolis, but it was the week before Christmas, in the middle of the war, and reservations were available only far in advance. By great good luck I finally got one for the Tuesday before Christmas, and in the heaviest snowstorm of the year finally reached my childhood home.

In a brief lucid interval amid the delirium of double pneumonia my father told me how glad he was that I had come. My throat ached because I could not say in return that I was on the road back to the real home, the Catholic tabernacle. I had delayed too long. For two days I waited in the vain hope that he might rally sufficiently for me to talk of such things, but he was too weak by then. For twelve years his legs had been confined to braces since the day when the vault door at the bank had been carelessly thrown back against him and had broken the bones in both his limbs. The same patience with which he had sat and read from his copious library through that long period remained with him in his last hours. Most of the time he was in a coma, induced by drugs. The golden hour to which I had looked forward— to announce to him my full reconciliation with the Church which he loved so much—was not to be; that hour was to be merged into eternity.

I wandered about the house, gazing upon the old familiar objects, listlessly opening some book which he had read over and over and reading the notes about poetry that he had so methodically but so feelingly recorded.

Mother agreed that I should be back with my family by Christmas Day, since the doctor thought my father might linger for a week or more. As I hurried through Grand Central Station on the morning which commemorates the Babe of Bethlehem, the organ was playing *Adeste Fidelis* and my heart burned with the recollections of the Christmases of childhood which had furnished such a bond between me and the man who was about to leave us. Hot tears were in my eyes and remorse was in my inmost being. This was not merely the sorrow which I have seen in the eyes of so many men at the departure of a dear one; it was the recognition that I had not lived up to the promise of my heritage. Toward the end of the following week he died. A reduced staff at the *Daily Worker* made it difficult for me to leave, and we agreed that I need not go. Return to Indianapolis for the four days that I knew my father lay dead in our old house—the New Year's holiday caused the long period before burial—I was conscious of each hour of the waiting and frequently telephoned my mother. Hundreds of people of all walks of life visited his bier, for he was widely known through his many years at the Fountain Square Bank. The newspapers stated that he had lived in that house for seventy years, and was the son of pioneers. But they could not tell the dramatic story of how he was winning a soul to Christ. I alone knew that in his death my father had speeded my new life.

Just then the conference of Teheran was rousing the hopes of the world for a long peace at the conclusion of the war. My picture post card view of the Soviet Union had now been dissipated, and yet Teheran renewed my hope that there might be an understanding among all mankind. How could I know that within two years the Soviet Government, through Jacques Duclos, would declare that accord to be only a "diplomatic document"? That the Soviet officials would tear up the treaty of Teheran with the same callousness with which the Kaiser had called the treaty with Belgium merely a "piece of paper"?

I was aware of the treachery afoot through memorandums I had received on the Balkans and Poland, but the Teheran accord seemed to be on such a large scale that I thought any nation that trampled upon it would fare ill. And so, with new vigor, I threw myself into the campaign to popularize the "Anglo-Soviet-American coalition" and "the concord of Teheran," and hoped that it would lead to real Catholic-Communist co-operation.

Right along, I was gaining strength for my Christian resolves by regular attendance at Mass. I would sit in the rear of the Annunciation Church remembering that I was like the Publican and thinking that my genuine humility at least was to my advantage and would work things out well. The supernatural life was beginning to exercise a dominant influence over me, and I was a man of benignity indeed after each Sunday morning at Mass. There is nothing more awe-inspiring but also more joyous than the Sacrifice of the Mass. He who offers Himself in Heaven for the salvation of mankind through that sacred sacrifice offers Himself here on earth for man's salvation. It is a revival of Calvary, and he who attends with belief stands at the foot of the cross and beholds that which was witnessed on the hill of Judea two thousand years ago. Heaven comes to earth.

From that altar and its holy drama come the moral guide-posts for life. Man is no longer merely the creature of intuition or instinct if he obeys the rule of the Cross and takes full advantage of all the Sacraments that center in the altar. These were the convictions which took possession of me by reason of my return to this much of Catholic practice. And I had an intense desire to receive the Eucharist again, to be united fully with Christ and the Church.

Always keenly aware of my moods, Margaret detected the transformation the Mass effected in me. It brought me a peace that "the Episcopal service never had," she told me later. Wondering what it could be, one day in October, 1944, when we were on a shopping trip to Bronxville, she suggested that we drop into St. Joseph's Church there.

It was there that the "miracle," as we called it, occurred. During the course of our prayers, Margaret sensed at once the real Presence and realized the difference from other churches. When we came out, she told me of this. Thereafter she went to Mass with me, and after the Christmas Mass of 1944 said simply: "I would like to be a Catholic." Joy was in my heart and she knew it.

We then planned that in the vacation of 1945 we would prepare the groundwork for our reception into the Church. But how should we go about it?

We were very much alone. There was no one in whom we could confide. Only to my mother, as I have said, did I hint that we would soon be in the Church. A Communist, even when far off the beaten track, has to proceed with caution. He may be watched and his mail may even be waylaid. I knew very well how messages had been intercepted by prying secretaries and secret reds. There was also the question as to whether we would be acceptable in the Church, for we were keenly conscious of our offenses.

There was really no doubt, though, how we would act finally. Monsignor Sheen had often been in our thoughts and our conversations. We had admitted the boldness with which he pressed his crusade for the Church. And I had never forgotten my meeting with him in 1936. As we discussed this matter late on a January evening in 1945, his pamphlet "Communism Answers a Communist" was on my desk. I had brought it out from the "archives" because of the new and final offensive on the "Catholic question" which I was initiating within the Communist organization. Perhaps the pamphlet reminded us of what we had already decided to do. At any rate, we agreed that we would write to Monsignor in our July vacation period, because, as we said, "He is our severest critic, and by going to him we shall show our Christian humility and the sincerity of our act."

The more we perfected our plans for becoming Catholics, the more I pressed for a closer relationship between Communists and Catholics. It was as though I were bent on giving the Communists a final chance. In the course of several luncheon meetings with Browder over the Teheran policy, he and I agreed that my recruit, Reverend Eliot White, should come out openly as a Communist. Heartened by this trend, I raised the matter of an outstanding Communist openly becoming a Catholic. "We will always be subject to suspicion so long as we cannot point to one Communist of standing who is a full-fledged Catholic," I said emphatically. I was doing some special pleading for myself, though on the premise under which I was proceeding, my arguments were valid.

Browder said noncommittally that he was "for it, if the morale of our comrades will not be injured." It was not the reply I had expected. It was, in effect, a refusal to consider Catholics seriously except fundamentally as enemies. But undaunted I raised the matter again two months later with both Browder and Dennis. It met the same fate. I was learning for the last time that even Communists who are playing with "revisionism" will not give any quarter to Catholicism, for they plan to stamp it out.

Knowing Marxist-Leninist philosophy as I did, my attempt to make Communists admit Catholics to membership on an honest basis was somewhat futile. Nevertheless, I looked upon it seriously as an acid test, and the negative responses I was getting indicated the old dishonesty of playing with the masses as with mice and then killing their beliefs and their hopes.

There was one more thing to do: take the whole matter in full dress to the National Committee. By way of preparation I began a survey of the entire Catholic press. Saying that the survey was for the Political Committee, I asked the help of the *Daily Worker* correspondents and certain district organizers in collecting the Catholic papers. They responded, of course, and sent in all the local Catholic papers month after month. With the information thus obtained, I went to the Political Committee and they set aside a special day for the discussion. On several occasions it was postponed, which indicated either a lack of interest or a desire to side-step the whole issue. But finally the day of discussion arrived.

In the report, which covered some forty pages and took an hour to deliver, I reviewed the growing antagonism once more between Catholics and Communists. Warning that there were thirty million Catholics in the United States— the "largest minority group," as I had said so often before— and that there were three hundred million in Europe, I stated that warfare with these millions would be tragic and that genuine collaboration was the goal to seek.

Within the Political Committee, the reaction was not encouraging. Foster, who was always bitterly anti-Catholic, said little, and what he did say was against any action. Minor tried to dismiss the whole matter by telling how well individual Reds and Catholics worked together. Browder was inclined to agree with Minor. Only Stachel took the subject seriously. It must be remembered that Moscow had recently been assailing the Vatican, and it was obvious to me that the overwhelming majority of the Committee interpreted this campaign as permanent warfare against Catholics.

Out of this meeting came a strange sequel, which neither the Political Committee members nor I had anticipated. But for me it proved to be a breath of liberation. It was simply a copy of a letter sent to me from the Most Reverend A. J. Muench, Catholic Bishop of Fargo, in which he spoke highly of my "intellectual integrity" as a young man.

This came about as follows: The only measures agreed upon by the Political Committee meeting on the "Catholic question" were that I should write a number of articles addressed to Catholics and that we should "study the question further." The latter phrase simply meant that the organization would mark time until Moscow, whose public declamations were now growing hostile to the Church, had fully developed its line. The articles prescribed were a one-way street—purely devices to confuse certain Catholics and broaden the antagonism to the Church. I essayed, nonetheless, to write one of these pieces for the *Daily Worker*. To make conciliation its theme and still remain within the boundaries set by the Political Committee's discussion, I chose a letter written to the weekly *Commonweal* which spoke somewhat sympathetically of the Communists. It was written by a person named McGuire.

Bishop Muench was quick to see the anti-Catholic feeling which might lie back of my article, and wrote a letter to the *Commonweal* cautioning the editors against encouraging effusions of the McGuire type in the Communist press. It was wise counsel. In the communication he also criticized what I had written, but at the same time referred to the activities of my youth and my former "integrity." The carbon copy arrived at the *Daily* one morning when I was in the throes of self-discussion about when and how I should return to the Church. It moved me deeply. For many long years I had stayed away from the altar of my fathers, and yet, this letter said that many still hoped for me and expected my integrity to win out. And Bishop Muench had not seen me since a conference on labor problems at Spring Bank,

Wisconsin, thirty-two years before. Moreover, the letter could be misued. Certain phrases torn from its context could be widely publicized as the commendation by a Catholic religious leader of a Communist, and yet Bishop Muench had such confidence in my integrity that he knew I would do nothing of that sort. These thoughts were like shafts of light, and they increased my mental alacrity in making preparations for the conversion. I felt humble in the sight of the Lord.

For fear some stenographer at the *Daily* had seen the letter and would report it in a distorted manner, I myself reported it to the ninth floor. A Communist, of course, has to do such things in self-defense. And now it was particularly vital that I be above reproach in my Communist reputation and conduct. At the least hint of divergence or disagreement, measures would at once be taken to "isolate" me, blacken my reputation, and even whisper suspicions about my personal responsibility and morals. Then, when my conversion was announced the Communist chorus could sing out that I had taken refuge in the arms of the Church because the Reds would not have me. That is the formula against dissidents. Lies have to be piled on lies. The amazing thing is that the Reds can actually induce certain "liberals," who would never submit to Communist discipline themselves, to join in this slander chorus.*

In spite of my preparation the procedure was not as we had planned it. Several totally unexpected barriers had to be surmounted and dates for action had to be changed. For any active Communist, imprisoned in his Red strait jacket, becoming a Catholic is a tremendous and involved undertaking. In this instance, the big new factor of the Duclos article came along to add more complications. Just in July,

* If Brooks Atkinson of the *New York Times* is assailed as a "gangster of the pen" and heaped with abuse merely for reporting on Soviet plans, imagine what would happen to a "deviating Red."

in which my vacation ordinarily occurred, the special national convention was to be held. I had been a delegate to each state and/or national convention since my entry into the Party, and I wanted to make sure that I was not so elected again. For if I were conspicuous in either convention I would be returned to the National Committee and probably to some special post-convention commission and that would hinder my plans to concentrate on the move to the Church. It might even postpone my breathlessly anticipated vacation.

By arranging for a transfer in membership from the Yonkers to the Mount Vernon branch, and not completing the transfer quickly, I could plead against my election from Westchester County. This I did effectively. Then I succeeded in getting hold of William Lawrence, at that time organizational secretary in the New York district, and got his consent to block my "pre-emption" in Manhattan. With a sigh of relief I saw that the final list of delegates did not have my name on it. That might still allow for a part of my vacation in July, since the convention proper occurred only on the last three days.

Hardly were these arrangements made when a new difficulty presented itself. This was the homely fact that my chief assistant, who had scheduled his vacation for August so that I might go in July, found that he could get a vacation spot for his family only in July. So I changed my vacation period. "At all odds," Margaret and I solaced ourselves, "this is not so bad as waiting until winter, which working on the National Committee might have entailed." We could scarcely wait until everything was over and our freedom from Communist bondage established.

Not until June had I told Margaret that I was definitely breaking with the Communist movement. Until then we simply said we were "returning to the Catholic Church at all costs." In the recesses of our minds we undoubtedly understood what that entailed, but I did not face it until just before the special National Committee meeting. The Duclos article itself had nothing to do with my decision, but a discussion I had with Foster about it did. In all conversions there is "a final straw" and this talk with the coming chief of the Communists furnished mine.

For many years it had been my custom to take a half-hour jaunt over to the secondhand book area on Fourth Avenue around four o'clock in the afternoon. This gave me a mental "breathing space" in the middle of the long day at the *Daily* just before the first make-up of the paper at five o'clock. On June 10—I'm almost certain that was the day—Foster hailed me at Twelfth Street and Broadway. He was homeward bound, since he always left early because of his heart trouble. He said that he had wanted to see me very much, and so proceeded to talk for more than half an hour. Most of the time he stood with one foot on the curb and the other in the gutter, as he had been when he first greeted me.

Of course, he plunged immediately into the Duclos article, and asked me if I had read his letter to the National Committee of January 20, 1944, which was then suppressed but was now endorsed by Duclos. I told him I had been permitted to glance through it for a few minutes back in 1944 but that I had no copy.

"That was a shocking, scandalous sample of bureaucratic procedure," he commented, bitterly. "But Browder never did understand democratic centralism; he didn't want to."

Since there was nothing I could offer on that subject, I remained silent. Foster went on: "Until the Soviet regime governs the earth, a state of war will exist. Every Marxist-Leninist knows that. Browder tried to create illusions which would have disarmed us for the struggle. He built up a rosy outlook on capitalism which just doesn't exist in reality.

Monopoly capitalism, in its crisis, will fight the Soviet Union and the monopoly capitalists know that as well as you and I. And the Soviet Union will have to undermine and destroy the chief example of that capitalism, American imperialism, and do a thorough job of it. Any other view is poppycock."

"Does that mean we are going back to the old so-called 'sectarian' days?" I asked doubtfully.

"Not exactly," he responded at once. "There will be truces, no doubt, in this war against American imperialism, but the objective must be made clear, that this American imperialism must be destroyed. Some of these monopoly capitalists, too, these Big Business men, will undoubtedly sell out the 'four freedoms'"—and he laughed dryly—"for Soviet trade just as some others sold out to Hitler."

Suddenly, to my surprise, he stated: "I have nothing to regret in what I have done." At first, this comment puzzled me, but I soon understood that he had been privately upbraiding himself for not having fought Browder to the finish in 1944, for he added: "Had I fought in 1944 I would have been expelled from the organization and declared a traitor to the workers."

His voice became high-pitched at that statement, as it often did when he was distressed, and I suddenly felt sorry for the man. He was so obviously a tool, preserved as a "Leftist" so that he might serve the Kremlin purposes when occasion required.

One more question—the sixty-four-dollar one—was still up my sleeve, "Will there be some possibility of working with the Catholics? There are a good many of them."

"Oh, fiddlesticks!" he replied, impatiently. "The two chief enemies of the Soviet Union and progress are American imperialism and the Vatican. They are eternal foes of Socialism and have to be fought endlessly. We've got to get out of our heads some of the illusions Browder planted there—and carry on war against American imperialism and the Vatican today and tomorrow and until victory over them is achieved." And lest I should misunderstand him he added, "Every Leninist knows that religion is a poison that has to be eradicated by argument or arms from the body politic—and the cornerstone we have to get rid of first is the Catholic mythology and the Catholic organization." Thereafter we talked about a number of other matters, but he had said enough for my final enlightenment.

Hurrying back to the office—for I was a little late—I almost bowled over Max Steiner, one of the officials of the New York district. "You look as though you had learned something important," he said lightly, noting my preoccupation and my apologies. "Yes," I replied, "Foster has just taught me a lesson I should have learned long ago."

Being a good-natured fellow, Steiner laughed heartily. But I had blurted out a powerful truth. What Comrade B. had told me in 1940, in connection with my article for *The Communist*, had been repeated by Foster: The Soviet Government and its Communist agents mean to wipe out all religion—by coercion if necessary—and warfare on the Catholic Church was the first objective. From my reading of Leninism and my knowledge of totalitarianism I should have realized that long before.

That night I went over the conversation with Margaret, and told her that a return to the Church involved a complete break with the Communist organization. This was perfectly agreeable to her, since she had never been active as a Communist, or even interested, and was much opposed to the Red view of women and motherhood.

How to make the break properly became a paramount consideration. Our family council of two pondered this dilemma for several nights. Few persons in the community knew exactly who we were, though we had made many pleasant associations and were well and widely known as good citizens. We could not take any of our neighbors into our counsels. The best way to avoid rancor on the one hand and the Communist lies on the other was to slip quietly out of our prison. The Duclos article and the violent discussions raging around it presented a splendid opportunity. Accordingly, in early July I requested the Political Committee to assign me to some labor union where I could act as editor—a union, of course, that was Red-led. In such a post I would naturally run into certain Catholic labor leaders I knew and could consult them about how to make my Red exit.

That request proved to be a blunder. The Political Committee reply came through Stachel, and he asked that we discuss it in the private sanctum. There he said: "We don't want to consider such a proposal. As a matter of fact, we are disturbed at the prospect of your leaving the *Daily*. You are our best all-around man—you can act as executive, reporter, editorial expert, writer of features—and have lately livened up our book reviews. You have always jumped in where a lift was needed. We can't think of your changing now. In fact, we have been talking about expanding your work under the new conditions."

This jumbled everything up; I said I would seriously consider what he had told me. Providentially, my wariness was increased by a series of suspicions just voiced about certain members of the Party. Notable was the persecution, though he did not know it was on, of Art Shields of the *Daily Worker*. Shields was a veteran reporter of the labor press and I had first known him years before when he and his wife were connected with the Federated Press. From the Communist viewpoint he had performed creditably as the *Daily's* correspondent in Spain and had stayed in Madrid until it fell. Since he did much feature work on the *Daily*, the editorial board and the Political Committee agreed to make him

Washington correspondent to succeed Adam Lapin. The latter had asked to return to New York.

Scarcely had Shields arrived in Washington when Lapin intimated that the new correspondent was lacking in "political stability." At first I thought little of this, since such words are often heard in Communist circles, but I noticed that the impression of his "political untrustworthiness" seemed to spread. A little investigation at the city desk and elsewhere revealed that all kinds of adverse reports on Shields were going regularly to the ninth floor. When I frowned on this procedure and spoke a word in defense of Shields to the board, the matter died down—for a very few days. When it flared up again I tried to tip Art off during one of his usual telephone calls from Washington. When he did not catch on, I advised him to present his case to the Political Committee. I got a chance to say that because he complained that something was going wrong with his work. He said "the desk" was criticizing him all the time, and he could not understand why.

When he came to New York to present his case to the ninth floor—by then, of course, he had guessed that it was a "political difficulty" that he was up against—he reported to me before and after. I knew that Dennis' advance ruling, to which Stachel reluctantly acquiesced, was that Shields be removed from Washington because of these suspicions with which he was never confronted and never even knew existed to the extent they did. When he came down from his interview or hearing he was delighted, for he had been given the impression that in a short time he could move his wife and son to Washington. Until the time I left, he never knew the formidable array of "political" accusations that had been built up against him. One day in the near future the managing editor of the *Daily* would simply receive a request to recall Shields from Washington on some superficial excuse. He would then be moved to a new post and kept under "observation."

This Gestapo or Gay-Pay-OO secretiveness, which tries a man and often finds him guilty without his knowledge, is not to be confused with the tyranny of petty minds which turns up in so many quarters. Human nature being what it is, there will always be some who, feeling threatened, resort to half-gossip and whispered insinuations in self-defense. But this Communist practice is something else again. It is an organized, well-recognized custom to which each and every member of the Red organization is subject in the name of political probity. Of course some are its victims more than others. But it is an extension of the police-state system of discipline to the United States.

This Shields case and several others like it counseled renewed caution in my own conduct. With August drawing near, Margaret and I drew up a list of everyone we knew in Crestwood and indicated the exact order in which we would let them know we were moving. It's not easy to pack up a whole family and get rid of a house without word of its getting around, and it was essential that not one hint get to the Communist headquarters.

I had one mighty source of strength, and that was a clear-cut understanding of what I was fighting. With the decision to break with the Communist movement the final scales had fallen from my eyes. The answer to the throttling of all dignity and decency in man that resulted from Communism was not the removal of all discipline. It was in the moral law, as voiced by the Catholic Church. The world-wide conflict, earth-shaking in its scope, lay between the slavery of the materialist state, which crushed out all semblance of dignity in man, and the eternal principles of those who held to a personal God and the eternal destiny of the human soul. The Catholic guides has warned the world that enslavement would be the outcome of the materialist philosophy of Marxism. They were now vindicated. If within the Communist party in the United States there could be such malignant terror—where there was no power—what must be the state of slavery in Soviet-dominated areas? So I asked, and the answer was quite obvious.

The omnipotent materialist state may seem to be having things much its own way, but that, we agreed, is nothing to paralyze us or drive us to despair. The Catholic Church stood against Atilla at the gates of Rome and against those greedy kings.

In August we wrote to Monsignor Sheen. We had delayed until the vacation was actually assured. The letter merely said that we would like to see him and asked him to phone us when he next came to New York. Day after day, and then the entire three weeks of the holiday went by, and he had not replied. We had sent the communication to the Catholic University, where his general mail was received, and it had not been forwarded to him during a long absence from Washington.

However, in the first week of September we did hear from him. He expressed the hope that our request to see him was for the purpose of returning to the Church. We replied in the affirmative, and on the evening of September 7, the eve of the Nativity of Mary, we met Monsignor at the Hotel Roosevelt. From the beginning our understanding was complete, and arrangements were made for Margaret to be instructed by Monsignor. With his usual zeal, he agreed to come into New York by plane from every city where he was lecturing so that the instructions could move with speed.

The fervor of our thanksgiving prayer that night was heightened by the straits from which we had escaped. Now there was a friendly hand to grasp, and someone with whom we could share our secret. We had let light into our cell.

In Crestwood Margaret carefully let this friend and that know part of our story, giving it out by degrees and with caution. And at the *Daily Worker* I criticized copy, made proposals and revisions on pieces to back the line—and fingered a rosary in my pocket as I did so. That continued for four weeks.

ELEVEN

Faith of My Fathers

BEFORE THE altar of St. Louis the family knelt—the father, mother and three daughters. Within the railing, vested in surplice and violet stole, sat Monsignor, in token of the Church's authority. The kneeling five then put their right hands on a great Book of the Gospels with golden edges, which Monsignor held. Together they repeated: "I (with the name of each), having before me the holy Gospels, which I touch with my hand . . . " and made the entire profession of Faith required of the convert.

It was a quiet hour in St. Patrick's Cathedral—seven o'clock of the evening of October 10. The little ceremony before one of the many altars was a small and obscure portion of the large edifice. The scattered sight-seers and silent worshipers were scarcely aware that an excommunication of three decades' standing was there and then being removed. One or two persons stopped for a moment to gape. After a while a few lingered, and by the time the ceremony was over, a little knot was there.

"*Miserere me, Deus,*" recited the Monsignor in his sonorous voice, reading from Psalm 50, the psalm of repentance. "According to the multitude of Thy tender mercies: blot out my iniquity." Then followed that prayer of the Savior's, "*Pater Noster qui es in caelis,*" and as the converts bowed their heads, "By the Apostolic authority, which I here do exercise, I absolve thee from the bond of excommunication."

A weight was lifted from our souls and peace and thanksgiving were in our hearts. One hundred years before—on

347

October 9—John Henry Newman had professed his faith at Littlemore, as the Church's lost daughter England began again to turn spiritually toward Rome. He must have experienced the hand of God upon him very like as we were doing so far away so many years afterward. To be a Catholic is to be of the Communion of Saints, and to be of God's centuries. St. Augustine was with us then, too, I thought— from out of the fourth century after Christ when the world seemed falling to pieces. And the patron before whose altar we had knelt was the gentle king of seven hundred years before to whose praise as a Christian man the non-Catholic historian has had to testify. Quiet continued in the cathedral as we walked to the baptismal font, where my dear ones would receive the waters of God, the Fountain of Grace. Though we trod softly, our steps through the aisle gave off echoes, so silent was the place.

Outside there was noise, confusion, the click of tickers, and the blare of radio announcements over this act. We had been obliged to release the news a few minutes before, for it had been discovered by the International News Service. Our original intention had been to acquaint the newspapers with the story the next day, when our marriage in the Church would be consummated and we had received Holy Communion. But the press would not let that schedule go through. Accordingly, our statement had been issued twenty-four hours earlier than anticipated.

The church was filling up as the baptism proceeded. Catholics were coming in to attend the Benediction of the Blessed Sacrament to be held later at the Lady's Altar in the rear of the church. And chaplains and army officers were around the high altar preparing for the ceremonies the following day connected with the consecration of Bishop Arnold as ecclesiastical superior to the Army chaplains. About two hundred people, on their way to the services, gathered around the baptismal font, as the baptism of an adult and three young girls at one time was unusual. The newspaper reporters, who were in the cathedral, thereupon reported the next day that two hundred of our friends were present. The only friends there, besides Monsignor, were Mr. and Mrs. James McDonnell, who had graciously consented to act as godparents for the newly baptized.

While the crowds attended the benediction service, Margaret and I went to confession. The blessing and forgiveness of God, and my mingled repentance and joy made the tears well from my eyes. Never have I been so regretful for the past and yet so relieved. Later that night Margaret said to me: "In that moment as you came out of the confession box, I knew for the first time the depth of your suffering for being cut off from the Faith; it was written on your tear-stained features."

That a leading Communist should become a Catholic was considered a unique bit of news, and the declaration I had made for all of us continued to be read on the radio, over and over again. The statement ran:

With deep joy, I wish to announce that by God's grace I have returned fully to the faith of my fathers, the Catholic Church. My wife, the companion at every step of my spiritual journey, and my three daughters have become Catholics with me.

Reason and faith have led to this happy step. From St. Peter to Pius XII, the Papacy has brought light to mankind, and despite all the pulls and tugs of history has continued its divine mission.

The voice of Catholicism is the guide to the winning of the real peace. The privilege of returning to the sacraments is one to be deeply prized; it is, after a long journey, the true returning home.

Communism and Catholicism are irreconcilable. Communism, I have found, aims to establish a tyranny over the human spirit; it is in unending conflict with religion and true freedom.

That was an adequate shorthand account of convictions at which I had arrived out of the tortured road away from the Communist camp. But what a long cause of thought and emotions were packed into those few words! "Hunger for the sacraments" is an expression heard often in Catholic sermons and read in Catholic writings. That is a literal term; it is a real hunger that haunts a man who is denied their grace. But all such pain was eased the following still morning of October 11, when Margaret and I received Our Lord at early Mass at the Lady Altar of the cathedral. Aside from Monsignor, who was the celebrant, only Mrs. McDonnell and our children were there. A few minutes before, Bishop John F. Noll of Fort Wayne had entered the cathedral to say Mass on a side altar, and he had said he would remember us then. I had known him years ago and I was happy to be able to greet His Excellency once more, and thank him for this graciousness.

"I feel as though I had just escaped from prison," I said, as we left for breakfast after the Mass. The long journey was ended. Once more within the fold of Rome I was at peace, and so with my whole family. Archbishop Spellman received us an hour later, and we then had the privilege of meeting twenty of the Bishops who were assembling for the consecration of Bishop Arnold. Our daughters were thus introduced to many representatives of the hierarchy in America on the very day of their entrance into the Church.

In the late afternoon of that day we went on to Notre Dame, where we were received with open arms the next morning. The name "Notre Dame" will always be synonymous with graciousness to us. It will be a second home. During the year which we spent on its campus we benefited by the Catholic atmosphere all about us and by the associations we made and the counsels we received. It was Monsignor who had thought of our going there when he was saying

Mass, and he had helped to arrange it through the courtesy of Father J. Hugh O'Donnell and the Congregation of the Holy Cross.

At Notre Dame—and now again at Fordham with the Society of Jesus—I learned once more the enormous social contribution of the religious orders of the Catholic Church. The Indiana university has so often been associated with football that it may come as a surprise to learn of its eminent position in scientific studies and discoveries. And not the least contribution to the same field was the achievement of one of Notre Dame's priest-scientists in the development of synthetic rubber. Behind the Catholic colleges and universities of this sort is the devotion of men and women who give up home and ambition for a life of voluntary poverty and service. There, where the religious life is encouraged, was the place to rehabilitate my own soul.

A Catholic has an obligation to live and act in a special manner. Since our name was so peculiarly associated with conversion to the Church, we had to be sure that our whims and wishes did not supersede our duties to the Catholic cause. It was no secret that two large newspapers were eager to have me become associated with them, or that I was deluged with requests to write all sorts of articles, booklets and manuscripts. It is no reflection upon any of these newspapers or publishers that I could not immediately join their staffs. It was, rather, that my responsibilities required association with a Catholic institution. That was where the kindness of Notre Dame was so providential. My year of silence and retreat there, teaching the future leaders of the nation's communities, was a boon and a blessing.

Since my departure from Communism led me back to the Catholic Church, it is as a Catholic that I must explain my position. My return to the Church was not a negative act. I was not a Catholic because I was anti-Communist;

it was the other way around. It was my returning faith that had said to me, in the words of Jesus: "*Ephpheta*—Be opened," and shed the light by which I fully perceived the slavery and war intent of the Soviet state. The bankruptcy of materialism had furnished the impetus to abandon Communism, but it was the grace of God that cured the paralysis of will that had postponed the act.

Faith does not arise from being *against* something so much as from being *for* something. Nor is the Catholic Church founded upon protest, upon negation, but upon the most positive of all concepts—the belief in the Almighty and His Divine Law. Therefore, the Church must combat the materialism that offends the spirit. Purely temporal things are defective and distorted, for they contain half-truths which often make them seem palliative to those whose emotions rule their will and blind their intellect. But there is no compromise in the Church's stand. Catholic faith and the Catholic view must be accepted as a whole.

We are aware at this moment of how valuable and to be cherished are the freedoms which we enjoy as Americans. We can observe what a curse would be the spear of that dark and dread totalitarianism which would substitute a police state for our liberties. We cannot be blinded to the chinks in our armor, to the drawbacks which make our free political system fall short of its responsibilities. They are created by and large through that very materialism which is the breeding ground for the police state. It obtrudes upon our view in every sordid aspect from the weakening of the family bond to power politics. If our American life were shot through with the acceptance of Catholic morality, it would provide a new strength and a new stimulus to develop our system in justice and charity.

The extension of Catholic concepts and conversions in America would be the salvation of our nation. Through the sacraments, the seven of them from the waters of Baptism to the oils of Extreme Unction, our citizens would be strengthened as individuals in that "peace which the world cannot give." Through the public precepts of the Church, more widely accepted, there would come about a brotherly solution of the labor questions and a moral answer to the other social problems which toss and torment our age.

I am the last man who would want to present a goody-goody version of the history of the Church's human side. Neither would that be in the Church's spirit. Catholic scholarship has acted in a far different manner, as you may note by consulting the monumental *History of the Popes* written by Ludwig Pastor under the blessings and co-operation of Leo XIII. The Church is the agency, though, which has saved over and over again what we term "Western civilization" and is the chief force that can save it again with our co-operation. Is there not something which should cause us to pause in the patent fact that there emerges out of the present wreck of human hopes in "the peace," the figure of the Catholic Church speaking the Christian, civilized message? None says so clearly as she "Love thy enemies" and begins to carry out this precept on a large scale. None preaches so concisely the message of justice to all peoples, an idea which is trodden underfoot by those who promised generations of peace at the meeting of Teheran.

Not so long ago in the *New York Times* magazine section a distinguished American, Raymond Fosdick, said that the world had reached a pass similar to the age in which St. Jerome and St. Augustine lived. Was not the logical thing to have gone on and asked for a return to that church which brought mankind out of the ruins of the Roman Empire, the Church of St. Jerome and St. Augustine? I think it was in the life of St. Ignatius Loyola, too, that the student will note the salvation of Europe from disintegration which his followers wrought, by making Catholics once more know and love Catholicism. The record of the Church is ever the rescue of man from his own wreckage.

Its Christian attitude toward conquered peoples alone would benefit all the world, our own nation included. There has been unleashed of late a bestial persecution of the German people, founded on the same savagery and insanity as Hitlerism stood for; millions upon millions of Christians are the victims, as they are driven across the face of Europe. America has this shame up to now, that it has allowed itself to be a silent partner to this rule of revenge. Why was Hitler destroyed if the same evils he represented are kept alive in the Russian act against these Germans in Austria, in the entire spoliation and bandit savagery against people who are not of a nation marked by the beast, no matter what certain gentlemen may say? The Papacy denounced such banditry, and has worked against it, and it is sad that its voice has not been heeded more fully by American leaders.

The Soviet leaders, who waxed angry over the "crime of Versailles," are staging scenes of degradation which would have seemed nightmares to the framers of that instrument of revenge. The Soviet armies are driving like cattle thousands of peaceful people, tearing them from homes held for centuries, and sending them tubercular and tortured into places which cannot contain them. And America has been up to now too complacent toward such criminality, which if unchecked will one day bring down fire from the skies on our cities and our children. The Catholic Church, at such a moment of betrayal of the peace, has emphasized that this would be the fate of all the comings and goings of the statesmen unless the name of God and His moral law are heard again at international council tables.

The Church can speak calmly though firmly, since its history exemplifies its age-long stand for justice amid every political and economic tempest, from the Huns to Hitler.

On March 14, 1937, when the Nazis were at the height of their power, Pius XI condemned their neo-paganism in one of the brave documents of the dark time, which had to be distributed secretly through the German cities. Almost at the same hour he issued, too, the encyclical against atheistic Communism, prophetic of the crude and cruel acts of the Soviet Union against the peace and the peoples since the war's end. How is it that such a system can spread so rapidly? asked the Pope. And he answered: "The explanation lies in the fact that too few have been able to grasp the nature of Communism." This leads even some of "the better-minded members of the community" to be won over to its tenets, despite the "repulsive crudity and inhumanity of Communistic principles and tactics."

With the rounded-out view traditional to the Church, this encyclical declares that it was the economics of extreme liberalism which brought on the evils breeding Communism, and did their utmost to "de-Christianize" the world. The fallacies of extreme individualism with its motto of "enrich yourself at all cost" have prepared the way for Communist propaganda directed from a common center and using any deception to further its cause.

We cannot deny that much of the acquiescence to Soviet violence and much of pro-Soviet appeasement have been founded on the bargaining and haggling theory of power politics. We witness, as a result, horrors extending across Europe and other centers of the world which have not been seen since the Seven Years' War. The Communists had a slogan once which they used extensively, at the time they feared the rise of the efficient German military machine: "Peace is indivisible." The rights of man, too, are indivisible, and it is to America's harm that they are being crushed underfoot in Poland, Bulgaria, Romania and other countries.

The Church's view against extremes and for moral law would provide a foundation for the peace which can't be discovered elsewhere. That peace is less secure today than in the debacle of 1920. And it is not to be wondered at that this restlessness of "the peace" is accompanied by the refusal to invoke the name of God at the council of the nations.

Such were some of the thoughts on the public character of the Church's service to mankind which were molded by my struggle to find peace. The terrible disillusionment, which should well be the title for our times, can be cured by no other precepts than those moral rules to which the Papacy points.

Within the life of our own nation, we could profit much by heeding the principles laid down in the great Papal encyclicals on "The Condition of Labor," the "Reconstruction of the Social Order," "Christian Marriage and the Christian Education of Youth." This is not the place to examine these good counsels. They are invaluable gems, though, for the guidance of our country in the perilous paths in which it is now beset. Ours is a great nation indeed, with its mighty productive genius, its heritage of freedom, its good-natured desire that men live at peace with each other. We can't gain the wisdom and the will to carry through these aims if we do not abandon the tearing down of the family structure and the chaotic view of labor and capital which still prevail. The Church so says, and the Church is deeply right.

In every social counsel of the Church there lies the merit of its stress on the moral duties and on the curbing of extremes. That is the true reply to the tyranny of Communism. The issue is not Communism versus fascism, but

Catholicism versus both Communism and fascism. Catholicism versus fascism—Red or Black or Brown.

The individual gains his salvation likewise in the treasures of the Church, in its fountain of living waters. There are hundreds of thousands of non-Catholic men and women in our country who want to live in the ways of God, who desire to be free in the sense in which those who know the truth are free. Each of them will find these desired things at the foot of the Catholic altar.

Come with me or any other Catholic on a visit to the Blessed Sacrament, and you will be aware of what I say. There, in the silence of the church, the individual soul greets His blessings. From that tabernacle pours forth the peace which is to be seen written in so many Catholic faces, the benignity in dealing with one's neighbor, the dignity of belief which makes for the fullness of the man. There is beauty in the air of faith and devotion around the Real Presence which even many non-Catholics observe; it is a mystery of which they become conscious. There is the most dramatic demonstration of the sweet appeal: "Come to Me all you who labor and are heavy laden, and you shall be refreshed."

Isn't it small wonder that there is such a trend toward the Church in our country? Men and women of intelligence, both of high and humble station, are listening to the Church and turning toward her tabernacles. They discover there the public morality which challenges this current barbarism miscalled "the peace," a more desolate and savage scene than we inveighed against after Versailles. They learn from it that cure for the individual's torment which satiety can't still and affluence can't ameliorate.

They glimpse a beauty in the Church which others stumblingly seek to describe. It is one of the happier ironies of our present day that literature, which tried so hard to deny

Christ in the name of sophistication, has been obliged to pay some recent tribute to the beauty of Catholicism. Franz Werfel, groping for real romance, must turn to Lourdes and the song of Bernadette. Dr. A. J. Cronin, searching for adventure, must locate it in the labors of a Catholic missionary. Even the Communist-controlled Anna Seeghers had to paint the refuge for her here in a Catholic church at night and in the silence of Father Seitz. The leading English stylist of our times, Evelyn Waugh, sees the hope of sinful mankind in the cup of the Catholic tabernacle, the Eucharist. In referring to these works, it is not for the purpose of commending them; it's not my function here to say "aye" or "nay" about them. What I do want to do is to signalize the overwhelming fact that the Catholic Church can't be passed by when beauty is sought even by many who do not understand and many who only partially understand Her divine mission.

This attraction which the Church exercises over men of "poetic" and creative minds is but a wan reflection of the spiritual beauty which exists for those who accept its tenets and live by its teachings. In almost every denomination which goes by the name of Christian, the service at some point breaks forth into the credo: "I believe in the holy Catholic Church." That is still the remnant of the heritage from the Church of Peter and the catacombs, of St. Benedict in the midst of the barbarian invasions, of the See of Peter today while the world looks out in horror at the waves of war and materialist degeneration. In that phrase, I think, there is the prayer that can lead mankind out of the trough of despondency and neurotic despair which so feature our current life. And the holy Catholic Church with its means of grace is the heir, too, let us not forget, of the Roman Sybils as well as of the Hebrew prophets and from that synthesis the moral guardian of what we know as "civilization."

It is the cardinal sin of Communism that it would destroy this source of beauty and moral strength. Red fascism, feeding on distrust and disorder, and uncertain of its future, strives to end all religion as the cornerstone of true order. Almost a century ago the great German Catholic social reformer, Bishop Wilhelm von Kettler of Mainz, wrote of the oncoming omnipotent slave state as the major menace to man as a religious being. I am indebted to the St. Paul weekly, *The Wanderer*, for this document of Kettler's, which its editors recently translated from the German. There was a mighty truth in his statement, for totalitarianism cannot, eventually, brook any semblance of freedom or religion, for it is itself based on materialism and absolutism and its only morality can be its own will and its own preservation.

During the last four weeks of waiting at the *Daily Worker* before my open act of conversion, I was treated to new information on the antireligious campaign of the Communists. This four-week period was required for Margaret's instructions in Catholic doctrine and belief. It is not possible to enter the Catholic Church as though it were some kind of club. The person entering must know why he is becoming a Catholic and must prepare himself by learning the principles and practices which make for Catholic worship and Catholic life. Normally this period is much longer; it may extend into months. But the urgency of our case and the necessity of being at Notre Dame for the November semester caused Monsignor to intensify Margaret's instructions. During that time the Party was feverishly working out a new scheme to incite certain groups of Protestants against the Catholics, as a means to debilitate and destroy all religious influence here. The comrade assigned by the Political Committee to work out this plan—which had been outlined before and partially carried through in support of the so-called *Protes-*

tant magazine edited by Kenneth Leslie—gave me a definite idea of what was up. The comrade had come to me for certain data he hoped to put into his report. In discussing what he wanted, he told me that the aim was to "intensify the penetration of the easygoing religious groups, such as the Episcopalians and Unitarians, and then work up anti-Catholic sentiment among more rigidly Protestant sects." (He used the word "anti-Vatican" for "anti-Catholic.") To a query of mine he laughingly acknowledged that the general idea was "along the lines of thought expressed by the rationalist, Edward Gibbon—that Catholicism really holds the nucleus of religious strength and that Protestantism's main mission is to destroy religion by undermining Catholicism."

The initial backing given by the Reds to Leslie and *The Protestant*, which was bitterly anti-Catholic and adhered to the Moscow line, was therefore being expanded. I was told specifically that as part of the campaign the comrades planned to encourage the anti-Vatican utterances of Bishop Bromley Oxnam, the Methodist bishop of New York. This was not surprising since Bishop Oxnam had been recommended by our Boston comrades while he was still in Massachusetts as one whom the *Daily Worker* should play up. "His anti-Vatican hatred," said the Boston report, "will make him staunchly pro-Soviet, and that can help Americans' education." Thereafter the *Daily Worker* was supposed to give the Bishop a special break. This, of course, was the Reds' estimate of the Bishop, and not the Bishop's idea of himself. But it is a good example of the methods to which they will resort to achieve their ends.

The proclamation of war upon the Catholics, of which the comrade had told me in October, was announced to the Party in the April, 1946, issue of *Political Affairs*. One of the main articles was "The Vatican's War on Peace." The irony of that title will strike every American, while Soviet

Russia, through its puppet Tito, is shooting down our air-
men and dumping them like refuse into a common grave.
The entire article is sly instructions to the comrades to
begin inciting the Protestants against the Catholics. The
"wealth" of the Church is played up, and there is the gibe
at Protestants that they have not demonstrated any "strong
and effective Protestant counteraction." There is the same
linking of "American imperialism" with "the Vatican"
which Foster spoke of to me. And, according to this article,
even "the current epidemic of conversions among notables"
is part of the American "imperialist" plot to strengthen the
Vatican as its ally. At every point, even to the Council of
Trent, the comrades are urged to stir anti-Catholic sentiment among Protestants as a means to destroy American
imperialism and add to the glory of the Soviet Union—
hailed, of course, as "the fortress of strength" for the
peoples. To the glory of our unity as a nation, I am satisfied
that this Soviet plot to cripple America with religious conflict will fail. The overwhelming majority of American
Protestants will recognize the evil that lies in such a course,
just as they have done in previous critical periods of our
history.

The move against the Catholic Church was much more
general than just this one new scheme would indicate. There
was the odd story of the Orthodox Church in Russia itself.
As managing editor of the *Daily Worker* I had received so
many reminders that the existence of this church was
"merely an expedient, to gain the good impression of such
countries as the United States," that I knew that explanation
by rote. Every leading comrade was fully advised of the
fraud involved in the claim that this Orthodox church had
"freedom of worship." They indicated this in the knowing
smiles, jests and cynical observations made whenever that
subject came up.

At one meeting at which this matter was discussed a well-informed comrade stated it in this fashion: "As long as people want to have religion and insist on it, we might as well control it. The Russian Orthodox Church is more controlled by the Soviet State than it ever was by the Czar. It can't make a move without the Government's consent. There are more ways than the crude use of open force to keep a hold on such an organization. In the Soviet Union, for instance, the price of electric current in the churches can be moved up or down by the governmental agencies, can be made prohibitive, too, if necessary." Then this comrade pointed with approval to an article in the *Christian Science Monitor* which stated that the Orthodox Church was being employed to extend Russian influence in the Balkans. Although that article was written in the form of a charge, he said it gave a correct outline of what was up in Yugoslavia and Bulgaria. The recent assaults by Russian Orthodox leaders upon the Catholic Church at moments when the persecution of Catholics was being unleashed by the Reds in eastern Europe are proof of its servant status. It continually echoes whatever the Soviet foreign office wants. The Russian Orthodox Church, as the leading comrades here are well aware, is as much a hand organ of the Russian state as it was under the Romanoffs.

When I quit the Communist party the Reds made an attempt to throw dust into the American people's eyes concerning their stand on religion. They asserted that any Communist could be a member of any religious body. The assertion was made through Elizabeth Gurley Flynn, who was chosen to attack me because she had been for years the most friendly to me. That is always the Red test of discipline.

Her assertion was utterly incorrect. For the ordinary worker, "the rank and filer," the Party follows Lenin's advice. That a worker is permitted to become a member even though he has religious sentiments, and once in the Party, the comrades will wean him away from religion. For anyone in a post of leadership, however, religious affiliation is strictly forbidden unless the Political Committee says that for "tactical purposes" he must join a religious group. But in order to do so, his basic atheism is first well established.

This atheism for all leading Reds is acknowledged by none other than Gil Green, speaking as secretary of the Young Communist League of the United States at the Seventh Congress of the Communist International in 1935. That was the "broadening" Congress, you will recall, the "democratic and People's Front Congress." But even there, when the Communists were trying to look "democratic," Green was compelled to testify publicly to the atheism of the Young Communists. In his report, which can be read in the *International Press Correspondence* for 1935, Green referred to the method of handling young people who want to go to church. He explained in detail how the genuine Young Communists work with them and stressed that in doing so the young Reds preserve their "aetheistic integrity."

In tracing the Communist course on religion, we are confronted with the same deep-dyed deception that stamps their other activities. Duplicity was created, it is true, long before the Communists came upon the scene. Its history is long and lugubrious. In the case of the Communists, though, it has been elevated to the importance of a first principle. "Democracy" is their term for dictatorship, "elections" are the imposition of hand-picked slates on nations and peoples, "defense" is aggrandizement by the Soviet Union, but air bases for the United States' security is "imperialist aggression," and democracy is "fascism."

On the very day when the publication of the peace treaties for certain European countries showed that the Truman-Byrnes leadership had given Soviet Russia new lands and peoples, the Soviet press assailed the United States for trying to think of its own security. *The Bolshevik*, organ of the Central Committee of the Communist Party of Russia, denounced the United States as "imperialist." In the very week when the United States Congress put the atomic bomb into the hands of civilians, the Soviet press assailed a growing "military caste" in the U.S.A.

During my last four weeks at the *Daily Worker* two cases developed that were illustrative of this general policy of deceit. One of them had to do with the further advance of Red Spain as a spearhead against "American imperialism" in Latin America. The other concerned Philip Murray, president of the C.I.O. The Spanish affair grew out of two incidents. One of these was the imprisonment of two "Republicans" in Franco Spain, about which the French Government and other agencies raised a great din. At the *Daily Worker* we were confidentially informed that these men were not Republicans at all but Communists who intended to destroy any Republicanism in Spain as soon as it manifested itself. Some interesting information was divulged during that case and the subsequent discussion about the formation of the "Republican Government" of Dr. José Giral. I learned that a Republican regime would never be allowed to progress very far in Spain before it would be given the same treatment as was given Dr. Subasitch in Yugoslavia, the Agrarians in Bulgaria and every other "liberal" force that co-operated with the Communists anywhere. The treatment was more urgent in Spain than in some other places, for Spain was to be used to batter down "Yankee imperialism," through the creation of unrest in Latin America.

It was no secret that the choice of Dr. Giral by the Spanish Republican refugees in Mexico was at first not pleasing to the Communists here. But after getting advice from abroad they decided to embrace the Giral cause in order to blast it into oblivion as soon as it had established itself in Madrid. "The

Giral regime can be another Kerensky regime," was the verdict.

During the month of August, 1946, Dr. Giral publicly assured a committee that his government would respect freedom of worship in Spain. But the Communists, committed to the obliteration of religion—particularly in Spain—know that Dr. Giral can guarantee nothing at all, not even his own political existence. The fate that the Reds have carefully prepared for him is to be their "prisoner," which is the term they used in discussions at which I was present. If he doesn't like that role, disruption and treachery within his own cabinet and country will speed him to the firing squad or continued exile.

As to Philip Murray, such suspicion as the Communists had of him came from his being a Catholic. They figured that this would someday lead him to break with them in the C.I.O. For a long period they had stated in reports that they would like to make him their "prisoner." This was not predicated upon Red dominance in the majority of the affiliated unions of that organization, but upon the key positions held by some of their concealed Communists, which made it hard for Murray to break with them.

Just before I left there was new uneasiness about him. Reports came in that he was appointing known anti-Reds to certain positions in the C.I.O. to offset the hidden Reds. And in certain unions, he was "yielding" to the advice of "hopelessly anti-Communist" Dave MacDonald, secretary of the Steelworkers, and was permitting anti-Communist clauses in those unions' charters or constitutions. As a result, some of the hidden Red leaders were being partially curbed. In general, Murray was not behaving entirely to the Communists' liking. Since I had written a number of pieces commending him for what they had regarded in the past as gestures toward the Left, I was now commissioned to look up data that could be used against him. Any evidences of "reactionary" utterances were to be prepared carefully and then kept "in storage." Whenever it became necessary to "caution" Murray or to castigate him, the data could be brought forth.

Although I did not discharge this commission, the proposal in itself proves that the Communists will tear down the free trade unions or subordinate them to subversive purposes whenever Moscow wants. Murray will become the embodiment of evil on the day when he refuses to go along with what the Reds think are the Kremlin's desires. With the same zeal with which they build up a union, they will tear it to shreds when that is the "line." In this era of increasing Soviet threats to the security of the United States, the Communist influence in the unions will constitute a grave menace to the American nation.

The course of the Communists within the unions is not covered by this account, for I have sought to avoid any accusations that might lead to the infusion of personal hatred in these pages. So likewise have I avoided any references to the Red infiltration of political organizations. Many specific names would have to be given, and I do not want to label men and women who may shortly change their minds even as I have done. Someday it may be possible to go into this fully.

Knowing that the Reds would be in the position of open seditionists through its war of nerves on the American republic, Moscow prepared in advance a document for Communists to employ during this anti-American period. It was a treatise on "Patriotism" that appeared in the *New Times* (the present name of the *Communist International* magazine). No attempt was made to deny the Communists' devotion to the Kremlin. On the contrary, the theme of the piece was that loyalty to the Soviet Union by an American or Briton was the highest form of patriotism to his own country because the Soviet Union seeks only the best for mankind and is the only country which is not "imperialist" in character! The logic is obvious. The Soviet Union knows what is good for the United States better than the American people themselves. Therefore, anyone attached to the Soviet Union knows more about it than the run-of-the-mill American patriot.

When I left the Party, the Communist official statement said that I was "frightened." That interesting word was hit upon to hide the fright which many Party members did feel at the reckless Kremlin attitude. A few days before I left, Sam Baron, the public-relations man for the *Daily Worker*, rushed into my office literally tearing at his hair.

"Can't something be done to stop these war editorials?" he groaned. "We are being deluged with letters, begging us not to stir up war between the United States and the Soviet Union. We are frightening the comrades." To which I wryly replied, "Don't you know the line?" And he rushed out of my room, shaking his head despondently. There isn't any doubt that many left the Party then, though the same thing has occurred with the shifting of other lines.

Unfortunately, the core remaining, dedicated to the ruin of America, will not be a laughing matter. Some periodicals have attempted to heap fun on the Reds for the rapid changes in line. But, as I have pointed out, these comrades are much better prepared for those changes than the magazine writers seem to think. They do have to sink their integrity to a low level, but they know what to expect and they are kept advised, at least the leading men are, of the shifts in other nations insofar as this can be done without revealing the whole conspiratorial apparatus. They are in dead earnest and they are armed with deceit.

Other newspaper writers have said of late: "Why, at the

most, there are only 70,000 Reds in the whole United States. They can't do any damage." Those gentlemen who write in that fashion could learn something from Stalin. At the time of the Trotskyite-Bukharinist trials, he said, "It takes a hundred men to build a bridge, but one can blow it up." That is the law of conspiracy. And the Reds' advantage in operating under it here is that they can depend upon the open-eyed innocence of many people who call themselves "liberal," but who follow the same materialist paths as the Reds themselves.

The existence of the Communist party in the United States is in itself a direct violation of the Soviet Government's agreement not to indulge in subversive propaganda or activities within our shores. The continuance of that Party is evidence that the Soviet Government can be trusted no more than could Hitler. Nor are the exhibits introduced in these pages needed to confirm this charge. The servility of the Communist party to the Kremlin has been demonstrated by every act in its history. Never has it or any of its organs criticized the Soviet leaders or Soviet policies. They are always right and the rest of the world always wrong. Never throughout its history has the Party deviated from the known will of the Kremlin. And the Soviet press and Government for their part have never criticized the Communist party for creating disruption in the United States. Indeed, that press and that government have thrown mud at countless personalities and institutions in America. But the Communist party here has always been immune from such assault, except when the organs of the Communist International occasionally admonish it to act more fully and efficiently for the Soviet Union.

The Catholic Church told us a long time ago of the peril that lay in atheistic Communism. Day by day we witness the darkness of its shadow across the world. And each day we can recall that it was the Church which continually warned mankind that this darkness would be the fruit of trust in the fleshpots of materialism.

Not so long ago there were thousands of us—and I was one of them—who expected that democracy would advance in Russia out of the Soviet regime and that all we had to do was to admire the Russian state and all would be well. But we did not measure the inherent autocracy that lies in the servile state. The Catholic Church did measure it, knew its evil, and bravely spoke out and informed mankind.

Any man who does not close his eyes, can know now that Russia has blocked the peace. The Soviet Government has prevented the passage of every agreement. It has claimed more and more loot in the true Hitlerite spirit. On February 9, 1946, Premier Joseph Stalin, who pledged "generations of peace" at Teheran, suddenly shouted in warlike tones. He accused the United States and Great Britain, nations which had been overeager to mollify and appease Russia, of preparing for war. In like manner did Hitler assail as "warmongers" those whom he was about to assault. And since that February day constant abuse against the United States has poured from the Soviet press. It dovetails perfectly with the information the Communist party here, the agent of the Soviet Government on our own soil, had received from the Duclos article. It expresses exactly the policy that I referred to in April in my testimony in Washington before the Committee on un-American Activities. It is a "creeping Blitzkrieg" which the Soviet leadership is pushing across Europe and Asia, designed ultimately to destroy the American nation because it is the greatest national depository of civil freedom. Even when the Soviet representatives in the United Nations express certain sentiments for "disarmament," these words prove as worthless as the guarantees of freedom in the Stalinist constitution of Soviet Russia. The continued maintenance of huge Red armies and the extension of terror in Bulgaria, Yugoslavia, Rumania, and Poland speak eloquently of the Kremlin's real purposes. From within Soviet Russia itself come continuous reports, secretly smuggled to the outside world, of new purges involving scientists, writers, and other intellectuals.

In the wise encyclicals of its shepherds, from Leo XIII to Pius XI, the Church has predicted that this would be the outcome of statism. It has been eminently correct. In the valley of the shadow of totalitarianism and total war through which the United States again passes, it would be well to acknowledge that fact and turn to the Church for further counsel.

Never has the Church said: "Be only anti-Communist!" It has emphasized instead that Communism arises from the defects and diseases of capitalism. In recognizing the perils of Red Fascism, we Americans will have to bestir ourselves to buttress our liberties by what might be called a "modified capitalism." Therein profit sharing on a legitimate basis, extension of security and a further cushioning and curbing of the business cycle can be outstanding features. Therein, likewise, the universal outlook of the Church can aid us to labor for the freedom of oppressed or handicapped peoples, including our late enemies in the war, and against the sin of racial discrimination.

For us as Americans the beginning of wisdom can be the acknowledgment of our own weaknesses, under which we have rather complacently watched nations robbed of their faith and freedom by the Russian totalitarian state. Persecution because of religious belief or patriotism runs rampant over Europe. The Russian secret police are in charge of Hungary and Poland, and are duplicated in terror in Yugoslavia. Our American mission, from our very strength, is to insist on the freedom of these peoples. We have expended lives and huge sums of money in order that the "four freedoms" might live, and now they are being killed off with our silent consent. Our own fine spirit of liberty, coupled with the Church's concern for the dignity of the human being, could combine to bring some semblance of justice into this bleak world that is at present hurrying toward another world war. But we can scarcely fulfill this mission so long as half our people spurn religious worship. In my humble opinion it is the Catholic spirit that can best help us to gain that spiritual strength which will maintain our Christian heritage.

From the Vesper service of my childhood days there swells out the hymn of Psalm 116: "*Laudate Dominum, omnes Gentes; laudate cum, omnes populi*—Praise the Lord all ye nations; praise Him, all ye people. For his mercy is confirmed upon us; and the truth of the Lord endureth forever."

INDEX

CPSIA information can be obtained at www.ICGtesting.com
Printed in the USA
BVOW08s1015260913

332222BV00001B/108/A

9 781419 160509